Statistical Problem Solving (SPS)

Statistical Problem Solving (SPS)

*A Team Process for Identifying
and Resolving Problems*

Hans J. Bajaria
Richard P. Copp

Multiface Publishing Company
A Subsidiary of Multiface, Inc.
Garden City, Michigan

Printed in the United States of America

Editor and production supervisor: Darlene Podgorski Copp
Cover designer: Vivian L. Bradbury
Composition, printing and binding: Braun-Brumfield, Inc.

The excerpts in Chapters 4 and 5 from *Applied Imagination: Principles
and Procedures of Creative Problem Solving* by Alex F. Osborn, 3rd revised edition, copyright 1963, Charles Scribner's Sons, are used by per-
mission from Macmillan Publishing Co., New York, N.Y.

Library of Congress Catalog Card Number: 91-91305
ISBN 0-9629223-0-7

Contents

PROCESS STAGE

CONTENTS

Foreword

In 1982, during my employment with a major manufacturer, we faced a complex problem. We had been successful in the implementation of Dr. Deming's suggested statistical process control methods and were beginning to receive quality recognition from our major customers. The application of statistical process control resulted in stable process output with timely feedback as special causes of variation appeared. Even with a stable process, we still faced an infrequent occurrence of marginal lining bond during the sintering process. The problem of incapability persisted despite the best efforts of our metallurgists, technical and manufacturing personnel.

No component with such a bond was considered acceptable, so the problem was severe. The only control method available was a destructive test, and gradually we were forced to increase the frequency of our checks from once/day to once/hour—with pressure to make them more frequent. This was a costly inspection proposition with slow feedback to the process.

In searching for a better solution—a permanent solution, I contacted Dr. Hans Bajaria and explained to him our dilemma. He smiled and hinted that our predicament was due to not fully understanding the "combination of variables" causing the problem. He indicated that there was a process to determine which methods are appropriate for individual problem situations. In our case, it could improve the capability by successfully reducing the common cause variation. The process is Statistical Problem Solving, or SPS.

Our plant manager agreed to give it a try. A cross-functional SPS team was formed and given one day of training by Dr. Bajaria. The SPS experiment was outlined and conducted in the production environment. Results were outstanding. They included a precise definition of the problem, discovery of the combination of variables at the root of the problem, achievement of a common team understanding, and correction of the problem, resulting in a reduction of inspection testing.

Ever since, I have discovered the power of SPS many times over during my career. I am convinced that, everything else being equal, the use of SPS in conjunction with SPC is the powerful statistical combination all industries need to enhance their rate of continuous improvement. I am thankful to Hans for exposing me to this reality.

O. P. Gupta
Vice President of Manufacturing
Operations and Total Quality
Zexel-Gleason USA, Inc.
Rochester, N.Y.

Preface

We began work on this book near the end of the 80s, a decade marked by widespread efforts to improve the quality of American products and services. Based on our experiences as problem solvers, we believed there was a need for more explicit, more practical guidance on how to solve problems efficiently and permanently.

Statistical Problem Solving (SPS) was conceived in response to a multitude of tough problems that few people were able or willing to deal with. As these difficult problems were solved, SPS evolved. Having used SPS to help solve several hundred real-life problems, we recommend it to any company seriously interested in solving their problems.

At its heart, SPS is a disciplined and cost-effective process for achieving improvements. In most cases, we believe it should be carried out through teamwork. Because there is ample literature on group dynamics, we do not attempt to give advice on team building or team maintenance. Instead, we suggest what we have experienced works within the context of SPS. These teamwork suggestions are itemized towards the end of most chapters, then summarized in Appendix C.

Over the years that we have been practicing and writing about Statistical Problem Solving, someone occasionally comments on the term **statistical** as intimidating. **Systematic** Problem Solving has been suggested as an alternative name. Obviously we have felt **statistical** is important to the SPS process since we have stuck with it. When problem solvers use statistics, they are statistical practitioners, not necessarily statisticians.

In fact, Statistical Problem Solving represents a deliberate effort to meld statistical science, physical science, and business realities. A healthy regard for all three helped to develop the problem-focused strategy and economic execution principles of SPS. (The latter are presented at appropriate points in the text and then summarized for quick reference in Appendix B.)

We have found that SPS students appreciate this synthesis of statistics and sense. Many are glad to learn how to use available statistical tools within a total problem solving routine. Engineers are comfortable with a coherent process that uses statistics but also relies on physical science and common sense. Plant personnel are pleased to discover that experimentation does not have to disrupt production.

Those familiar with design of experiments (DOE) may recognize aspects of it within Statistical Problem Solving. While DOE is often valuable, performing a designed experiment is not the goal of SPS. The SPS path heads towards a solution, which may or may not require structured experimentation. The center of SPS attention is always **the problem**. This single-minded orientation prevents a possibly costly preoccupation with particular methods or techniques.

Since we do suggest which methods are useful at which points in the problem solving process, we have included descriptions of many problem solving tools, statistical or otherwise. Readers are forewarned, however, that it was not our intent to write a textbook and hence we have tried to keep such discussions as brief as possible. For readers who need more depth, we have added references at the end of each chapter.

When asked to classify this book, we refer to it as a **management** book. Because managers are usually in the position to commit time and resources to problem solving projects, we are eager to get their attention. Probably of greatest use to managers are the first three chapters. They describe the practical and philosophical underpinnings of Statistical Problem Solving, summarize its stages and steps, and suggest how to conduct problem selection. Some managers may prefer to skim over the more technical content of Chapters 4–8, but we urge them to read Chapter 9 on implementing solutions. Even the best investigations and the most promising solutions are useless if implementation isn't given full management support.

Practitioners seeking better direction for their problem solving efforts will want to study the entire book. Following our presentation on how to use SPS in the body of the book, Appendix A describes actual experiences with SPS. These case studies are intended as useful snapshots of "SPS in action" to clarify many finer points that come alive only while solving real problems.

One of the strengths of SPS is how it facilitates communication on the complexity of a problem situation. Once problem solvers can productively communicate about a problem, the situation becomes simpler. Another strength—which our reviewers tell us to stress—is the **hands-on, workable** nature of SPS. Employees at all levels in an organization can learn to use SPS with little technical training.

When you start on a problem, you never know how complicated it will be to solve. As the saying goes, simple solutions seldom are. But even when the problem turns out to be an easy one to resolve, SPS guides you down the shortest and most economical path to an effective solution.

Acknowledgments

In many ways a book is like a stage play. The authors—the actors on the stage—are only one part of the total production. Although only the authors' names appear on the cover, the support and contributions of many friends and associates are essential in completing the work.

Darlene Copp played a central role as our editor. Her persistence and encouragement kept the momentum going as we juggled the many demands of careers and families. She frequently researched information for us. Her many ideas about the book's organization and features will aid our readers. Most important was her ability to transform our often weak and ambiguous expressions into clear and vivid prose. Finally, she guided the major task of transforming the manuscript into the final product.

We received tremendous help from Raj and Rina Bajaria in creating all the figures and tables. Their unfailing patience with our constant revisions and corrections was always appreciated. Raj's technical expertise helped us take productive advantage of the latest technology in producing the manuscript. Rina's skill in creating figures was exceptional. Niru Bajaria was especially helpful in preparing and getting manuscripts to our reviewers, as well as maintaining communication with them when we were unavailable.

Over a period of three years, a loyal and understanding group of colleagues carefully reviewed our manuscript as it developed—chapter by chapter, figure by figure, table by table. Though we missed our own deadlines, we were never held up waiting for their comments. The importance of our reviewers' improvement suggestions and positive feedback cannot be overestimated. As users of Statistical Problem Solving, they gave us the essential view from the trenches, keeping us honest and tempering our claims. These special friends are:

Marty Gettings
Director of Marketing, Datamyte Division of Allen-Bradley
A Rockwell International Company

Thomas Hughes
Director of Quality and Productivity Technology
Allied-Signal, Automotive Sector

Rob Kinnear
Quality Engineer
A-line Plastics

Vance Shutes
Quality Control Manager
R & B Manufacturing

Gary R. Spooner
Quality Assurance Manager
Walker Manufacturing Company

Dennis Swary
Quality Manager
Owens-Illinois, Closure Division

We next gratefully acknowledge a second group of reviewers, those who read the complete manuscript a few months before typesetting began. Their willing support along with their favorable responses propelled us through the final stages of book production. They are:

Professor George E. P. Box
Center for Quality and Productivity Improvement
University of Wisconsin—Madison

Conrad A. Fung
Asst. Professor, Department of Industrial Engineering
University of Wisconsin—Madison

James S. Gleason
Chairman and President
Gleason Corporation
O. P. Gupta
Vice President, Manufacturing Operations and Total Quality
Zexel-Gleason USA, Inc.

William H. Mixon
Vice President of Manufacturing
CR Industries

Carl E. Raglin
Chicago General Manager
Union Camp Corporation, Container Division

We especially appreciate the contribution of Conrad Fung, whose insightful and pointed remarks after a painstaking review of the manuscript helped us to make several significant clarifications in the book.

We are thankful as well to the many students of SPS courses, the employees of Holley Automotive Division, and Multiface clients, in particular those of Pennsylvania Pressed Metals, the Container Division of Union Camp, and Allied-Signal, Automotive Sector. By sharing their problems with us, they gave us opportunities to learn more effective problem solving. Their questions helped us to refine our own thoughts about SPS. By working on their real problems while writing this book, we were reminded not to emphasize theory but to stay focused on practical results and the bottom line.

A special acknowledgment is reserved for the Federal-Mogul Engine and Transmission Products plant in St. Johns, Michigan. It was here that the process of Statistical Problem Solving was initiated. Since that time, Federal-Mogul Corporation facilities have contributed in a major way to develop SPS practice.

Finally, we must gratefully recognize the patience of our children—Seema and Sona Bajaria and Matthew and Kevin Copp. The book stole countless hours of time away from our families. We hope that in some way our book will contribute to a brighter future for them and their generation.

Hans J. Bajaria
Richard P. Copp

Chapter 1

Meeting
A Need

Issue:	Any quality improvement program requires solving problems at some stage. Problem solving can be expensive and frustrating. What is needed is an efficient and effective strategy to identify and solve problems.
SPS Response:	Statistical Problem Solving (SPS) is a disciplined process for finding the least-cost, straightest path to problem resolution.
SPS Result:	Permanent problem solutions with virtually zero expense for investigation and minimal implementation expense.

Improvement and Problem Solving
Go Hand in Hand

Everywhere we look, there is the need for improvement—in products, in services, and even in the quality of decision making. When pursuing improvement, we inevitably meet obstacles, which makes problem solving an integral part of any improvement effort. It follows that effective problem solving skills are essential for successful improvement programs. In fact, there is a growing awareness that problem solving skills are in short supply throughout business and industry.

Several improvement systems with an emphasis on product quality emerged during the eighties. In striving to adopt any of these, companies formed improvement teams and carefully followed prescribed steps, yet their success has been erratic. Sound strategies for company-wide quality improvement are well established. The challenge remaining is to successfully apply problem solving methods within a total improvement framework.

To find solutions to the toughest improvement problems, an effective diagnostic process is necessary.

Problems Waiting for Solutions

> We are all continually faced with a series of great opportunities, brilliantly disguised as insoluble problems.
>
> — John Gardner

Major technological and administrative problems remain unsolved throughout industry. They are solvable, but too often those responsible for improvement are uncertain how to deal with challenging problems.

Unfortunately, many problem solvers believe their success rate cannot be improved upon. Any attempt to scrutinize their problems, perhaps with the use of scientific tools, meets with their resistance. Common objections are "we already tried that," "what do you know about this anyway," "you don't understand the situation," and "there are too many variables!"

Troubleshooters are sometimes successful by virtue of common sense or by playing their hunches. But what about the persistent, wearisome problems that don't go away no matter how many hunches are played out? These are the chronic problems— typically accepted as unavoidable.

Besides chronic problems, many others exist that are not even perceived as problems. These are "hidden" problems, and as detrimental to the continuous improvement goal as chronic problems. We fall back on euphemisms to rationalize the existence of such problems. "Nature of the beast," "state of the art," "acceptable yield," and "industry standard" are some of the common excuses for not achieving real improvement.

Still other problems are "buried" in traditional accounting procedures. For instance, scrap may be viewed as a problem only if it exceeds the budgeted (allowable) amount for scrap. Or, the amount of cash tied up in accounts receivable may be viewed as no worse than it has been historically.

Because resources for problem solving are limited in any company, accurate selection of the top problems is crucial to achieving improvement. Selecting which chronic problems to attack first and uncovering hidden problems are major concerns in Statistical Problem Solving.

Hunches Versus Science

Trial-and-error problem solving may from time to time bear spectacular successes, but more often than not it will result in failure.[1]

The difference between the occasional lucky success and consistently solid success is the difference between "hunching" and science. Conventional problem solving efforts often boil down to the pursuit of a hunch. Following their hunches, some troubleshooters claim a fairly high success rate. Nevertheless, hunching cannot be taught to others by any precise discipline.

Ask two intelligent people about the nature of any problem, and you will get two different answers. Likewise, for a well-defined problem, ask them for a solution, and you will get two different ones, each containing some truth. *Only a systematic, disciplined approach for defining and solving problems will consistently and efficiently reveal the real nature of a problem and its best possible solution.*

Relying primarily on instinct, the huncher hits upon a solution, often involving new hardware, and then sets out to *prove* the solution works through collecting and studying output data. It might be said that hunchers investigate by implementation. Their investigations become very biased since, once money has been spent, they must defend their solutions. In contrast, the scientific problem solver collects and analyzes data from existing hardware; if new hardware is indicated, analysis can support its likelihood of solving the problem. The cost of implementation is justified *before* that cost is incurred.

Figure 1.1 illustrates the very different paths followed by scientific problem solving versus hunch-based problem solving. The scientific path is superior in that (1) its solution has a higher probability of success, (2) there is considerably less cost involved, and (3) if an attempt fails, the scientific problem solver systematically moves to the next step, whereas the huncher becomes discouraged or defensive. With hunching, each hunch carries with it a price tag. Along the scientific path, a minor inves-

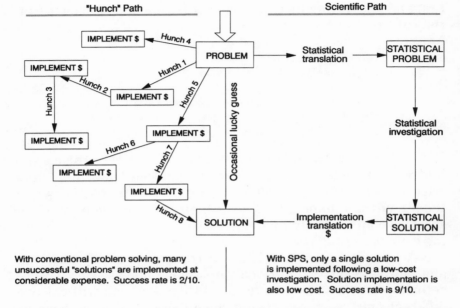

Figure 1.1 Contrasting the different paths followed by scientific problem solving versus hunch-based problem solving

tigation expense may be incurred, but no implementation dollars are spent until after a solution is found.

Statistical Thinking

To guess is cheap. To guess wrongly is expensive.
—Chinese proverb

It must be clear how wasteful and inadequate hunching is in eradicating deep-seated, complex problems. **A major reason for continuing problems is the general lack of statistical thinking.**

At its simplest level, statistical thinking refers to the use of data to analyze and solve problems. Without a reliance on data, problem solving is hunch-based. At a more difficult level, statistical knowledge is needed to understand why there is a problem with the product.

Our first awareness of any problem is typically diffused, with bothersome symptoms capturing our attention. By beginning problem solving with facts (data), statistical thinking clarifies our understanding of the problem. At each successive step of the problem solving process, statistical principles act like a funnel, directing the process towards a successful solution.

Problems are either acute or chronic—an important distinction in understanding why some problems are more difficult to solve than others. With *acute* problems, the process was producing consistently good product, then "something changed" and suddenly there was a problem. This is commonly termed a problem of **instability**.

Discovering what changed may take some detective work. Any systematic problem solving procedure is usually up to this task. Occasionally, however, an acute problem may involve a complex combination of variables. Such complexity is characteristic of all chronic problems.

In the real world, the majority of problems are *chronic*. The process has *always* produced some bad product. This is a problem of **incapability**. Unraveling the complexity at the root of chronic problems requires more sophisticated thinking than is adequate for most acute problems. **Statistical thinking discovers the variables that combine favorably or unfavorably to create good or bad product.**

In Statistical Problem Solving we call this the science of "backward thinking." We begin an investigation where we see the problem—with the product—and then "back in" to the process. "Forward thinking" relies primarily on common sense, engineering principles, and practical experience, which collectively represent knowledge of the process. Very often process knowledge is sufficient to solve problems. However, when you are aware of a problem but have no clue how to solve it, statistical thinking refines process knowledge and accelerates common sense.

The Strategy of Statistical Problem Solving

Statistical Problem Solving (SPS) is a systematic process for finding the most efficient path to problem resolution and permanent improvement.[2] The following contributors form an essential foundation for SPS success:

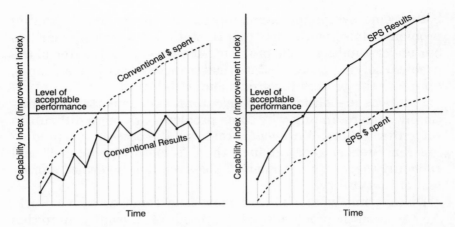

Figure 1.2   Illustrating the relative difference between conventional and statistical problem solving for continuous improvement

- the combined experience of a team,
- product and process knowledge,
- the discriminating use of statistical methods,
- an adherence to economical execution principles in the problem environment, and
- participant learning simultaneous with problem solving.

Figure 1.2 contrasts the success of typical, nonscientific problem solving with the success of Statistical Problem Solving. As illustrated, the conventional approach produces erratic results, marked by occasional success. SPS, however, produces steady incremental improvement. The figure highlights another very important difference between the two approaches: By confusing investigation and implementation, conventional problem solving can be very costly. In contrast, SPS always works with a least-cost philosophy.

As an improvement strategy, Statistical Problem Solving incorporates several strengths:

- SPS combines mathematical efficiencies with business-oriented execution methods.
- SPS creates a useful synthesis of existing quality improvement tools to increase the rate of problem solving success.
- SPS eliminates the tendency for collecting and analyzing massive amounts of data, reducing the cost of investigation.

- SPS minimizes interruptions to production and does not waste process output.
- SPS seeks a solution *first* within the existing process or system, reducing the cost of solution implementation.
- SPS quantifies the degree of expected improvement before spending valuable resources to carry out a solution.
- SPS improves understanding of the process, allowing better control of process output variation.
- SPS facilitates productive teamwork and creates a unified direction within employee-involvement groups.

None of the individual methods in Statistical Problem Solving are new. What makes SPS unique is a structured approach to problems that strategically integrates the best scientific tools available and insists on economical execution.

The Stages of Statistical Problem Solving

At the core of Statistical Problem Solving are its *five steps* for handling the many variables that characterize most problems. These steps are introduced in the next chapter, and then each step is treated individually in subsequent chapters. Effective problem solving, however, begins before the first SPS step and continues after the last SPS step. To capture the entire problem solving process, we use *three stages*:

1. Product Stage
2. Process Stage
3. Implementation Stage

Problems are selected and defined during the first stage. The focus of this stage is on *product*, whether that be goods, services, information, or performance.

Selecting a problem is primarily a management responsibility, as explained in Chapter 3. Defining the selected problem becomes the first task of the SPS team. Whenever the team uncovers several subproblems, however, and which one to attack first is not clear-cut, management should participate in the definition step. Selecting the subproblem to solve should have management concurrence. (Subproblems are discussed in Chapters 3 and 4.)

Effective problem selection and definition is crucial to successful problem solving. In defining the problem, it is determined to be acute or chronic. Properly executed, this stage may consume as much as fifty percent of problem solving attention. If the product stage is neglected or rushed through, problem solvers may find themselves backtracking to the first stage before they are successful in resolving the problem. In addition, the clarity created by thorough problem definition makes the path to the solution straightforward or sometimes even makes the solution itself obvious.

The problem is typically solved during the second stage. The troublesome *process* becomes the focus of an investigation for which the SPS team is responsible.

SPS steps are designed to discover and verify which variables, or combination of variables, are causing the problem. To use a familiar investigative analogy, suspects are identified, interrogated, and tried. At the end of the trial, guilt is pronounced and the culprits are sentenced. Sentencing in the problem solving sense means rehabilitation—discovering how to control variables to enhance the process.

The third stage ensures follow through. Only through a creative *implementation* will the solution discovered during the second stage result in permanent improvement. Responsibility for the successful completion of this stage reverts back to management. The SPS team decides how to translate the statistical solution they discovered into an actual, verifiable solution, but management must support the implementation by committing the necessary resources.

Figure 1.3 depicts how the five steps and three stages of Statistical Problem Solving relate. Their combination forms a complete problem solving process for continuous improvement. This process may be cyclic in nature. Insufficient clarity at the end of the product stage, lack of a solution after the process stage, or difficulty during implementation will require problem solvers to loop back to a previous stage/step and continue the problem solving effort. (See the glass blemish case study in Appendix A.) Figure 1.3 also suggests the primary and overlapping responsibilities for each stage.

The *purpose* of each problem solving stage has a convenient medical equivalent.

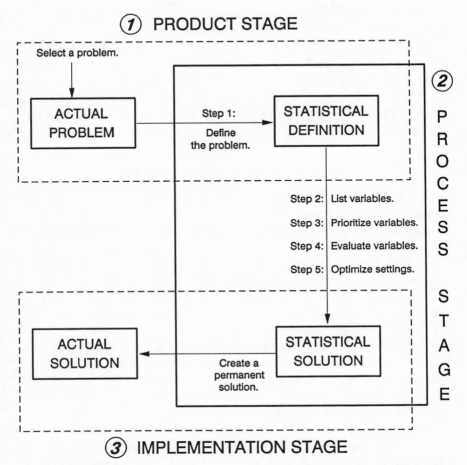

Figure 1.3   SPS stages and steps combine to form a comprehensive problem solving process for proactive companies: Broken lines enclose management responsibilities. Solid line encloses team responsibilities.

Product stage: Describe the sickness.
Process stage: Determine the treatment.
Implementation stage: Follow the treatment.
Each stage relies predominantly on one particular discipline to accomplish its purpose. In brief, these are:
Product stage: Statistical process control
Process stage: Experimentation
Implementation stage: Behavioral science

Successive chapters describe how these sciences aid the purposes and challenges of problem solving.

SPS is designed to move through the problem solving stages without having to know each science in depth. The emphasis is always on *using* the science. As will be stated often throughout the book, SPS focuses on the problem, not on the techniques. In its use of backward thinking, SPS relies on the use of all sciences and all skills as needed.

The SPS Approach to Training

Introducing SPS into an organization naturally means some education and training. When people are expected to do new things, they must be taught what to do, how to do it, and why it is important.

Training is a strategic concern that will greatly influence the success or failure of any new program. Many companies follow a path they perceive as rapid and simple: hire a trainer for mass training sessions. Management hopes the training will take hold and their personnel will practice the new skills. But, once back on the job and faced with challenges, most employees abandon the new skills and revert back to their former ways. Then the training was essentially a wasted expense. Even worse, big promises followed by false starts alienate employees and damage management's credibility.

Training in problem solving actually offers some unique challenges and opportunities. Real problems are seldom simple, yet classroom training examples are typically oversimplified. A classroom setting can never provide instruction in the kind of real-life examples that students will eventually face. Thus, on their own, the students will be ill-equipped to deal with real live problems.

Understanding how adults learn represents another training challenge. Most adults must see immediate relevance in what they are learning. If they don't, they will lose interest or even resist learning. Classroom examples from a different industry will usually fail to hold their attention, or examples from a different discipline will seem irrelevant to them. For instance, a manufacturing engineer in a forging plant may hear an example from an assembly process and think, "That's an easy application for assembly, but forging is far more complex." Or, a design engineer hearing about a manufacturing problem may think, "That's a good technique for manufacturing, but it won't work for a design problem."

Training is a significant expense, no matter how the training is conducted. An instructor must be paid, materials purchased, and students lose time from their jobs. Travel expenses may also be incurred. Therefore, training dollars must be spent productively. Training should be treated as an investment; results should have an immediate and continued positive impact on the bottom line.

The SPS approach to training can offer immediate benefits to a company. Real problems can be solved *during* training. The training of small groups focused on solving a real problem is far more effective than hours in the classroom hearing about problem solving methods. As the familiar Chinese proverb goes:

> Tell me, I will forget.
> Show me, I may remember.
> Involve me, and I will understand.

Every problem is unique, yet all problems have common elements that present opportunities to teach problem solving principles and the SPS process.

SPS training begins after selecting a problem and forming a team. Initially, the SPS facilitator gives the team a very brief overview of the SPS approach and steps. Then, as opportunities arise while working on the problem, the SPS facilitator briefly explains SPS concepts and tools. Training segments might thus include a five-minute explanation of an execution principle or twenty minutes to introduce a specific statistical technique.

Explanations should not become bogged down in mathematical details nor drift away from the specific issue at hand. Team members will typically show interest in methods applicable to their problem, but will become impatient hearing about unrelated procedures. **Solving the problem is always the primary focus of the training.**

The outcome? A problem solved, money saved, and a group of employees trained to be more effective problem solvers.

Figure 1.4 represents the *infusive approach* to training used by SPS. A pilot team is formed and solves a problem. The initial

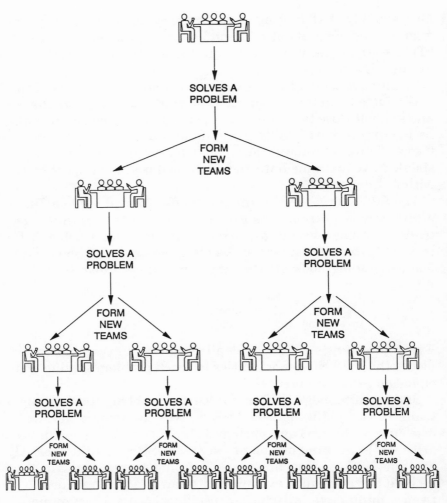

Figure 1.4   People learn SPS by doing, giving rise to more teams.

team members become the core members of new teams, exposing more people to SPS. As those teams solve their problems, they in turn form additional teams. In this gradual manner, SPS is infused into an organization. Results are experienced as people are effectively trained.

Over time, individuals will emerge who have a special talent for leading SPS. They are candidates for the role of SPS facilitator and would benefit from additional training in statistical methods and problem solving. Such training is selective and therefore strategic.

Conclusion

If most companies are experts in their particular product, why do they have problems? Expertise alone is obviously not enough to either prevent or solve problems. Problem solving skills and methods are also needed.

Many quality improvement experts have dismissed the subject of solving problems by equating it with the waste of fire fighting. Instead, they advocate problem prevention within the context of various improvement programs. No one can deny the value of prevention. As long as we live in an imperfect world, however, problems and problem solving will be inevitable.

The methods for problem *solving* and problem *preventing* are the same. But before you know how to effectively prevent problems, you have to learn how to solve them.

Easy problems take little more than patience and common sense to solve. The more organized that problem solvers are in tackling problems, the more successful their results are likely to be. That's why problem solving systems with prescribed steps are helpful. Statistical Problem Solving (SPS) offers several advantages over most commonly used problem solving systems.

In its first stage (**product**), SPS guides the problem solving team through a thorough description of the selected problem. The problem is recognized as either acute (a problem of instability) or chronic (a problem of incapability). The precision of the definition step affects how successful the rest of the SPS process is. In fact, problems are often solved in this initial stage.

In its second stage (**process**), SPS guides the team in identifying and examining the many variables affecting the troublesome process. Most problem solving systems include a step for determining root causes, but offer little assistance in how to accomplish that. SPS provides a systematic process, the appropriate tools, and economical guidelines.

In its third stage (**implementation**), SPS advocates creativity and long-term thinking to ensure that verified solutions are permanent.

What's been missing in many improvement programs is a

13

structured, scientific process for dealing with complexity. Once that process is mastered, problem solving can be applied to a whole range of improvement opportunities presented *in the form of problems.*

Statistical Problem Solving can successfully tackle the difficult problems, often described as chronic or unsolvable. Genuine improvement can be realized once these types of problems are eradicated. Describing the uniqueness of SPS and how it works is the subject of this book.

References

1. Steven R. Phillips and William H. Bergquist, *Solutions: A Guide to Better Problem Solving*, San Diego: University Associates, Inc., 1987, page 8.

2. Hans Bajaria saw the need for a systematic way to solve chronic problems in the early years of his consulting practice. In 1981 he began to evolve and use a methodology for efficiently handling difficult problems. In 1987 Bajaria and SPS practitioner Richard Copp co-authored a paper to introduce Statistical Problem Solving as a proven improvement tool: "Statistical Problem Solving (SPS)," Technical Paper 870274, 1987 Society of Automotive Engineers (SAE) International Congress & Exposition, February 23–27, Detroit.

Chapter 2

Dealing With Complexity

Issue:	Problems occur when there is too much variation in the output of a process. Discovering the actual sources of excessive variation out of the many possible sources is the central challenge of problem solving.
SPS Response:	A five-step process begins by defining the problem in terms of unwanted variation. A systematic path is then followed to determine which variables and their combinations are creating the undesirable variation. To shorten the path to problem resolution, the most strategic problem solving tactic is chosen as soon as possible. Tactics run from tightening control of an existing system to creating a new system.
SPS Result:	Sources of undesirable variation are understood in the shortest possible time.

Reducing Variation

Most of us understand intuitively that an essential aspect of good quality is consistency. We expect that certain products are always on the shelf at the supermarket, that we will generally receive prompt service at the bank, and that each new roll of film we buy will produce accurate colors. Consistency means that the output of a process or the delivery of a service is predictable and therefore manageable.

Those companies able to deliver products and services that consistently meet their customers' expectations are most successful. Internally, those organizations whose systems and processes are predictable experience greater productivity. *Many problems occur precisely because results are inconsistent—that is, the results have excessive variation.*

During the 1980s it became universally recognized that reducing variation is synonymous with improving quality. **When the causes of variation are understood, problem solving is most successful.** Understanding variation allows us to control and reduce undesirable variation, thereby producing the consistency associated with excellence.

All products, whether goods or services, have features or attributes that are important to the user. Such properties might be the feel of a fabric, the time it takes to receive a mail order, the accuracy of a bank statement, or the sharpness of a television picture. Producers have developed targets for the features of their products that they believe will satisfy their customers' expectations. Both a target value and some acceptable range of deviation from that target are usually specified.

For instance, a manufacturer may set a target to respond to product complaints on the same day they are received, but will allow up to five business days to respond. An automobile manufacturer will specify a target effort for depressing an accelerator pedal with some allowable deviation from that target. If too little effort is required, the weight of the driver's foot will cause excessive speed; if too much effort is required, the driver's foot will quickly tire.

For problems of excessive variation, the scientific approach is especially effective in improving the consistency of existing technology. Such improvement is crucial because the same level of technology is available among the competitors within most industries. Those who optimize their existing systems and processes, however, become the most competitive.

Even if new technology is found necessary, it too must be optimized, based on a whole new set of variables to understand. In aiming for improvement, why prematurely invest in new technology when better management of existing process technology can achieve the same end?

The Problem of "Too Many Variables!"

A typical initial reaction to a problem situation is to express frustration with "too many variables!" Many shoot-from-the-hip problem solvers do not make a systematic effort to deal with the variables at all. They simply take random shots at the problem and hope that one of their shots will be successful.

More organized problem solvers embark on a process-of-elimination course. They think the most scientific way to proceed is to hold everything else constant while changing one variable at a time. Once they have tried each variable in a series, they believe that all the variables have been examined. In fact, however, only a fraction of the possible variable *combinations* have been tried.

The process-of-elimination approach is similar to trying to open a lock with a single key. Each key on the ring is tried until the one that opens the lock is found. Occasionally, this effort will work. Most problems, however, resemble combination locks. They require that many variables be tried in the correct combination to open the lock. A major limitation of typical problem solving is its reliance on trial-and-error methods. By missing important variable combinations, there is a good chance a problem solution may never be found.

Table 2.1 illustrates how it is possible to try all variables, yet miss most of their combinations. To improve the yield of a chemical process, four variables are important: time, temperature, catalyst concentration, and rate of agitation. If the problem solver decides to look at each variable at the standard setting and one alternative setting, there are sixteen possible combinations.

The problem solver begins by gathering data on the yield under current process conditions (Cell #1). Then, while holding the other three variables constant, a test is conducted at the longer time, moving from Cell #1 to Cell #2. Next, the temperature is changed while holding the other three variables constant, moving from Cell #2 to Cell #4. The problem solver continues in a similar manner until each variable has been tried at its alternative setting and data are available for Cells 1, 2, 4, 12, and 16.

Even in this straightforward progression, only five of the possible 16 combinations have been tried. If the problem solver's budget allows only a limited number of tests, there is a more valid set of combinations—based on a working knowledge of statistical experimental design—than the problem solver may have selected, but there are also tradeoffs. Statistical Problem Solving minimizes the tradeoffs of trying only some of the possible variable combinations, as will be discussed in Chapter 6, Prioritizing Variables.

Table 2.1 Conventional investigation of four variables shown against the background of all their possible combinations

		Temperature = low		Temperature = high	
		Time = 5 min.	Time = 10 min.	Time = 5 min.	Time = 10 min.
Agitation rate = fast	5% Catalyst Concentration	Current Process Cell # 1	First Try Cell # 2	Cell # 3	Second Try Cell # 4
	1% Catalyst Concentration	Cell # 5	Cell # 6	Cell # 7	Cell # 8
Agitation rate = slow	5% Catalyst Concentration	Cell # 9	Cell # 10	Cell # 11	Third Try Cell # 12
	1% Catalyst Concentration	Cell # 13	Cell # 14	Cell # 15	Fourth Try Cell # 16

⬚ Missed combinations during an investigation

When relying on the typical problem solving mode, most problem solvers do not even proceed in the straightforward manner of the above example. Confusion often develops due to their haphazard manner of conducting tests. For instance, hunchers frequently make major changes in their strategy in the middle of an investigation. Pressures such as time, new information, "remembering" other important variables, or failure to qualify their measurement method may affect their efforts. Confused investigations may be further aggravated by variables interacting and yielding unexpected results.

Our chemical process example (Table 2.1) limited the investigation to only four variables, with each considered at just one alternative setting. With more than four variables and the possibility of many alternative settings, the number of variable combinations rises exponentially and rapidly becomes unmanageable.

The distinct power of Statistical Problem Solving (SPS) lies in its ability to handle the unmanageable. The SPS prioritization step is designed to deal efficiently with "too many variables" by reducing them to a manageable number. Experienced problem solvers know that only a few of the "too many" are important, and only those top few require thorough evaluation.

One company that has incorporated Statistical Problem Solving into its overall quality improvement program explains why:

> Using SPS, GCG partners can understand and work on the multiple variables that normally interact to add complexity to a process. This approach connects the fundamentals expressed by leading statistical experts in a way that allows us to apply these principles simply and effectively in all functions and at all levels.[1]

The Steps of Statistical Problem Solving

Statistical Problem Solving strategically applies statistical methods to reduce inherent variation in process output. Leading quality experts attribute at least 85% of quality deficiencies to chronic problems (common cause variation).[2] SPS successfully attacks that 85%. Acute problems (special cause variation) are responsible for the remaining 15%. When these have no obvious solutions, SPS successfully attacks them as well.

As an improvement science, Statistical Problem Solving deals with process variables by identifying, prioritizing, and evaluating them, followed by optimizing their approximate best settings. Through five logical steps, SPS rapidly finds the variable combination to solve the problem at hand. These steps, and the corresponding chapters in which they are discussed, are:

1. DEFINING the problem in statistical terms (Chapter 4).
2. LISTING all variables suspected of contributing to the problem (Chapter 5).
3. PRIORITIZING the suspect variables for investigation (Chapter 6).
4. EVALUATING the top few prioritized variables and their interacting effects (Chapter 7).

5. OPTIMIZING the process by finding the best variable settings (Chapter 8).

The strategy of SPS depends upon a *systematic, disciplined process* in which results for each step must exist before moving on to the next step. As a consequence, each SPS step must be carried out with considerable care.

At the same time, an important goal in problem solving should be to follow the shortest possible path in finding a solution. Each step of Statistical Problem Solving has the power to shorten the problem solving path. Before reaching Step 5, the problem solution often becomes obvious to the team. Table 2.2 illustrates this concept. In Example 1, for instance, problem definition on a grinding problem revealed the cause was obviously an unstable

Table 2.2 Each SPS step has the power to shorten the problem solving path. (i.e., Not all problems require strict execution of all SPS steps.)

SPS STEP	EXAMPLE 1: Grinding Operation with 10 % scrap	EXAMPLE 2: Chemical Process with 80 % yield	EXAMPLE 3: Mechanical Assembly with 10 % failing final test
1. Define the problem.	Use SPC chart to identify unstable condition due to poor adjustment strategy.	Existing data shows unacceptable yield. p-chart is in control.	Scrap and rework costs at end of assembly line are stable and unacccceptable.
2. List suspect variables.		Brainstorming yields 4 variables: time, temperature, agitation rate, and catalyst concentration.	Cause-and-effect diagram is used to list variables. 12 dimensions are on the list.
3. Prioritize the variables list.			Use of subjective rating and ranking narrows the list from 12 to 4 dimensions to evaluate.
4. Evaluate variables and interactions.		Designed experiment executed to evaluate variable effects.	Disassemble and measure components. Use multiple regression to evaluate dimensions.
5. Optimize variable settings.			Monte Carlo simulation to find optimal dimensions and tolerances.
Solution Implemented.	New standard operating procedure using NLG stabilizes process, 100% pass rate.	Process is run with variables at new settings, yield up to 97%.	Component part blueprints are changed to yield 100 % good assemblies.

target due to untimely adjustment by the operator. New adjustment rules using narrow limit gaging (NLG)[3] solved the problem without continuing through the next four SPS steps.

The goal of SPS is a solution to the problem, *not* the completion of all five steps.

Deciding on the Problem Solving Tactic

Within the context of strategic problem solving, a tactic is *the mode of procedure for achieving a desired end*. Problem solvers should be aware of four basic tactics:

    1. Control the existing system.
    2. Optimize the existing system.
    3. Redesign the existing system.
    4. Create a new system.

Knowing which tactic fits the situation can productively influence each of the five SPS steps, *shortening the time it takes to solve the problem*. The problem solving tactic should thus be decided on as soon as possible. The following example illustrates how the tactical approach affects competitiveness.

As represented in Figure 2.1, a welding process is producing output where strength is an important product attribute. There is a problem with the existing technology as currently managed

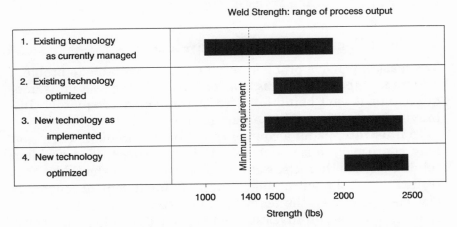

Figure 2.1 Relative improvement as a result of better understanding of process variables and process technology changes

21

(#1). A substantial portion of the output, ranging between 1000 and 2000 lbs., falls below the minimum requirement of 1400 lbs. If the existing technology is optimized, the process output will range from 1500 to 2000 lbs. The optimized process (#2) is obviously better than the original process (#1) since it does not produce any output below the 1400 lb. minimum requirement. **What makes the output range narrower in the optimized process is better understanding and control of its variables.**

Hunchers might solve this problem by implementing new technology (#3 in Figure 2.1). Although the new technology solves the problem, it means a major implementation expense, along with a considerable delay in realizing the solution. If optimized (#4), the new technology far exceeds the requirement. From a competitiveness perspective, optimizing the existing process is the best alternative since the solution occurs immediately upon understanding the process variables, without an additional investment.

The problem solving tactic can be discussed as a conclusion to Step 1 (definition) or at the start of Step 2 (listing). If the tactical approach is clear, identifying it results in a more efficient listing of suspect variables. If an early choice of a tactic is not possible, the decision is deferred until later. In subsequent chapters we will suggest how a problem solving tactic may be selected at different points in the investigation.

Tactic 1: Control the Existing System

The least expensive problem solving tactic available to problem solvers is *improved process control*. The existing system is adequate, but it isn't being followed or controlled adequately. Improving control is most often applicable to small problems.

To illustrate, using a control chart during problem definition may confirm a cause that was already suspect. The problem solving path is then clear-cut: The proven cause should be controlled in a foolproof manner. If a permanent control scheme is also clear-cut, then the team can jump straight to implementation. If, however, an investigation is needed to determine workable process control methods, then the team begins listing variables, SPS Step 2.

For one manufacturing problem, interpreting a control chart pattern revealed that ink viscosity was linked to print density. What was not clear, however, was the variable or variables responsible for the inconsistent viscosity. Was it the ink quality, amount of water added, agitation variables, or other variables? An SPS investigation of suspect variables was needed to determine how to control the process better.

In another manufacturing problem, a machine counted 25 pieces at a time for bundling. Most of the time the machine was accurate; but when the count was off, two consecutive bundles were affected. For example, a pattern of 25, 26, 24, 25 might appear. Over time, a direct link was observed between an occasional pause of the rollers that advanced the bundles and the off-count bundles. No further investigation was needed. Regular lubrication of the rollers was implemented as an effective solution.

Tactic 2: Optimize the Existing System

Control charts may reveal in-control conditions, but a mismatch exists between product specifications and process capability. "Sometimes it works and sometimes it doesn't" is a colloquialism to describe this problem condition. The majority of the output is acceptable, but not all of it.

The challenge in solving this type of problem is to unlock the combinations of variables responsible for both good and bad output. A large number of problems—and the most difficult—are of this type. The culprit is a gap between the *current* knowledge of correct settings and acceptable ranges for key variables and knowledge of their *optimum* settings and ranges. SPS steps are designed to discover and close this knowledge gap.

Tactic 3: Redesign the Existing System

A process may be defined as the series of steps to perform a task, accepted and understood by all concerned. Processes are often either inadequately defined or never defined at all. This may be especially true as small entrepreneurial businesses grow fast or as big companies or big departments undergo change. With this problem solving tactic, possibilities for *formalizing* the system are considered, and variables are listed (SPS Step 2) accordingly.

Product or process design changes also fall into this category of solutions. An off-target condition while developing a particular product characteristic, such as strength, might necessitate redesigning the product. Or, problem definition may reveal a built-in inadequacy in a machine, calling for a redesign of the system to alleviate the shortcoming.

In one manufacturing application, two papers were glued together to produce a cardboard product. During problem definition it was observed that edges were mismatched due to the operator's habit of "eyeballing" their alignment. A control chart showed that the mismatching occurred throughout consumption of the paper roll. The problem solving team easily determined how to improve the paper matching. The crude eyeballing had to be replaced by a more precise alignment technique.

In some cases, the need for redesign becomes obvious during consideration of the control and optimization tactics. In other instances, the need to redesign the existing system is not certain until after the control and optimization tactics are actually attempted.

Tactic 4: Create a New System

It may become obvious during problem definition that the current technology cannot deliver the desired results. For example, an off-target problem was discovered during a vibration test. The critical component could not be enlarged or reshaped to increase its strength due to space constraints. The problem solving team was forced to consider new materials for the process. They had to move from an inexpensive investigation of *existing* process variables to the much more costly effort of creating *new* variables.

Strategic Considerations

Any particular problem might be solved by more than one of the problem solving tactics. The same problem could be solved equally well, for instance, by improving control of the process or by redesigning the process.

To illustrate, an out-of-control condition was detected by control charting a manufacturing process. Preliminary investigation found that a fixture plate was loosened by the impact of every machine cycle. The problem solving team could have considered this a problem of process control and subsequently concentrated on maintenance variables during their investigation. Or, they could have approached the problem as one of system design. They then would have concentrated on which variables to include in a redesign of the process to prevent the plate from loosening.

The tactics of system design and new technology may also prove equally effective in solving problems. For instance, a forged part was found incapable of meeting a minimum strength requirement. Changing the design could have solved the problem. Or, converting to a powdered metal process, instead of forging, also could have solved the problem.

In selecting among problem solving tactics, strategic concerns can help with the decision making. In general, consider problem solving tactics in this order:

1. **Control the system.** Remove process instability through improved control.
2. **Optimize the system.** Reduce inherent variation by optimizing existing process variables.
3. **Redesign the system.** When neither improved control nor optimization will solve the problem, improve the design of the system.
4. **Create a new system.** If a good design, well controlled and optimized, does not deliver the desired results, then consider new technology.

This order of preference is based on SPS execution principles, to be introduced in later chapters. In short, problem solvers should always first seek an inexpensive route to problem solution. SPS philosophy prevents an investment in new technology before improvements in the existing system are investigated.

The Teamwork Factor

The necessity of a team approach for successful problem solving is illustrated by the well-known story of the five blind men and the elephant. Challenged to describe the elephant, each examined a different part of the beast. The first, holding the tail, said the elephant is like a rope. The second, grasping a leg, stated the elephant is like the trunk of a tree. The third declared that it must certainly be like a fire hose, for he had found the trunk. The fourth believed the elephant was like a tanned hide, for he happened upon an ear. The fifth exclaimed that all the others were wrong! Feeling the elephant's massive chest, he *knew* the elephant to be like a great barrel.

In fact, all five men were both right and wrong. Each man's perception was true, yet an accurate description of the elephant was found only in a synthesis of the experiences of all five.

So it is with effective problem definition and analysis. Each person affected by a problem has a different perspective on the nature of the problem. Their viewpoints are based on their own particular knowledge, experiences, and responsibilities. Since each of these different perspectives contains an element of truth, it is a basic SPS tenet that synthesizing group knowledge leads to effective problem solving. Team effort protects against individual bias.

Recognizing the value of each person's experience provides an additional benefit. By being fully involved in the problem solving process, team members are more likely to fully support implementation of the solution.

Conclusion

Inconsistent results produce problems. Narrowing the range of variation in either products or services is thus a primary improvement goal. In turn, understanding the causes of variation is the fundamental aim of successful problem solving.

Recognizing and dealing with the process variables affecting variation in the output is the nuts-and-bolts challenge of effective problem solving. Often there are many variables, too many for a trial-and-error approach to problem solving. *Combinations* of variables and *interactions* among variables further complicate problem solving. If important variable combinations or interactions are missed during the problem investigation, a solution may elude the problem solving team forever.

Statistical Problem Solving is designed to handle the complexity of chronic problems, as well as many acute problems. It works from the premise that only a few of the many variables affecting a complex problem are important in successfully solving the problem. SPS begins by defining the problem as one of instability (acute) or incapability (chronic). It next identifies, prioritizes, and evaluates the variables causing the undesirable variation at the root of the problem. SPS then works at optimizing the settings of those variables proven to be crucial to a permanent problem resolution. These tasks are distinguished as five steps in the SPS process. How many of the steps are actually needed to solve a problem varies from situation to situation, although most difficult problems require the completion of all five steps.

To find a permanent solution as quickly and efficiently as possible, SPS encourages the selection of a *problem solving tactic* early in the problem investigation. Four basic tactics are available to problem solvers: control, optimize, redesign, or adopt new technology. Improving the existing system through one of the first three tactics is always preferable when using the low-cost SPS approach. For cases when the existing system is inadequate to solve the problem, SPS can help in justifying an investment in new technology to create a new system.

References

1. *Global Manufacturing and Us*, Gleason Components Group (GCG), Summer 1988, page 13.

2. W. Edwards Deming, "On Some Statistical Aids Toward Economic Production" in *Interfaces*, the Institute of Management Sciences, Vol. 5, No. 4, August 1975. Also, J. M. Juran and Frank M. Gryna, Jr., "Quality Improvement—Management-Controllable Defects" in *Quality Planning and Analysis*, 2nd ed., New York: McGraw-Hill, 1980.

3. Ellis R. Ott, "Narrow-limit Gaging" in *Process Quality Control*, New York: McGraw-Hill, 1975.

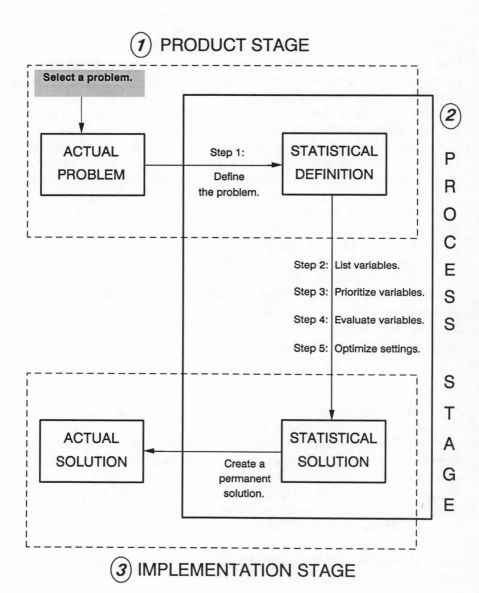

Chapter 3

Selecting
A Problem

Issue:	When many problems exist, which to attack first may not be clear. Further, without a problem selection strategy, critical problems may go unrecognized.
SPS Response:	SPS supports a proactive response to identifying and prioritizing problems to work on. It stresses understanding both instability and incapability as contributors to chronic problems. It uses the p + c + Pareto chart to reveal critical problems.
Result:	Determination of which problem solutions will contribute the most to overall improvement.

Why Look for Problems?

Businesses range from those acutely aware of their problems to those that think they have no problems. Regardless of a company's level of problem awareness, their competition does not stand still. If a business is profitable, someone has an eye on it and is maneuvering to capture a share of its market. Thus, successful companies continuously improve their quality and productivity. And improvement itself is not enough; the improvement must occur at a rate faster than the competition's rate of improvement.[1]

Continuous improvement requires the constant recognition and solution of problems. Poorly directed problem solving, however, only wastes effort and slows the rate of continuous improvement. Problem selecting is just as important as problem solving; it is a preliminary and necessary activity for success in Statistical Problem Solving.

True problem selection is proactive. In *proactive* companies, management is aware of both existing problems and the problems that can arise as the company, its industry, and economic conditions change. In *reactive* companies, problems are attacked only because their symptoms are so acute. Problem solving is little more than fire fighting that controls problem symptoms, but never eliminates problem causes. Reactive companies are typically complacent when acute symptoms are absent. Potentially major problems may be developing that they are totally unaware of.

For instance, one company's final product had a chronic 10% reject rate. Since shippable product could be sold at a price that absorbed the 10% scrap, the problem got little attention. In fact, it was not even perceived as a problem. However, when a competitor entered the market with a superior product, customer expectations were raised. To prevent customer complaints, only final product that met the new industry standard was shipped. As a result, the scrap rate skyrocketed from 10% to 60%! But it was too late to understand and solve the problem. The company was sold and employment dropped to 15% of its original level. The consequences of being reactive instead of proactive can be serious indeed.

How Are Problems Found?

Some problems are obvious. Some are hidden and not recognized until someone does some digging. Other problems are buried, intentionally or unintentionally disguised. Bringing buried problems to light disturbs company politics. No one can measure the loss due to hidden and buried problems, but it is great. Bold leadership is needed to dispel the fear that causes problems to be suppressed.

Table 3.1 lists some of the more common problem areas to look for continuous improvement opportunities. Once proactive companies have solved their obvious problems, they look for less obvious improvement opportunities. For instance, they consider automation for material handling or for real-time process corrections. Or, they investigate how to reduce the number of steps in a process or how to use space more economically. They might

Table 3.1   Problem areas to look for continuous improvement opportunities

Customer Satisfaction	Traditional Loss	Nontraditional Loss	Administration	Business
Nonconforming product	Scrap	Market share	Accuracy of quotations	Regulatory requirements
Late deliveries	Rework	Space utilization	Schedule changes	Import/export regulations
Safety	Damage	Energy resource utilization	Excessive downtime	Market position
Reliability	Waste	Capital equipment utilization	Excessive setup time	Tax burden
Maintainability	Unreported losses of time and material			
Storage requirement		Material utilization	Invoices returned for credit	Balancing expectations among customers, shareholders, and employees
Fraudulent charges		Material movement within facility	Computer report discrepancies	
			Absenteeism	
			Safety incidents	

also look at controlling process variables instead of product variables.

Identifying Problems

In the business world, improvement is measured and seen in financial terms. Ultimately, the bottom line must be favorably affected. If the right problems are selected and solved, the financial index of a business will be favorably changed. But bottom-line performance is too broad to direct the activities in selecting and solving problems. To get there, other indexes are needed.

To select problems *and to track progress*, useful indexes fall into five general categories:

- Business indexes
- Quality indexes
- Productivity indexes
- Cost indexes
- Waste indexes

Business indexes allow one business to be compared to another according to market share, market position, return on sales, or gross profit margin. Quality indexes measure a product relative to customer expectations. Included are the capability indexes (C_p, C_{pk}, etc.), first-time pass rate, and warranty claim rate.

Indexes of productivity measure how fast and efficiently a product is produced. These include machine utilization, inventory turns, uptime, and direct labor hours per unit produced. Cost indexes translate business activities into financial terms. Energy costs, maintenance costs, and burden rates are examples.

The waste indexes encompass all the above categories, but are expressed as loss or failure to reach a goal. Included are scrap rate, unscheduled overtime, rework costs, downtime, and inventory shrink. Any of these indexes can be used to select candidates for improvement.

A word of caution. Almost any single index can be improved at the expense of other indexes. For example, if cost-cutting pressures are strong, a procurement group might re-source business to lower bidders. But if a lower bidder has an inferior product, production efficiency and quality might be adversely affected. The net cost to the business thus increases despite the fact that the cost of purchased materials decreases. Due to a causal link between the two indexes, one goes up as the other goes down. Juran discusses this problem as *suboptimization* within companies.[2]

When a particular index is given new emphasis, other indexes might deteriorate due to simple neglect. Therefore, *a minimum of two indexes* should always be used to track improvement—the specific index to be improved, plus one other.

Ideally, three indexes that reflect local interest, global interest, and financial interest should be tracked. For instance, if problem solving is to increase the first-time pass rate (FTPR) at a final test, the FTPR monitors the local interest and directly measures the SPS team's success. Global interest is monitored by tracking non-routed operations upstream of the final test. The team is thus prevented from improving the pass rate by increasing the cost in the processes that feed the final test. Rework and scrap costs are used to monitor the financial impact of the team's efforts.

The ultimate goal is better performance of the business as a whole, not optimization of one index. Profitability is the true test of effective problem solving and the continuous improvement it supports.

Prioritizing Problems

Walter Shewhart, a pioneer in the field of statistical quality control, advocated that problems causing *instability* be removed before problems occurring under stable conditions. Under unstable conditions, correct operating settings cannot be discovered because underlying scientific laws do not apply in the presence of instability.

Problem solvers must be aware that when instability is present, it is difficult to apply physics, statistics, social science, or *any* science. The Shewhart principle thus helps guide the order in which problems should be solved. The tool for assessing process stability is the statistical process control (SPC) chart; its use is discussed at length in Chapter 4.

If not removed, instability can disrupt problem solving efforts. Work on a chronic problem occurring under stable conditions (a problem of incapability) is easily sidetracked when the system is unstable.

While the Shewhart principle addresses under what conditions problems occur, the Pareto principle addresses the relative extent of various problems. The Pareto principle is also called the 80/20 rule. Simply stated, 80% of the loss due to problems is caused by only 20% of the problems. Consequently, if efforts are directed at the *right* problems, the total impact of *all* problems can be reduced substantially. Attacking only 1 out of 5 problems can bring the greatest return. The tool for determining the critical 20% of problems is the Pareto chart, also discussed in Chapter 4.

For the most effective problem selection, the Pareto principle and the Shewhart principle should be considered together. The combination p + c + Pareto chart, introduced in Chapter 4, is a very useful tool during problem selection. It helps assure that the right problems are worked on.

Quality Versus the Grade of Quality

When improving *quality*, the focus is undesirable variation; the product is not consistently meeting the customer's expectations. The existing design and process must be optimized. When improving the *grade of quality*, what is already meeting customer expectations is raised to the next level of excellence. Product features must be added, materials upgraded, or new technology adopted.

Consider a ballpoint pen. The user wants it to write smoothly without skipping, to be free from leaks, and to have a reasonably useful life. Some users, however, want additional satisfaction from their pen in the form of beauty or prestige. The difference between a $.69 pen and a $69.00 pen is the *grade* of quality. Juran distinguishes between quality of conformance and quality of design.[3]

Whether to improve quality or the grade of quality is a management decision that greatly affects how the creative resources of the business are directed.

Who Selects Problems?

Problem selection should be viewed as an important part of business strategy. The thought processes and tools of problem selection consequently belong in the managerial domain. Problems selected must make good business sense, at a company-wide level. Obligations to customers, employees, shareholders, and society at large must all be considered. Only upper management can integrate all these broad concerns into problem selection.

At the same time, most important problems require cooperation between management levels, among departments, and within departments. Unless problem selection includes collaboration, the required support may not exist.

SPS advocates this organizational strategy: a participative environment to select the problem, an interdisciplinary team to solve it. *In a participative environment, the employees' intimate knowledge of daily operations combines with management's broader perspective.* Employees are encouraged to bring problems to management's attention. Management sets priorities and selects problems based on which solutions will be most beneficial to the business.

When only one level of an organization selects a problem, the outcome is likely to be undesirably biased. For instance, if management alone selects problems, their distance from day-to-day operations may result in their missing important problems. In fact, because employees are often afraid to reveal problems, the problems may actually be hidden from management.

On the other hand, employees may select problems as part of employee involvement programs or by default. Employee selection, however, is usually limited by an incomplete awareness of business performance. The employee perspective may be too narrow to effectively prioritize problem solving resources. Without management direction, employees will naturally work on problems close to them out of self-interest. Problem symptoms that make their jobs unpleasant will get attention. Although they may solve some problems, they may unintentionally divert resources from more pressing problems.

Some form of a management council with representatives from all functional areas can provide the most effective guidance in problem selection. Juran suggests a *quality council*, usually composed of senior managers, to identify problems in a project-by-project improvement approach.[4]

In all companies, problem selection occurs naturally through existing structures, such as monthly staff meetings or daily production meetings. These structures are predisposed to select immediate and urgent problems, real as they are. Through the long-term perspective of a council, however, those problems that promise the greatest improvement impact for the company as a whole can be identified. It is this form of leadership in strategic problem selection that marks proactive companies.

What's the Problem?

A symptom is evidence of the problem.

We experience problems through their symptoms. Some problems require measurement to reveal their symptoms. Valve leakage or small cracks in forgings are examples of symptoms uncovered by testing. Many other problems exhibit symptoms that are available to the senses. They can be seen, felt, smelled, heard, or tasted. No measurement is required to reveal the problem.

For example, in a process that sticks three layers of paper

together, bubbles sometimes appear between the layers. Bubbles are an obvious symptom. They may appear along the edge of the paper, in the middle, or both. They may be evident between layers 1 and 2, between layers 2 and 3, or both.

The symptom, however, rarely tells the whole story. When bubbles are present, it is more likely that delamination will occur. Delamination is a *subproblem* that requires a special test to discover. The delamination can also occur at several locations: at the edges of the paper, in the middle, between layers 1 and 2, or between layers 2 and 3.

There may be many *variables* affecting the subproblems. For instance, the operator may not be maintaining the correct combination of glue, pressure, temperature, and speed. Due to humidity, the moisture content may be too high. Or, glue may be building up on the rollers, causing instability in the process.

For successful problem selection, symptoms, subproblems, and contributing variables must be understood as distinct aspects of the problem. Figure 3.1 illustrates the way in which variables and subproblems combine to create symptoms. With SPS, problems are selected at the symptom level, dissected at the subproblem level, and attacked at the variables level.

Problem selection should begin at the symptom level. Discovering subproblems and the variables affecting them usually requires diagnostic work by an SPS team. This diagnosis occurs during problem definition (SPS Step 1) and listing variables (SPS Step 2).

> **The primary problem is a description of the problem that is broad enough to include all potential subproblems and suspect variables.**

When problem selection begins at the subproblem level, attention may be diverted from the primary problem. This is "the headache" that stops production, offends the customer, or attracts management's attention. Zeroing in on a particular subproblem during problem selection is risky. If that subproblem is the wrong one, the team assigned to it may succeed in solving it, but not necessarily in getting rid of "the headache."

Primary problems and their subproblems are discussed further in Chapter 4 on defining problems.

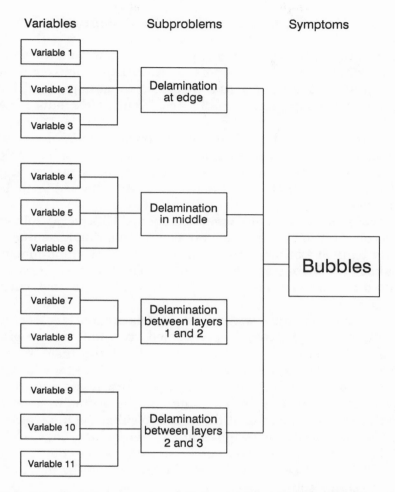

Figure 3.1 Symptoms may result from various subproblems, each of which can be caused by many variables and their combinations.

Symptom and *primary problem* are closely related terms. In many cases, they may be two sides of the same coin. Rather than attempt to distinguish their usage rigidly, it is more helpful to describe their usage operationally. By solving problems, symptoms are removed. Symptom is thus a useful term for problem *selection*, while primary problem is a useful term for problem *assignment*.

How Should Problems Be Assigned?

The SPS team should ordinarily be assigned a primary problem, as experienced by its symptoms, or its most obvious evidence. Depending on the information available to management, however, problem assignment might also occur at the subproblem level.

In our paper production example above, an SPS team was assigned to discover why bubbles were forming between the paper layers. That's problem assignment at the symptom level. But consider a small manufacturing plant plagued with late deliveries.

Discussion by plant management identified several subproblems contributing to the late deliveries, including absenteeism, poorly trained workers, various quality problems, and machine breakdowns. Using the Pareto principle, the managers pinpointed machine breakdowns as responsible for the majority of late deliveries.

Particular machines within the process created *another level of subproblems*. Process logs revealed that Machine 4 broke down most frequently. Further analysis of the machine was needed to understand the variables causing the breakdowns—which was the problem assigned to an SPS team. Figure 3.2 depicts how problem selection began at the symptom level but moved problem assignment down to the subproblem level.

Problems should be assigned at the subproblem level *only* if valid data support the choice of a particular subproblem. In our example, the process logs verified Machine 4 as the focus of an SPS investigation.

What if annoyance with absenteeism had prompted the managers to incorrectly assign it as the subproblem to work on? Even if the SPS team had successfully reduced absenteeism, the late deliveries would have continued since machine breakdowns continued to occur.

In this example, the information needed to identify and prioritize subproblems was known by the plant management. In a large organization, however, a management group would probably not have direct information about possible subproblems. Problem assignment would then remain at the symptom level to insure focus on the primary problem.

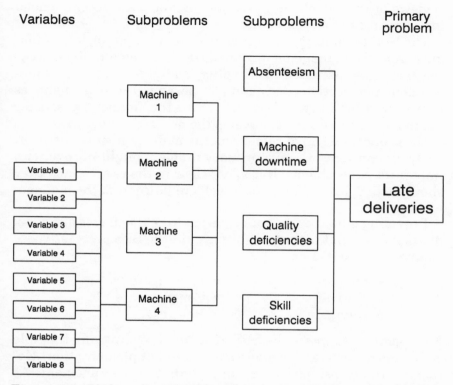

Figure 3.2   If close enough to operations, management can select at the symptom level but assign at the subproblem level.

Technically, problem selection ends when a problem is assigned to an SPS team. Members for the SPS team might be nominated along with the problem assignment, or the team might be formed at the local level. How SPS teams are formed will also be influenced by size of the organization. Team formation is discussed under "The Teamwork Factor" in this chapter.

What Is Management's Role in SPS?

The SPS team operates autonomously as long as the path to the solution remains clear. Interaction between the management council and the SPS team may take different forms. Periodic reviews of the team's progress, for instance, are recommended for companies of any size.

The SPS team might also seek additional input or later guidance from the management council. Deciding on a problem solving tactic (as discussed in Chapter 2) might require the management perspective. For example, perhaps the team believes that new technology is necessary. Are the financial resources available? Is there time to develop the new technology? Answers to these questions must come from the management council. Or, early diagnostic work on a primary problem might uncover two important subproblems. If it is not clear to the team which they should attack first, they should seek guidance from the management council.

Providing guidance and information to SPS teams is one of six distinct *roles* that management plays in the SPS process. These can be summarized as:

- Support.
- Motivate.
- Navigate.
- Participate.
- Congratulate.
- Reward.

Management *supports* the SPS effort by providing any tangible resources needed for the investigation and implementation. *Motivation* comes primarily through words of encouragement. As described above, management *navigates* when it guides decision-making during the problem solving process.

Every manager should *participate* in the SPS process by working on an SPS team at least once. Only through participation will managers really understand how messy problems can be.

To *congratulate* team members is to express appreciation for their efforts. A few sincere words go a long way. Finally, when team members are successful, *reward* should be tangible if it is to be meaningful. Increased profitability through successful improvement projects should be shared.

The Teamwork Factor

POINT ONE: Forming the right team is important for SPS success. The team should not be a group of people thrown together haphazardly because they have extra time to work on the problem. **Careful member selection is crucial because the success of the total problem solving effort depends upon the team members' combined knowledge of the problem.** Having a sufficient base of knowledge to solve the problem must thus be the primary goal in team formation.

Team size depends on the particular problem, the size of the company, and the demands of the investigation. Executing SPS requires different knowledge and information for each step. Consequently, **team membership is dynamic**, with members added and released as need dictates. The team may be relatively large when defining the problem to provide the broad perspective needed then. By the evaluation step, however, the team should be more focused, with the investigation requiring the work of only a few team members. Typically a core team follows the problem from definition through solution implementation. People with special expertise join the team on an ad hoc basis.

For a manufacturing process problem, the full team might consist of a production operator, a quality inspector, a supervisor, a process engineer, a metallurgist/chemist, a design engineer, and a downstream user of the process output. A typical design problem team might include a design engineer, a reliability engineer, a marketing representative, a draftsman, and a quality engineer. For administrative problems, teams may be smaller with at least two members related to a functional area, plus a downstream user of the administrative service. Table 3.2 suggests the possible makeup of teams for manufacturing, design, and administrative problems.

The team's process expertise *combined with SPS skills* refines knowledge of the problem and moves it to the level of understanding needed to permanently solve the problem.

POINT TWO: While knowledge of the process is a prerequisite for team membership, formal training in SPS is not. Instead, teams need an SPS facilitator, someone experienced in the SPS approach and proficient in problem solving skills. The facilitator helps the team work together effectively by: (1) acting as an SPS resource, (2) keeping the team focused on the problem, and (3) functioning as an impartial moderator if disputes arise.

41

Table 3.2 Possible makeup of SPS teams for design, manufacturing, and administrative problems

Team member classification	Design engineering problem e.g., Improve durability	Manufacturing problem e.g., Improve pass rate	Administrative problem e.g., Reduce accounts receivable
	SPS Facilitator*	SPS Facilitator*	SPS Facilitator*
" Upstream supplier "		Material supplier Component supplier Upstream operation setup person*	Order processor* Customer purchasing agent Sales representative
Process managers/ operational personnel	Design engineer* Draftsman*	Operator* Setup person* Supervisor	Billing clerk*
" Downstream user "	Manufacturing engineer* Service engineer	Downstream operation setup person	Customer service representative*
" End user " representative	Marketing representative	Sales engineer Marketing person	
Special experts	Quality engineer* Reliability engineer Packaging engineer	Manufacturing engineer* Maintenance person Metallurgist Inspector Material handler	Computer system expert

*Denotes a member of an SPS core team. Others called in on an "as needed" basis. All teams should have an SPS facilitator as a member and advisor.

Conclusion

Problems are never in short supply. Some demand our attention, usually to our discomfort or dismay. Others can safely be ignored, despite their nagging presence—like a leaking faucet. Still other problems smolder beneath the surface, lurk in a corner, or lie dormant. These last problems need to be exposed.

Companies differ in how they approach problems. Reactive companies act on problems out of necessity or when pressured to act. Due to either arrogance or inertia, they suppress or deny many of their problems. Proactive companies are more decisive in eradicating their problems.

With so many types of problems vying for attention, proactive companies must select among them and set up problem solving priorities. We have suggested that management is best suited to the problem selection task because their perspective is company-wide. If management fosters a participative environment, their decisions benefit from the knowledge of people closest to the problems.

Indexes provide a starting point for problem selection. They reflect the basic concerns of any company, including market share, quality, productivity, waste, and financial return. Work in one area of concern should not cause another to suffer. Consequently, for any particular improvement effort, at least two different indexes should be monitored.

Since work on chronic problems cannot progress under unstable conditions, problems of instability should ordinarily be attacked first. Those responsible for problem selection should understand and apply the concepts of instability and incapability. An additional concept of importance is the Pareto principle, or the 80/20 rule. By illustrating which problems create the most loss, the Pareto chart is an indispensable tool for picking the right problems to solve.

Problem *selection* should begin at the symptom level, with the most obvious evidence of the problem. Likewise, problem *assignment* should focus on the primary problem, which is the broadest possible description of the problem. In some cases, the management council might recognize the subproblems involved and have ready access to information concerning them. Problem assignment might then occur at the subproblem level, shortening the path to problem solution.

Every organization must develop its own strategy for directing its problem solving resources. It is only important that management identify which problem resolutions will derive the greatest benefit for the company as a whole.

References

1. J. M. Juran, *Juran on Leadership for Quality: An Executive Handbook*, New York: The Free Press, 1989.

2. J. M. Juran, *Juran on Planning for Quality*, New York: The Free Press, 1988.

3. J. M. Juran and Frank M. Gryna, Jr., *Quality Planning and Analysis*, 2nd ed., New York: McGraw-Hill, 1980.

4. *Juran on Leadership for Quality*.

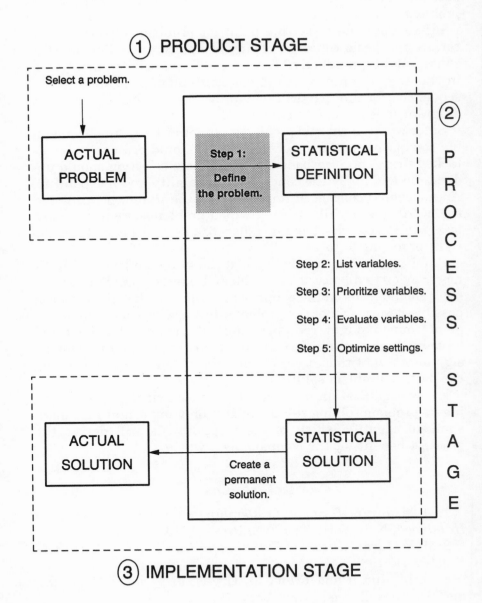

Chapter 4

Defining
the Problem
(SPS Step 1)

Issue:	All problems exhibit physical evidence. Many problem solvers use it as a starting point for their investigations. Still other problem solvers begin by attacking assumed causes. Successful results, however, depend on a precise, focused problem definition.
SPS Response:	SPS forces problem definition in statistical terms. The SPS team answers four interrelated questions, each calling for specific tactics: 1. WHERE is the problem? 2. WHAT are the problem symptoms? 3. WHEN do the symptoms occur? 4. HOW EXTENSIVE is the problem?
SPS Result:	A statistical problem definition that (a) helps to narrow the variables list in SPS Step 2, and (b) focuses and directs the following investigation.

Uncovering the Problem

When things go wrong, blame comes quickly. "It's a material problem." "A tooling problem." "A temperature profile problem." In each case, the finger is being pointed at *suspected causes* of the problem, not well-established causes nor even the problem itself.

When a suspected cause of a problem is declared to be the problem, efforts to find a solution usually head off in the wrong direction. Even if the problem solver successfully eliminates the cause, it will not necessarily follow that the problem itself will go away. **The focus must be on the problem.**

Precise problem definition is a challenging task. Perhaps because it is challenging, too often it is skipped in a rush to identify root causes. Experienced problem solvers recognize, however, that problem definition is vital to their success.

> The formulation of a problem is far more often essential than its solution, which may be merely a matter of mathematical or experimental skill.
> —Albert Einstein[1]

In fact, thorough problem definition may lead directly to a solution, one that becomes obvious as the problem is progressively described. At least, as John Dewey has often been quoted, "A problem well stated is half solved." A complete description of the problem reduces how long it takes to find and implement a solution, an economic concern for all problem solvers.

In grappling with problems, people have a tendency to become embroiled in technical details or preoccupied with pet theories about causes. As a consequence, they narrow their focus on the problem much too soon. With "hunchers," no investigation of the actual problem via problem definition ever occurs, only a later investigation of their implemented solution.

Many group problem solving procedures perpetuate nonstatistical thinking by stressing the brainstorming of "alternative solutions" after only a cursory discussion of possible causes. (This might be viewed as "team hunching.") Problem definition is skimmed over and huge assumptions are made about causes. Instead of investigating the problem, the group immediately heads towards "selecting the best solution." Such problem solving approaches may be quite adequate for problems with few variables or to achieve team-building goals, but their nonscientific slant limits their usefulness.

Difficult problems cannot be solved by finding "a fix." Looking for a fix can limit the scope of an investigation, excluding the actual solution early in the problem solving effort. With SPS, the initial attempt to define the problem is broad enough to prevent errors of omission. Carefully considering the four aspects of problem definition presented in this chapter can prevent costly mistakes later in the problem solving process.

> In my own experience in solving problems and watching others solve them, by all odds the most

difficult step in this process is the first one—defining the problem. The difficulty arises in part because of a confusion between *symptoms* and the *problem*. . . Sales have fallen off, a schedule for delivery has not been met, an angry customer is on the phone, the production line has broken down, there is a fire in the shop, or whatever. But it should be noted that none of the things mentioned are really the problems to be worked on—rather they are the *symptoms to be removed.* . . . It is far more costly to be working on the wrong problem and to discover this only after expensive action steps have been taken, than to make an initially greater effort to define the problem correctly.[2]

Statistical Problem Definitions

In following the shortest, most economical path to problem resolution, Statistical Problem Solving defines problems through a four-part diagnosis:

1. Deciding on a point of attack (the WHERE question).
2. Describing problem symptoms (the WHAT question).
3. Identifying symptom patterns (the WHEN question).
4. Determining problem size (the HOW EXTENSIVE question).

The results of this analysis create a *statistical problem definition.*

The SPS goal is to define the problem as a process output characteristic with undesirable variation. Process output to be scrutinized might include a shaft diameter out of blueprint limits, a too-noisy electrical motor, a car dashboard with visual blemishes, or overdue insurance payments by a mortgage service department.

The inability of a process to hit a target or fall within a desired range is the central concern in formulating a statistical definition of the problem. As a first investigative step, SPS quantifies undesirable variation.

For example, in a problem with a shaft diameter, simply stating that it is outside of the blueprint limits is not sufficient definition. Suppose the specification is .250, plus or minus .005 inches. To quantify the undesirable variation, definition should

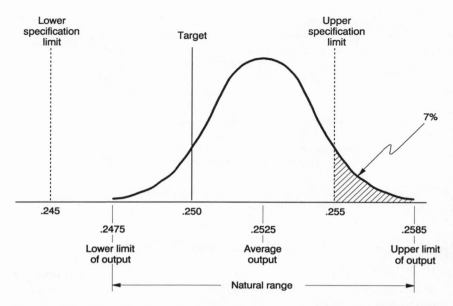

Figure 4.1 Distribution of shaft diameters showing approximately 7% of process output outside of the specification limits

include what *proportion* of the output is out of limits and what the *natural range* of the output is. About 7% of the shafts are out of limits, with shaft diameters ranging from .2475 to .2585 and centered at .2525, as illustrated in Figure 4.1.

Table 4.1 depicts all the possible combinations of outcomes for the "where," "what," "when," and "how extensive" questions, revealing 324 possible definitions! Yet, only a few of these will yield a fruitful starting point, leaving over 300 possibilities for a false start. This chapter describes how in-depth, systematic problem definition points out the most direct path to successful problem resolution.

WHERE Is the Problem?

To improve quality, some companies start at the beginning of their major processes and systematically move downstream, fixing things along the way. Others start at the end of the process and work upstream. The less organized simply turn their people loose to take random shots at problems.

Table 4.1   Possible combinations of outcomes for the four elements of a
statistical definition in SPS

Where is the problem?	What are the problem symptoms?	When do the symptoms occur?		How extensive is the problem?
		Location	Spread	
1. Where problem is obvious.	1. Primary problem alone	1. On target	Capable	1. Big
		2. Off target	Capable	2. Medium
2. Upstream from where problem is obvious.	2. Unlinked subproblems	3. Unstable	Capable	3. Small
3. Downstream from where problem is obvious.	3. Linked subproblems	4. On target	Incapable	4. Minute
		5. Off target	Incapable	
		6. Unstable	Incapable	
		7. On target	Unstable	
		8. Off target	Unstable	
		9. Unstable	Unstable	

$3 \times 3 \times 9 \times 4 = 324$ possibilities

Experienced problem solvers begin by asking, "Where's the problem. Let's go see it." Likewise, the SPS investigator starts at that point where the problem first becomes obvious, then works within that operation, moving upstream or downstream as the investigation directs.

SPS also stresses working from the end-user's perspective in answering the WHERE question. Consider a cracker manufacturer trying to reduce variation in cracker thickness, assumed to be the cause of cracker breakage during packaging. From the end-user's point of view, thickness is relatively unimportant, but broken crackers are aggravating. The investigators should have begun at the point in the process where the crackers actually break—the most downstream operation.

Ideally, SPS begins at the most downstream operation feasible where the problem is still obvious. It is a common mistake to blame the upstream operation in defining a problem. A supervisor or operator complains, "If they didn't send me that junk, I wouldn't have any problem."

Such complaints are particularly true within the customer-supplier relationship. The customer pressures its supplier to improve in prescribed ways, without firm evidence that such upstream improvement will benefit the product. In fact, troublesome processes often are not due to the condition of input materials. Even if material is the problem, it may be more efficient to change the process to operate well regardless of material condition.

Figure 4.2 illustrates three possible ways the process can affect input and subsequent output materials. Input materials can be good, bad, or anywhere in between. Process operations may have no effect on the input, it may damage the input, or it may adapt to ("forgive") the deficiencies of input materials. Table 4.2 shows the possible material conditions, the effect the process has on the material, and the condition of the output. With a "forgiving" process, the output is always acceptable, regardless of the condition of the input material.

Exploiting the forgiving potential of a process usually results in considerable cost savings. Only if it is not possible to make the process forgiving should effort be moved upstream to tighten the quality control of the input material. The choice between controlling upstream versus forgiving downstream creates what we call the "forgiving principle."

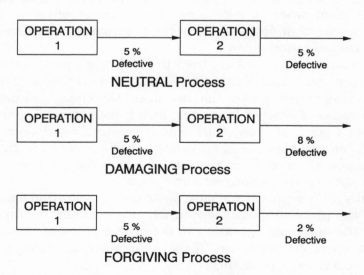

Figure 4.2   Three ways a process can affect the input material

Table 4.2   Output condition as the result of the interplay
between process type and input materials

		Process Type		
		Forgiving	Neutral	Damaging
Input Material Condition	Good	Good	Good	Poor
	Marginal	Good	Marginal	Poor
	Poor	Good	Poor	Poor

A common experience illustrates the practicality of the forgiving principle. Imagine yourself driving down a narrow road
with no shoulder. You suddenly come upon a rough section of
road. How do you respond? Most of us slow down to minimize the
shock. Slowing down to compensate for an inferior road is an
application of the forgiving principle. Certainly, the road needs
repair, but we do not stop our car and stubbornly wait for the
road to be repaired. The act of repairing the road—when it's
feasible—is analogous to improving upstream operations.

Opportunities to apply the forgiving principle are most often
discovered when viewing a problem from the end-user's perspective. A case study involving the appearance of a car dashboard
supports this claim.

Because dirt causes a bumpy texture in the paint, one solution
was to maintain cleanliness throughout the upstream operations. On the other hand, parts could be cleaned before painting,
a moderately expensive application of the forgiving principle.
From the end-user's viewpoint, however, it was found that a
decorative foil applied to the dashboard often masked imperfec-
tions in paint texture. Pursuit of the forgiving principle meant
discovering how to apply the foil so it is consistently forgiving of
the paint problem.

The forgiving principle advocates the following course of action: When it is known that the upstream operation is contributing to the problem, make your process forgiving for the short term. Then work with your supplier to control upstream in the future.

Many familiar processes are designed with the forgiving principle in mind. Grinding, tumbling, and coining operations all seek to take inconsistent input and produce more consistent output. However, because these operations are usually viewed as expensive "added" operations, they are introduced into a process only when absolutely necessary. Although unrecognized, many other operations may have the potential to be forgiving; they must be studied to discover how they can be made forgiving. We will return to this concept in later chapters.

Precisely because processes can affect output in various ways, it may not be obvious where the problem lies. Data may have to be collected and analyzed to determine exactly which physical location in the process should be attacked. Figure 4.3 shows that sampling should occur at the point where the problem first becomes obvious. Additional sampling at the next upstream operation helps to determine the actual problem location. At the sampling points, data can be collected and analyzed in three basic ways.

First, random samples of both input and output materials can be checked and compared. We call such samples "basket checks" and have found them useful to quickly obtain needed information. If data from the basket checks are not discriminating enough, statistical control charts before and after the trouble-

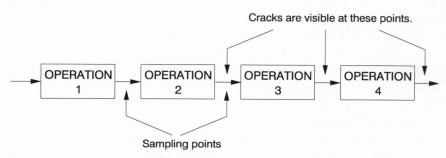

Figure 4.3   Sampling to determine problem location

some operation may reveal the problem location. Finally, it may be necessary to follow samples through the process operations to isolate the "before" and "after" condition of specific units of output. Once the nature of each process operation is understood, where the problem is becomes clear.

Summary: WHERE Is the Problem?

Problem definition begins at the point where a problem first becomes obvious. From there, three avenues of attack are possible. First, the process step that actually produces the problem output becomes the object of the investigation. Second, the relationship between incoming materials and the problematic process step is examined; if warranted, the investigation moves upstream. Third, definition focuses on downstream processes, exploring ways to make them "forgiving" of the problem. In stressing the end-user's needs, SPS tries to answer the WHERE question by moving the investigation as far downstream as possible.

WHAT Are the Problem Symptoms?

Although the question "What are symptoms of the problem?" seems straightforward, it may not get a clear answer. To illustrate: A team was formed to solve a problem with an assembly containing a diaphragm. At their first meeting, the SPS facilitator—a member of the team—asked, *"What's the problem?"*

A virtual barrage of theories about causes, ways to proceed, and possible solutions came from the team. To complicate things further, all of these causes, methods, and solutions were confounded together. Members of the team were not even aware that their responses were so unfocused. Answers to "What is the problem?" included:

> "We're cutting the diaphragm when we crimp."
> "We have to do a designed experiment."
> "Sometimes the diaphragm pulls out."
> "We need a new material."

"We have to find the window of acceptable crimping pressure, so what sample size do we need to prove that we have the right pressure?"

The question was asked several more times, but only causes and hunches were suggested. Finally, the question was restated and the correct answer came, "Oh, we are failing the burst test." That was the problem!

Problem solvers should first describe the problem by its most obvious evidence, or its symptoms. An SPS definition identifies the undesirable variation in process output or product characteristics. For example, an important dimension in a machining operation is frequently off target. A huncher might say, "The problem is that the fixturing has too much clearance." In fact, the fixturing is a suspected *cause*. The troublesome process output characteristic (or *symptom*) is an off-target dimension.

The initial response to the WHAT question should therefore be very general. As SPS problem definition progresses, it becomes more focused and specific.

> In problem-definition, we should begin with a wide focus and then use a narrow focus to define the subproblems. As Professor John Arnold of Leland Stanford has said: 'Knowing what you are looking for helps you to recognize it when you see it. But in the case of innovation, how do you know what you are looking for? You don't, unless you state your problem so broadly, so basically, so all-inclusively and generically, that you do not preclude even the remotest possibility—so that you do not precondition your mind to a narrow range of acceptable answers.'[1]

Another example will highlight the importance of beginning problem definition in general terms. A problem solving team was formed to investigate a gear that was causing high rework and scrap. As with our earlier example, when asked "What is the problem," the team provided a flood of answers:

"We have nicks on the teeth."
"The parts are too big."

"Certain teeth are warping and twisting during heat treat."
"The parts are not round enough."

Again, after much discussion the correct answer emerged: The
parts would not pass through a functional gage. Although the
primary problem was in the back of each team member's mind,
until it was explicitly stated, the group could not reach a consensus on the problem. Before that, each only argued in favor of
a pet theory. With a general starting point, one that encom-
passed all theories about the problem's symptoms, finer problem
definition could proceed.

Primary Problems and Subproblems

Starting with a broad point of view, the problem that is most
apparent is designated the primary problem. In the examples
above, "fails the burst test" and "won't pass through the gage"
were the primary problem descriptions.

Not all problem solvers clearly identify the primary problem.
Those that do, however, often stop at this point. They fail to
realize that the primary problem should be broken down into
possible subproblems. Problem solvers must further determine
how the subproblems relate to the primary problem and to each
other. Recognizing subproblems and their relationships is essential during problem definition. Figure 4.4 depicts how the
WHAT question unfolds.

Unlinked Subproblems

One possibility is that the primary problem is composed of several subproblems, each of which contributes to the primary problem but is unrelated to the others. We refer to these as "unlinked
subproblems."

Returning to our gear example, the team went on to list these
subproblems: size, roundness, taper, tooth form, and nicks. Before the SPS team effort, different individuals had been assigned
to solve the problem. Depending on their bias, each had picked
a different subproblem to work on, without considering the pri-

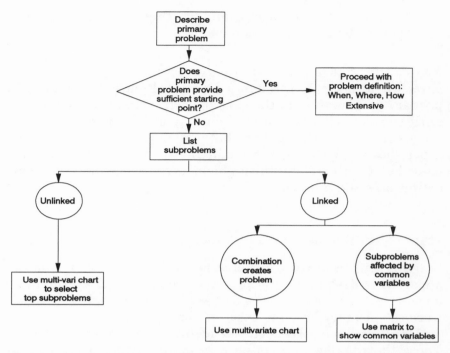

Figure 4.4 Possible outcomes when answering the SPS question "What are the problem symptoms?"

mary problem. Some success was thus achieved on specific sub-problems (for instance, the incidence of nicks had been reduced), but the primary problem remained unsolved.

Attacking different subproblems will lead problem solvers along *haphazard* routes. Instead, an SPS team lists all the sub-problems and examines their relative contributions to the primary problem. This careful activity leads to the selection of the correct subproblem or combination of subproblems as the object of the problem investigation. In our gear example, the team decided they did not have enough knowledge to reach a consensus about which subproblem to pursue. Better data were needed.

By inspecting small production samples every few hours, the necessary new data were collected. The operator recorded three phenomena: whether the part passed the functional gage, whether there were any nicks, and those dimensions that al-

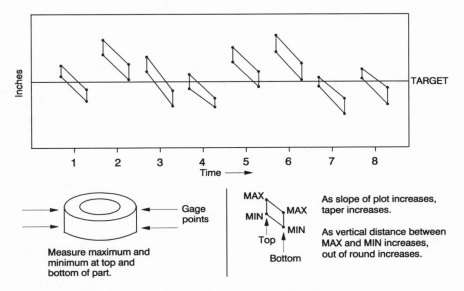

Figure 4.5   Multi-vari chart of gear dimensions

lowed for the calculation of size, roundness, and taper. Dimensional data were displayed on a multi-vari chart, as shown in Figure 4.5. The new data clearly revealed which subproblem—taper, as indicated by the steepness of the slope in Figure 4.5—was contributing the most undesirable variability. The multi-vari chart also helped to answer the WHEN question for this problem, as discussed later.

This gear example is typical of problems with "envelope" characteristics. That is, a problem can develop due to one or more of several independent physical conditions. When using geometric dimensioning and tolerancing (GD&T), an envelope or boundary of the ideal part is typically specified. It consists of the "virtual conditions" of the part's various features.[3] When a situation causes output to miss the envelope, the subproblems must be identified and analyzed to find which sources of undesirable variation are violating the boundaries.

Linked Subproblems

A primary problem may also be composed of two or more subproblems that are related or "linked" in one of two basic ways.

57

First, the subproblems jointly create the undesirable effect when they occur in a certain combination. Second, the subproblems are mutually affected by process variables they have in common.

The first type of linked subproblems is illustrated by a cylindrically shaped component that has to satisfy two requirements, length and diameter. Sometimes the component causes a high noise level in an assembly—the primary problem. The SPS team suspects length and/or diameter variation as subproblems contributing to the noise.

As depicted in Figure 4.6, when the length and diameter combine as large and small or small and large, respectively, the assemblies will be noisy. If each subproblem is examined individually, no relationship to the primary problem is apparent. Thus, these two subproblems must be solved simultaneously by first understanding their dependence on each other. A later solution must eliminate the undesirable combination.

The second way subproblems may be linked is illustrated by a screw machine situation in which two troublesome part features

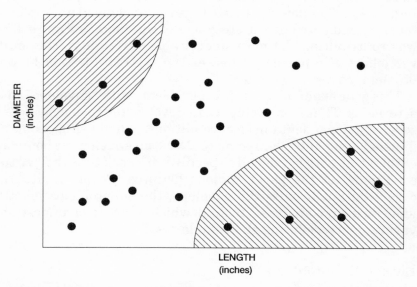

Figure 4.6 Scatterplot of diameter and length for problem components shows troublesome regions (shaded).

Table 4.3 Matrix indicating both common and unique variables suspected to affect two subproblems on a screw machine

	Subproblem # 1	Subproblem # 2
Material size	■	
Material hardness	■	■
Coolant	■	■
Spindle speed	■	■
Tool Material		■
Tool adjustment	■	
Depth of cut		■
Feed rate		■
Collet	■	

are machined at different stations. Each feature is affected by the same variables, and each is also affected by variables unique to that feature. To clarify this problem situation, Table 4.3 lists both the common and the unique variables affecting each sub-problem.

When two or more subproblems are linked in this way, the investigation must track effects of the variables on all the sub-problems. The ultimate problem solution may necessitate a compromise. That is, the improvement desired for each subproblem may need to be negotiated and balanced among all the subproblems involved. Such compromise realizes the ideal situation may not be attainable all at once.

For example, two important valve characteristics are no leakage and adequate flow capacity. Design factors affecting leakage are A and B, while those affecting flow are B and C. When B is at its preferred setting to minimize leakage, it also reduces flow. The problem solver must thus select a level for B that results in a compromise between the desired leakage and flow values.

The "WHAM" processes make up a special category of linked subproblems. These are manufacturing processes that produce several product characteristics simultaneously. Stamping, forging, screw machining, and casting are all examples of WHAM processes. Subproblems in this category are linked because their product characteristics cannot be controlled individually. Changing any process variable affects the whole process. Consequently, a clear understanding of how each variable affects each subproblem is essential.

Summary: WHAT Are the Problem Symptoms?

When beginning to define a problem, the SPS team is careful to isolate the affected process output characteristic, such as part roundness. With that as their focus, the team defines the primary problem in broad terms. They later refine their definition by examining possible relationships among subproblems.

There are three possible outcomes in asking the WHAT question: First, a clear statement of the primary problem itself may provide sufficient definition. Second, the primary problem may involve two or more subproblems that are unlinked, and thus can be solved individually. Finally, the primary problem may include linked subproblems, demanding that the investigation proceed with careful consideration of subproblem relationships.

WHEN Do the Symptoms Occur?

Perhaps the most complicated issue to address in defining a problem concerns *when* problem symptoms occur. Fundamentally, this question separates stable—natural—situations from unstable—unnatural—situations. Or, the variation causing the problem is a result of either **incapability** *(a chronic problem)* or **instability** *(an acute problem)* or possibly both.

Instability can create difficulty for the problem solver in both capable and incapable processes. For a capable process, instability itself creates the unwanted variation and is the very root of the problem. If the instability is removed, the problem goes away.

For example, in a powdered metal compacting operation, about 8% of production was rejected for not meeting a weight specification. During the problem definition stage, an average and range chart was plotted that revealed an instability in the average chart. Working with the control chart, the SPS team identified several causes of instability. When the causes were eliminated by some hardware changes to the compacting presses, the problem was solved.

Many problems, however, are the result of incapability; the troublesome variation occurs under *stable* conditions. Ideally, problem solving strategy would first remove any instability, then attack incapability. But real problems are not always so straightforward. With a problem of incapability, instability occurring during the investigation can interfere in three possible ways.

First, the pattern of instability is actually a part of the system, predictable but not removable. The problem investigation must thus proceed in spite of it. Manufacturing plants, for example, experience chronic instability in their shipment schedules. Consider a goal to increase the quantity of product shipped.

Because of the way people treat monthly goals, the last week of the month routinely has the greatest amount of product shipped. If weekly shipments were plotted, that week would certainly show as a "blip" on the chart. Although the control chart pattern appears unstable, it is actually the *natural* pattern for that system. A moving average chart might disguise the blips, allowing the team to monitor their progress without being distracted by the end-of-the-month blips.

Instability is also a natural part of the system in processes where a wear condition exists. Process output will change as tools wear or reagents are depleted. The challenge for problem solvers is to recognize and minimize the effect of the instability both on operations and on problem solving efforts.

Second, incapability may cause one problem while instability causes another, diverting attention from the problem of incapability. Typically, the "fire fighting" of instability disrupts progress on long-term capability improvement. In a forging operation, for example, nicks and excess flash were two different problems. Problem definition revealed that the majority of defects were due to the flash condition, whereas the nicks resulted from an unstable condition. It later became clear that causes of the two problems were independent of each other.

Scientific or technical factors sometimes dictate how to proceed. In this forging case, how to attack the two problems is primarily a management decision, as discussed in Chapter 3. Management may decide to solve the flash problem first, the nick problem first, or both together. Instability interferes with problem solving if it is allowed to disrupt the priorities set by management. Confusing problems of incapability with those of instability also detracts from problem solving efforts.

Third, instability can change the underlying system of causes, thwarting the investigation. For example, delamination was occurring in a paper coating process. An SPS team decided to investigate the process parameters they believed important. They were unsuccessful at first in finding the best setting for each parameter. Then they noticed that the paper was curling and causing delamination at all combinations of settings. As a frequently occurring problem of instability, the curling prevented the discovery of correct process settings.

The cause of the curling was identified as a buildup of glue on a roller due to improperly maintained equipment. Once the glue buildup was removed, the SPS team succeeded in finding the best setting for each parameter. Maintaining roller cleanliness was thus added as another important parameter.

There are cases in which the concern for stability is irrelevant. In product development, for instance, time order and thus stability is essentially meaningless.

In general, instability that is not recognized and *either* removed *or* fully understood can frustrate efforts throughout the problem solving process. Further, instability can potentially sabotage implementation efforts.

The Shewhart Principle

Dr. Walter Shewhart reasoned that no valid conclusion about a system of causes can be reached in the presence of instability.[4] Thus, when solving a problem, causes of unnatural behavior must be removed—or at least understood—before process capability can improve. The distinction between instability and incapability is an important one, but not widely understood by problem solvers. Even those who do understand it fail to recognize its importance and rarely follow its precepts.

The tactics and statistical tools for solving problems of instability are fundamentally different from those used to solve problems in a stable system. The Shewhart principle is thus especially important during the definition step. **If problem definition reveals that the problem occurs due to instability, the tactics of statistical process control must be used to understand and, ideally, remove the instability. If the problem is occurring in a stable process or the instability cannot be removed, the problem solver will proceed with SPS.**

The set of tools used to evaluate process stability is known as statistical process control (SPC). With SPC, stability is assessed by looking at the process output over time. Process behavior is expressed by plotting on a chart, in time order, a summary statistic of repeated small samples of output, such as the proportion defective. Limits are calculated and drawn on the chart, providing boundaries between what is considered natural and what is considered unnatural. Such a time-ordered graph with limits indicated is called a control chart.

In assessing process behavior over time, understanding the *pattern* of the process output can provide clues about the nature of the problem. Typical control chart patterns are illustrated in Figure 4.7. They include rising or falling trends, cycles, sudden shifts, or random instability. The time interval between occurrences of the problem often sheds light on the system of causes responsible for the problem.

Examining natural and unnatural patterns on control charts may reveal that those variables affecting unnatural behavior may be quite different from those affecting natural behavior. The liner delamination example above is a case in point. Unnatural behavior may be due to variables A, B, C, and D, while natural behavior may be affected by variables C, D, E, and F.

If no distinction is made between the natural and unnatural, a total of six variables, A through F, must be investigated. Categorizing patterns as stable or unstable reduces the number to four: Investigate A, B, C, and D for a problem of instability, or C, D, E, and F for incapability. Applying the Shewhart principle, the unstable symptoms must be removed first whenever possible.

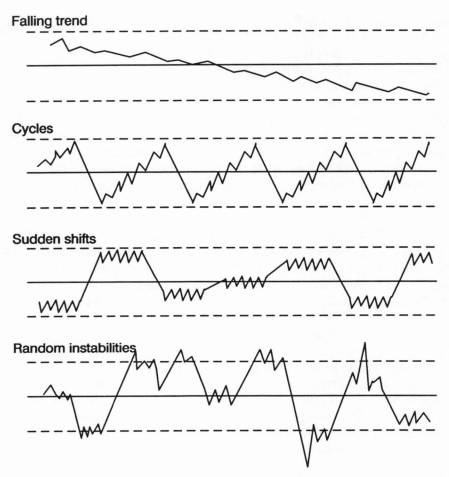

Figure 4.7   Typical control chart patterns

Two Kinds of Control Charts

Table 4.4 lists major control charts. The many types fall into two categories, variables charts and attributes charts. A variables control chart displays summaries of data from process output that can be measured on a continuous scale, such as a dimension or a temperature. Variables charts are typically used in pairs, with one showing the closeness of the output to the

Table 4.4   Major control charts

VARIABLES CONTROL CHARTS

Charts indicating location: Charts indicating dispersion:

Average ($\bar{X}$)   Range (R)
Median ($\tilde{X}$)   Standard deviation (s)
Individual (X)   Moving range (mR)
Moving average (m$\bar{X}$)
Cumulative sum (CuSum)

ATTRIBUTES CONTROL CHARTS

Fraction nonconforming (p)
Number nonconforming (np)
Number of nonconformities per unit (c)
Average number of nonconformities per unit (u)

SPECIAL APPLICATION CHARTS

Multi-vari chart
Multivariate chart

---

target, and the other showing the range, or the spread, of the data. Attributes control charts express the proportion of output that is considered conforming or not conforming to the requirements.

A simple example will highlight the distinction between the general categories of variables and attributes control charts. The specification for a shaft diameter gives a target dimension of .250 inches with a tolerance from .245 to .255 inches for the lower and upper limits. Using a variables control chart, the actual dimensions of the shafts are recorded and graphically displayed. The variables control chart is indifferent to the specification limits; it simply displays the actual condition of process output.

In contrast, the p chart—an attributes control chart—classifies process output as conforming or not conforming to a descriptive acceptance standard. For instance, if a crack occurs in a forging process, the part is unacceptable when compared to the acceptance standard of crack-free parts. The p chart reveals the proportion of nonconforming output resulting from the process. With variables charts, simple calculations along with a quick analysis of the chart are necessary. The results of this process capability analysis[5] can provide an estimate of the proportion not conforming.

Variables Control Charts

Data typically group around some central value with variations from that value becoming less and less frequent as the distance from it increases. Figure 4.8 tallies the shaft diameters from our previous example with a target value of .250 inches. Most of the shafts are produced in the .251 to .254 range. Although rare, there are shafts as low as .248. Likewise, some parts are seen at .258, if only a few. The shape of the tallied data forms a distribution.

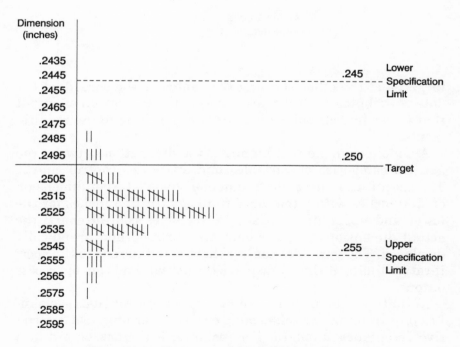

Figure 4.8   Frequency tally of shaft diameters

In general, a distribution is described by where it is located—where most measurements are concentrated—and its spread, the range over which the data are dispersed. (Other describable aspects—symmetry or flatness, for example—are not relevant to our present discussion.) The most common measure of a distribution's location is the average. The spread—or dispersion—can be measured by the range, the distance from the highest to lowest value. Dispersion can also be measured by the standard deviation, a common statistic in quality control.

The amount of spread in process output should affect which control chart to use. The degree to which consecutive units of output are alike characterizes the process output. When units are virtually identical, we call the process *homogeneous*. Stamping and grinding are examples of processes with homogeneous output. The individuals, or X chart, is the most appropriate variables control chart for a homogeneous process.

If consecutive units are not alike, we call the process *heterogeneous*. Torques and noise levels in assemblies are examples of heterogeneous output. Here the variables chart should actually combine two charts. One indicates the location of the process output distribution and the second reveals the spread of the output. The most commonly used combination variables chart is the average and range chart, as depicted in Figure 4.9.

In combination, the average chart reveals where the process is running relative to the target value, while the range chart shows the degree of output consistency. The particular pattern in Figure 4.9 shows a change in both the average and the range with respect to time. The pattern challenges the problem solver to understand the phenomenon creating it. In this case, the pattern was due to machine warm-up. As the machine ran, the average gradually shifted upward while the consistency of the output improved, as reflected in the downward trend of the range chart. Heat was later identified as the important variable causing the phenomenon.

Tracking both the location and spread of output, the variables control chart combination is a powerful definition tool. When process output fails to fall within acceptable limits, it will reveal whether the deviation is due to (1) off-target output, (2) output that has excessive spread, or (3) a combination of both. Present-

Average chart

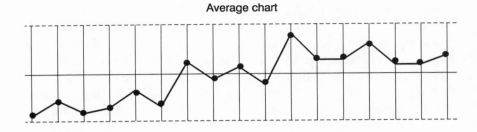

Range chart

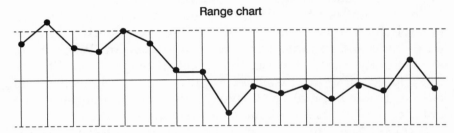

Figure 4.9   A typical average and range control chart combination

ing data in time order, the variables chart also indicates whether the location and spread are stable or unstable.

As a tool to discover how the process output is exceeding the acceptable range, the variables control chart can discriminate between nine possible situations, as listed in Table 4.5. Only the first category in the table—a stable, on-target process with acceptable spread—will consistently produce acceptable output.

Attributes Control Charts

The family of control charts for variables data allows investigation of a wide range of problems. The charting of variables data, however, is not appropriate to all problem situations. When the charting of pass/fail data is necessary, control charts designed for attributes data are needed.

Just as the simultaneous use of more than one variables chart is helpful, the p + c + Pareto chart combination is valuable in defining an attributes problem. The p chart and c chart indicate the quality of process output in different ways. Measuring the proportion of nonconforming units in the output, the p chart

Table 4.5   Possible outcomes when answering "When do the symptoms occur?"

	Condition of target	Condition of range	Condition of output
1	Stable and on target	Stable and capable	Acceptable
2	Stable and off target	Stable and capable	Unacceptable
3	Unstable	Stable and capable	Unacceptable
4	Stable and on target	Stable and incapable	Unacceptable
5	Stable and off target	Stable and incapable	Unacceptable
6	Unstable	Stable and incapable	Unacceptable
7	Stable and on target	Unstable	Unacceptable
8	Stable and off target	Unstable	Unacceptable
9	Unstable	Unstable	Unacceptable

provides a direct indicator of business loss due to the problem. The c chart reveals the number of nonconformities within a given unit of output. It is thus a more sensitive measure of output quality.

The automobile, a complex product with many possible non-conformities, illustrates how the p chart and c chart form an ideal combination in assessing product quality. At the end of the assembly line, some cars are shipped while others are repaired. For example, 4 out of 100 cars are found to have one or more defects and are repaired. The proportion repaired (4%) is recorded on a p chart. When a random sample of 100 cars is carefully scrutinized, however, a total of 37 defects are found in the 100 cars. The defects per unit (.37) is recorded on a c chart. The two charts each give a different quality impression of the cars.

To those who might view the p chart and c chart as just two different ways to measure the same thing, consider this reality: The quality of a process may degrade significantly without an increase in nonconforming units. Thus, the number of units rejected can remain stable, while the quality of each unit is deteriorating. The latter is vital information for those pursuing continuous improvement.

The Pareto Principle

> Twenty percent of the customers account for 80% of
> the turnover, 20% of the components account for
> 80% of the cost, and so forth.
> —Vilfredo Pareto, 1911[6]

Problem solvers are intuitively influenced by reasoning that captures the Pareto principle. This 80/20 rule was first described as universally applicable by J. M. Juran.[7] The Pareto principle holds there are many contributing causes for any problem, but only a few of them are primarily responsible. Juran tagged those primary causes the "vital few." The essentially inconsequential remaining causes are the "trivial many." This concept is graphically represented on the Pareto chart, as exemplified in Figure 4.10.

Attacking the biggest contributors to a problem first is a basic Pareto tenet. In Figure 4.10, the subproblem "taper," responsible for 70% of the total problem, is obviously one of the vital few. If this subproblem is diminished by 90%, the total reduction in the problem occurrence is 64% overall. If, however, the subproblem "warped tooth" is reduced by 90%, it will improve the total problem by only 3.6%.

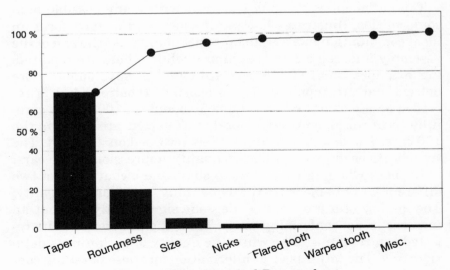

Figure 4.10   A typical Pareto chart

The resources necessary to attack one of the vital few are usually no greater than would be needed to work on one of the trivial many. Or, the effort required to solve a subproblem may be unrelated to whether it is one of the vital few or the trivial many. This is a key point in deciding on the use of limited problem solving resources. SPS strategy insists on getting the biggest bang for your company's buck.

Synthesizing the Pareto and Shewhart Principles

The p + c + Pareto chart combination addresses the Pareto and Shewhart principles simultaneously. When there are many subproblems, or categories of defects, the problem solver must decide which to work on first. Our earlier forging problem of nicks and flash required a decision on whether to first attack instability or incapability.

While management must set problem solving priorities, it is usually best to follow the Shewhart principle. Attack the source of instability first, even if it is not the top subproblem on the Pareto chart. Once the primary problem is seen under stable conditions, then Pareto is applied by turning attention to the most frequently occurring subproblem.

In Figure 4.11, instability is revealed by the c chart, but was not detected in the p chart. That instability should be eliminated before the top subproblem in the Pareto chart is dealt with. Regardless of the chosen tactic, the p + c + Pareto chart provides the necessary information to make a good decision.

There are four possible situations that can be defined by the p + c + Pareto chart combination. Each calls for a specific course of action, as described in Table 4.6.

SPC: System or Investigative Tool?

Control charts are very useful in answering the WHEN of SPS problem definition. If problem definition indicates the process is unstable, the appropriate control chart becomes the primary tool of the SPS practitioner. Understanding the underlying causes of a particular pattern seen on a chart, however, is often extremely difficult. In the listing and prioritizing steps of SPS, the top few

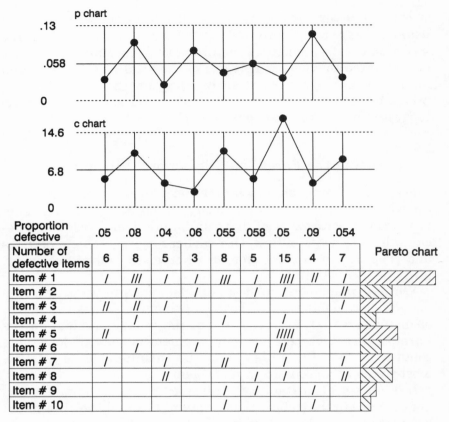

Proportion defective	.05	.08	.04	.06	.055	.058	.05	.09	.054	Pareto chart
Number of defective items	6	8	5	3	8	5	15	4	7	
Item # 1	/	///	/	/	///	/	////	//	/	
Item # 2		/		/		/	/		//	
Item # 3	//	//	/						/	
Item # 4		/			/		/			
Item # 5	//						/////			
Item # 6		/		/		/	//			
Item # 7	/			/	//		/		/	
Item # 8			//			/	/		//	
Item # 9					/	/		/		
Item # 10					/			/		

Figure 4.11   Sample p + c + Pareto chart combination

suspect variables are identified. They are then tracked on the control chart to determine if they cause the instability.

Using SPC for problem definition is "investigative SPC," as described in Figure 4.12.[8] The more prevalent use views SPC as a system of control. Process output is displayed on control charts, and operators use chart signals to decide on corrective actions. Common remedies include adjusting a setting, changing a tool, or performing some maintenance.

In our experience, very few processes can be controlled in such a straightforward manner. In fact, those processes that do lend themselves to being easily controlled usually do not need to be charted. There are practical, productive alternatives to perma-

Table 4.6   Problem definition possibilities with the use of the p + c + Pareto chart combination

	p chart in control	p chart out of control
c chart in control	Work on major output characteristics determined from Pareto chart	Work on that output characteristic which causes p chart to be out of control
c chart out of control	Work on that output characteristic which causes c chart to be out of control	Analyze p + c + Pareto chart to determine which output characteristic needs to be worked on first

nent control charts. These include automated adjustment based upon chart data, statistically sound rules for operator adjustment, and scheduled process interventions based on chart studies. Examples of the last are tool changes and preventive maintenance.

With conventional SPC, many plants are covered with control charts. To minimize the resources needed to daily maintain the charts, companies may next computerize the charting activity. The benefits of computerized charts rarely justify their cost. They also often reveal on-going unnatural process behavior that operators are unable to correct. As in all such troublesome situations, skilled SPS investigation is necessary to resolve the chronic out-of-control conditions.

SPC should be used foremost as an investigative tool. Only if investigation reveals that a permanent chart is part of the solution should charting become standard operating procedure. In fact, cases calling for permanent control charts are rare. Discussion of solution implementation in Chapter 9 will suggest appropriate use of the permanent control chart.

Summary: WHEN Do the Symptoms Occur?

By addressing the nature of process changes over time, the WHEN question separates natural from unnatural process be-

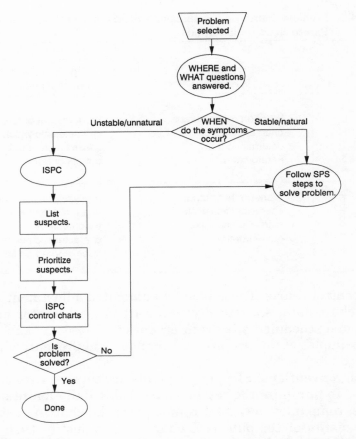

Figure 4.12 The role of investigative statistical process control (ISPC) in problem definition

havior. In general, the statistical definition of a problem describes how a given process output characteristic fails to fall within a desired range. The WHEN question looks at that failure specifically with respect to time. Does the failure occur under stable conditions (i.e., *chronically*), or does it occur due to process instability (i.e., *intermittently*)?

For variables data, the failure to fall within the desired range can occur due to the process output being unstable, off target, or incapable. The WHEN question looks at the pattern of the process output location (target) and spread (capability) over time. It thus scrutinizes, first, if the process is stable and, second, whether the problem is a case of being off target, incapable, or a combination of the two conditions.

For attributes data, the WHEN question tracks the various subproblems over time. It thus helps determine the stability of each subproblem (applying the Shewhart principle) and helps identify the top few subproblem categories (applying the Pareto principle). For both variables and attributes data, the WHEN question generates a cascade of useful information from relatively small amounts of data. Aided by one or more control charts, problem definition becomes very precise and the problem solution becomes approachable.

In many problems, the WHEN question overlaps the WHERE question. The two may be addressed simultaneously by charting the process output condition in more than one process location. Through the strategic placement of control charts, important relationships among process variables and successive process operations can be profitably understood.

HOW EXTENSIVE Is the Problem?

HOW EXTENSIVE is the most straightforward of the four SPS definition questions. While the least complicated to formulate, the HOW EXTENSIVE answer is significant in determining the approach to be taken in the SPS prioritization and evaluation steps.

Falling along a continuum, problem magnitude can be divided into four categories: big (more than 25% of the output is unacceptable), medium (5–25%), small (0.5–5%), and minute (less than 0.5%). The most valid way to assess problem magnitude is by reviewing control chart data. Often such data will be available from the earlier WHERE or WHEN investigations.

A large problem magnitude often indicates one or two dominant variables acting independently. Typically, those managing a process have limited knowledge about the effect of process variables. In the prioritization step (Chapter 6), therefore, screening experiments to change the process variables over a wide range are most appropriate.

On the other hand, a small problem magnitude is generally an indication that suspected process variables are interacting. Problem investigation must then consider variable interactions, to be discussed in Chapters 6 and 7. Prioritizing variables through subjective methods is usually successful for small-magnitude problems. Evaluating the variables is typically conducted by observing the variables over a relatively narrow operating range.

The characteristics of medium-sized problems resemble problems of both large and small magnitude. One or two dominant variables may be at work, but variable interactions may be contributing to the problem as well. Subjective rating is often adequate to prioritize the variables. If it is not, data from a process log can often help with prioritization.

When the problem magnitude is minute, SPS investigators actually try to *create* defects. The solution for minute problems lies in moving away from those variable settings that caused the problem to worsen. Since the solution is reached through extrapolation, a basic understanding of the underlying physical principles governing the process is required.

Using control charts, there are basically three ways to describe problem magnitude. The first is to compare the overall variation with the product requirements. Typically the average and range charts will provide the needed information to perform capability analysis, the results of which can be expressed as proportion defective. Second, the magnitude can be expressed by the proportion of process output that is unacceptable. The p chart or np chart reveals such proportions. Third, the degree of unacceptable output can be described as deficiencies per unit and indicated on the c chart or u chart. While an important factor, an understanding of problem magnitude alone is not sufficient in formulating strategy for the prioritization and evaluation steps. Team consideration of SPS execution in a given environment is equally influential.

Summary: HOW EXTENSIVE Is the Problem?

The best tool in determining the extent of the problem is the control chart. Problem magnitude influences the choice of both approach and methods for the prioritization and evaluation of variables. The size of the problem also suggests whether or not hardware changes will be part of the solution.

Multistream Processes

A special case often encountered in problem solving is the multistream process. For the sake of productivity, certain functions are repeated within a machine, producing several parallel streams of output with each cycle. Such machines may be multispindle, multistation, or multicavity. When an output problem occurs, numerous questions come to mind: Which stream of product is creating the problem? Is one at fault? Two? All of them? Is one less consistent than the others?

Dealing with problems in multistream processes requires the simultaneous consideration of WHERE and WHEN issues. Because of the complexity of such investigations, existing data are rarely sufficient for understanding the problem. Consequently, SPS with a multistream process almost always leads to the careful collection of new data.

The time order of the new data and its stream of origin must be known. Recording the data on a control chart, the natural process behavior is separated from the unnatural. Output from the various streams are checked for equal consistency. Finally, the output streams are compared to see if they are equally targeted.

Two statistical procedures are often used to make these comparisons: Bartlett's test compares the consistency or range in each stream, while analysis of variance (ANOVA) compares the averages of each output stream to check for equal targeting.[9] A less rigorous comparison of separate streams can be made by checking consistencies with a range chart and targets with an average chart.

Figure 4.13 shows the progression of logic to follow in defining a problem with a multistream process. Definition must include whether the problem is due to variation within the streams or variation between the streams, known as stream-to-stream differences. Once it is known where the problem is located, problem investigation can continue through the next SPS steps.

The Teamwork Factor

POINT ONE: When defining the problem, the SPS team should make no assumptions about possible causes. They should also resist the temptation to suggest solutions at this early stage in

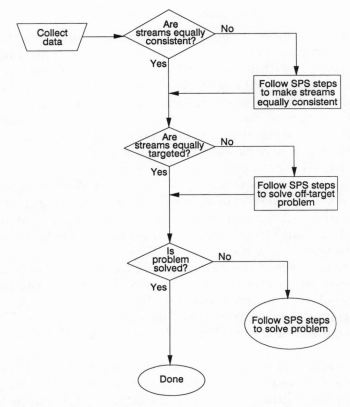

Figure 4.13   Defining problems for multistream processes

the SPS process. If they jump ahead to causes and solutions, they may allow the bias of a dominant team member to control the investigation. For effective definition, the team should stick to the four SPS questions and focus on the process output characteristic manifesting the problem.

POINT TWO: SPS training does not attempt thorough instruction in how to perform statistical methods. When productive problem solving is the goal, classroom training in statistical methods is largely ineffective. Once back on the job, students still need guidance in the practical aspects of applying the methods.

SPS team members need not be experts in statistical methods. To explain, consider a problem solving team that includes a metallurgist because material considerations are important.

Metallurgical knowledge is necessary to finding the problem solution, yet all team members need not be trained in metallurgy. Instead, the team turns to the metallurgist for guidance on material issues. Likewise, team members need only a general understanding of the statistical methods used in SPS. The facilitator guides their use of statistical methods on an as-needed basis and is the source for any additional statistical knowledge called for.

It is equally unnecessary to train all SPS team members in a general problem solving course. The presentation of concepts and methods irrelevant to their own situation is a waste of time. Once again, expertise in problem solving procedures resides with the facilitator.

POINT THREE: The SPS facilitator must be skilled in statistical methods, problem solving strategies, and group dynamics. Preparation of facilitators should be aimed at rounding out their understanding of these subjects.

As technical advisor to the team, the facilitator must be proficient in those statistical techniques commonly employed for SPS. These include statistical process control (SPC), contingency table analysis, correlation and regression analysis, design of experiments, the analysis of variance, multiple regression analysis, and Monte Carlo simulation. A variety of statistical training is available through colleges, universities, continuing education arms of professional organizations, and consulting firms. Short courses detailing SPS steps and strategies are also available from a number of sources.

In addition, SPS facilitators are responsible for guiding group activity. Besides being able to conduct effective meetings, they must display a sensitivity to interaction among group members. Drawing out quiet team members and throttling back dominant members are necessary skills. If necessary, facilitators can also upgrade their knowledge of group dynamics through commonly available short courses. In general, however, facilitators should concentrate on keeping the team focused on the problem at hand. Focus on the problem helps to create unity within the group, which normally enhances relations among team members.

One of our book reviewers shares this past experience with quality improvement project teams: *"It's amazing how unfo-*

cused and undisciplined our problem solving thought process can be without the proper direction. Many organizations underestimate the importance of a well-trained and disciplined team leader. Part of our failure in the past were team leaders ill-prepared for the task."

POINT FOUR: The facilitator is more than a teacher of SPS. The facilitator is also a student of the team in learning the specifics of the problem at hand. This dual role eliminates the distance that often exists between trainers and trainees. The SPS facilitator can thus productively function as a full member of the team.

Team members are also both teachers of their own area of expertise and students of all other team members. The dual role in this case helps to create an atmosphere of mutual respect within the group.

Conclusion

The essential first step in solving any problem is creating a clear definition of the problem. Inadequate problem definition is often the culprit in the ultimate failure to solve problems. One common pitfall is confusing the problem with suspected causes of the problem. The four questions of the SPS definition step force the team to focus on the problem itself.

Although the problem definition questions have been presented sequentially here, in practice the four are discussed simultaneously. Their analysis results in a four-part definition consisting of: (1) the precise physical location to begin investigation, (2) a distinction between the primary problem and its subproblems, (3) the condition of the problem with respect to time, and (4) the most productive investigative approach based on the magnitude of the problem.

Appropriate control charts are the best tools for defining the problem. Investigation begins by attacking the problem where it is most obvious. When problem location is not obvious, the tactical placement of control charts at suspected operations within the process will reveal that information. The chart at the problem's location is then used to determine problem symptoms, the pattern of problem occurrences with respect to time, and problem magnitude.

SPS Step 1 yields a *statistical* definition of the problem. For example, a sensor was failing a final test at the end of the assembly line. SPS definition focused on the sensor electrical function as the process output characteristic to examine. Based on final test data, it was decided to investigate upstream in the process where several linked subproblems contributed to the primary problem. The process was incapable (spread of process output always too great) with an unstable target (process output sometimes off target). With process output approximately 10% defective, the problem was judged to be medium-sized. Such precise problem definition guided the SPS team in executing subsequent SPS steps.

Examples throughout this chapter have illustrated how the four individual problem definition questions can be answered. Each of those examples are presented again in Table 4.7 within the context of a complete statistical definition.

Table 4.7   Complete statistical definitions of examples cited in Chapter 4

Where is the problem?	What are the problem symptoms?	When do the symptoms occur?		How extensive?
		Location	Spread	
Gear example: Begin at point where problem is obvious.	Primary problem is failure to pass through gage. Many unlinked subproblems. Top subproblem is taper.	Stable Off-target (i.e., Average taper is too great.)	Stable Incapable	Small
Grinding example: Begin at obvious point.	Primary problem is size out of limits.	Unstable target	Capable	Small
Sensor example: Move upstream.	Primary problem is high reject rate at final test. Numerous linked subproblems. One sensor output was selected as top problem.	Unstable target	Incapable	Medium
Burst test example: Begin at obvious point.	Primary problem was failure to pass a burst test.	Off-target (i.e., Average burst pressure too low.)	Incapable	Big
Productivity example: Begin at obvious point.	Numerous linked subproblems.	Off-target	Incapable	Medium

Because of the technical issues involved, precisely defining problems demands considerable skill. Problem definition may also require a lot of work. The effort expended at this stage, however, will reduce the work later in the problem solving process. In fact, for some problems the definition may suggest the solution.

SPS begins with a very general description of the problem to ensure that possible solutions are not excluded early in the problem solving process. Through carefully approaching (WHERE), identifying (WHAT), pinpointing (WHEN), and measuring (HOW EXTENSIVE) the problem, SPS narrows its focus. This focus productively directs the next steps in the SPS process.

References

1. Alex F. Osborn, "The Creative Problem Solving Process" in *Applied Imagination: Principles and Procedures of Creative Problem Solving*, 3rd revised ed., New York: Charles Scribner's Sons, 1963.

2. Edgar H. Schein, *Process Consultation: Its Role in Organization Development*; Reading, MA: Addison-Wesley Publishing Co., 1969, pages 47–48.

3. Lowell W. Foster, *Geo-Metrics II: The Application of Geometric Tolerancing Techniques*; Reading, MA: Addison-Wesley Publishing Co., 1982.

4. Walter A. Shewhart, *Economic Control of Quality of Manufactured Product*, New York: D. Van Nostrand Co., Inc., 1931; reprinted by the American Society for Quality Control, Milwaukee, 1980; pages 355 & 418–419.

5. J. M. Juran and Frank M. Gryna, *Juran's Quality Control Handbook*, 4th ed., New York: McGraw-Hill, 1988.

6. Michael Jackman, *The Macmillan Book of Business & Economic Quotations*, New York: Macmillan Publishing Co., 1984.

7. J. M. Juran, Frank M. Gryna, Jr., and R. S. Bingham, Jr., *Quality Control Handbook*, 3rd ed., New York: McGraw-Hill, 1974, pages 2–16 to 2–19.

8. Hans Bajaria coined the term "investigative SPC" and its acronym ISPC in 1988 to recognize SPC's problem solving uses.

9. Acheson J. Duncan, Ph.D., *Quality Control and Industrial Statistics*, 4th ed.; Homewood, IL: Richard D. Irwin, Inc., 1974; Bartlett's test, pages 709–711; one-way analysis of variance, pages 609–631. Note: These are both common statistical procedures and discussed in most statistical textbooks.

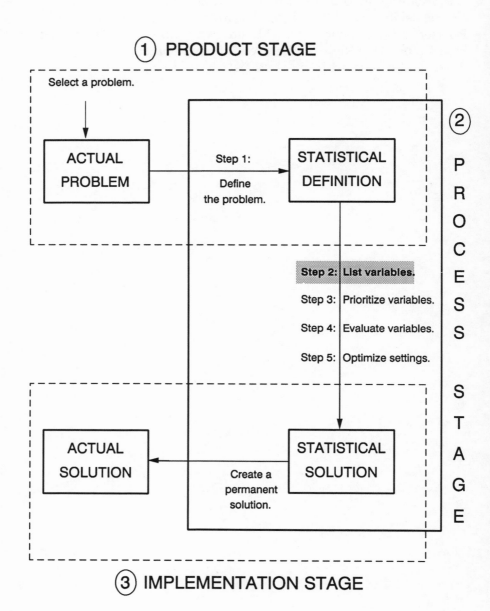

① **PRODUCT STAGE**

Select a problem.

ACTUAL PROBLEM

Step 1:
Define the problem.

STATISTICAL DEFINITION

② **P R O C E S S   S T A G E**

Step 2: List variables.

Step 3: Prioritize variables.

Step 4: Evaluate variables.

Step 5: Optimize settings.

ACTUAL SOLUTION

Create a permanent solution.

STATISTICAL SOLUTION

③ **IMPLEMENTATION STAGE**

Chapter 5

Listing
Variables
(SPS Step 2)

Issue:	Problems are affected by so many variables that tackling them often results in confusion. In the face of such complexity, most problem solvers do not take the time to develop an orderly list of variables. Instead, they investigate the variables haphazardly. Even worse, some problem solvers try out solutions before even considering variables. Money is spent without solving the problem.
SPS Response:	A list of all variables possibly contributing to the problem is developed. SPS promotes productive listing by using: METHODS OF IDENTIFICATION to insure that the list is *complete*. Brainstorming, cause-and-effect diagrams, and process flow diagrams are used. RULES OF SELECTION to help keep the list *manageable* and *feasible* for investigation. Cost and ease of investigation are primary concerns.
SPS Result:	A complete yet manageable list of variables for possible investigation.

Innocent Until Proven Guilty

Once the problem has been thoroughly defined, the stage is set for considering variables that might affect the problem, both favorably and unfavorably. The objective of the listing step is to identify which variables bear upon the problem at hand. The next SPS step, prioritization, will select the top few variables. Step 4, evaluation, experiments with the top few to understand their impact on the process output. The success of experimentation, however, rests on a thorough listing of all suspect variables.

To avoid the fallacy of assuming a certain variable or variables are guilty of causing the problem, all identified variables must be thought of as "suspects." Uncertainty is the very reason the problem is being investigated. There is first of all uncertainty about which variables are important. Then there's uncertainty about exactly how the key variables and their combinations affect the output.

The distinction between suspect and guilty is by no means trivial. A biased investigation diminishes the validity of results for each SPS step, jeopardizing successful problem resolution. Practically speaking, an assumption of guilt moves the investigation immediately and prematurely into the implementation mode. The investigators concentrate on "fixing" instead of experimenting with, referred to as "trying." Hardware expenses may be incurred with no resulting improvement in the problem condition.

For instance, in a problem with an assembly the condition of a certain component was thought to be guilty in creating the problem. To correct the faulted condition, an operation was added that resulted in both a capital expenditure and an increase in piece cost. With expenses already incurred, results could not be objectively evaluated. When the implemented solution was not successful, a variety of rationalizations were used. Do they sound familiar?

"We needed that operation anyway."
"If you don't try anything, you won't learn anything."
"This is the price of progress."
"You'll see the results as soon as we fix the mating component."

The waste of premature implementation highlights the fundamental SPS goal to minimize the cost of problem solving.

When variables are viewed as suspects, problem solvers use their creativity to evaluate the effects of the variables without permanently implementing changes. SPS investigations provide information about how successful any changes would be. It can then be decided if implementation expenses are justified before any dollars are spent. Proof of likely success before implementation is obviously valuable in the production environment.

In the development environment, product and process variables must be created. Since the objective of development *is* implementation, the distinction between "trying" and "implementing" is particularly difficult to maintain. Further, because development projects are fully budgeted, all implementation expenses are accommodated, desensitizing the development team to possibly excessive costs.

In fact, many ideas are implemented in the development environment without being properly investigated. They then become permanent features of the design or process. It would be virtually impossible to later remove them since all the design validation testing hardware would have included the features in question. In the assembly example above, which occurred during development, the added operation was never removed from the process. The added expense thus became permanent.

With SPS, proposed design and process expenses can be justified by examining variables before deciding to incorporate them. In this way, SPS helps minimize both development expenses and the final cost of the product and process.

Variables as Knobs

As presented in Chapter 4, SPS begins by describing the problem as a process output characteristic with undesirable variation. A classic process is depicted by the process flow diagram in Figure 5.1. As shown, the process output is affected both by variables within the process operation and by characteristics of the input materials. Referring to the various types of variables generically as "knobs" is helpful in applying SPS to problems in all environments: manufacturing, product design, service, and administration.

A knob is anything that, when turned, has an effect—positive or negative—on the process output. A knob changes operating conditions. A television, for example, has knobs that affect video reception, including color, tint, brightness, sharpness, and contrast. By turning any one of these knobs, the quality of the picture changes. Some factors are more difficult to control but also affect the perceived picture quality. These "knobs" would

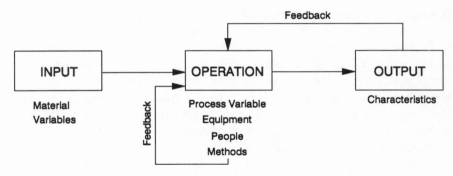

Figure 5.1   The classic process

include the size of the picture tube, the amount of light in the room, and the distance between the viewer and the screen. "Knobs" beyond the viewer's control, such as a storm or an airplane, change the picture quality as well.

Knobs are the variables, the parameters, the controls, the factors that must be understood to solve problems. The SPS knob terminology evolved from the necessity to communicate technical realities in an unintimidating way. Just the mention of statistics has been known to scare away both technical and nontechnical personnel. Because "knob" is intentionally colloquial, everyone can relate to it. For multidisciplinary teams especially, a common language is helpful in clarifying major issues and goals.

Building on the general term "knob," additional terms can help pinpoint the investigation of variables. The following knob terminology is useful in creating the SPS variables list.

PRIMARY KNOB   A variable that is fundamental to a process, possibly affected by one or more subknobs.

SUBKNOB   A variable that affects another variable, or knob. For example, fluid pressure and piston area are both subknobs that determine clamping pressure, the primary knob.

SUSPECT KNOB   A variable selected for investigation.
                Or, a knob to "try."

GUILTY KNOB   A variable identified for implementation.
                Or, a knob to "fix."

HARD KNOB | A variable that can be touched, measured, adjusted, or acted on in some way. For example, speed can be increased or decreased by turning a knob.

SOFT KNOB | A variable in the form of a possible action. For example, should we offer a 5% or 10% discount? A discount is intangible.

TURNABLE KNOB | A variable that is relatively convenient or inexpensive to change.

UNTURNABLE KNOB | A variable that either cannot be physically changed or is not easily changed due to excess expense. For example, humidity can only be controlled through expensive air conditioning.

FORGIVING KNOB | A knob that is easily, quickly turnable and can be used to compensate for the effect of an unturnable knob.

Using this knob vocabulary, it is possible to clearly describe a variety of problems. Even more important, the knob terminology helps separate *investigating* from *implementing*. We express this difference as "trying" or experimenting with a knob versus installing or fixing a knob. Trying is inexpensive and temporary, while installing is costly and permanent.

Two distinctions created by the knob terminology are significant for SPS goals. The investigative preference for *turnable* knobs over *unturnable* knobs is stressed in the first SPS rule of selection. The relationship between the *primary* knob and its *subknobs* is the focus of the second rule of selection. (SPS rules of selection are introduced later in this chapter.)

Identifying Variables

The goal of the SPS process is a thorough evaluation of the top few knobs from among the many knobs that are suspected to affect a problem. Each part of the process helps to sort out the important knobs from the unimportant knobs. The definition step produces a precise description of the problem that provides focus for the next step. Without focus, the listing step could easily generate an unmanageable list of suspect knobs, containing many unreasonable suspects.

Selecting a problem solving tactic (as introduced in Chapter 2) before beginning the listing step provides *additional* focus in identifying suspect variables. For example, if a team decided to improve control of the existing system, they might list eight suspect knobs. If they decided to optimize the existing system, they might list six knobs. If there were no problem solving tactic guiding the team, however, up to 14 suspect knobs might be listed.

In our experience, 60–70% of the time a problem solving tactic can be selected prior to the listing step due to the clarity created by problem definition. It is easier to select a tactic in the design and development setting where control of instability is usually not an issue. In complex manufacturing problems, control, optimization, and design factors come together. The combination of those factors makes early selection of a tactic more difficult. With or without a problem solving tactic to guide them, the team needs reliable methods for identifying variables.

Listing tools should assure the list is complete while aiding the facilitator in keeping the team focused. It is all too easy for any group of people to waste time on irrelevant and fruitless tangents. The methods for identifying variables described below—used individually or in combination—guide SPS teams through the listing step.

Brainstorming

> It was in 1938 when I first employed organized ideation in the company I then headed. The early participants dubbed our efforts "Brainstorm Sessions"; and quite aptly so because, in this case, "brainstorm" means using the *brain* to *storm* a problem.[1]

Alex F. Osborn, whose study of creative thinking dominated his life's work, was the originator of the popular brainstorming technique. The primary purpose of brainstorming is to encourage a free flow of ideas. In the words of Osborn:

> The *spirit* of a brainstorm session is important. Self-encouragement is needed almost as much as mutual encouragement. A perfectionism complex will throttle effort and abort ideas.[1]

Through its goal to create an atmosphere of trust, brainstorming promotes the interplay of team members' ideas. *An open, free exchange of ideas often leads to new and better ideas.* Osborn stressed that brainstorming was never intended to be a replacement for individual ideation. As he explained: *"Group brainstorming serves solely as . . . a means of generating a maximum number of potentially usable ideas in a minimum of time."*[1] Individual efforts at problem analysis must precede and follow brainstorm sessions. Each person is on the SPS team for his or her own unique knowledge and perspective on the problem under analysis.

Understanding and following four fundamental guidelines is essential to brainstorming success. They were identified by Osborn as follows:[1]

> *Criticism is ruled out.* All judgment is postponed until after the brainstorming session.
>
> *Free-wheeling is welcomed.* All ideas are accepted, regardless how wild they sound; they can be tamed down or dismissed later.
>
> *Quantity is wanted.* The more ideas, the better the probability that useful ideas will emerge.
>
> *Combination and improvement are sought.* Participants may suggest how the ideas of others can be improved or how two or more ideas might be joined to create a new idea.

It is important to list *all* ideas. No partiality can be shown in recording the results of the brainstorming session. If participants notice some ideas are not being listed, their enthusiasm for suggesting more is dampened.

The SPS question to be brainstormed is: Which knobs might be investigated to help solve the problem? Once the brainstorming session has run its course, the facilitator should give each team member a chance to make a final addition. The aim is to insure no valuable knob is neglected. Still, in our experience, a member may approach the facilitator after a session ends with an idea that was not thought of earlier. Or perhaps the idea was not offered for some reason, usually political. The facilitator must then diplomatically introduce the idea at the next meeting.

Many training experts advise that the group should depart after the brainstorming session and reconvene sometime later to screen and organize the ideas. Two sessions emphasize the distinction between *soliciting* ideas and *judging* ideas. Realistically, however, this may not always be possible. Whether they continue in session or meet again later, the SPS team must check all proposed knobs against two criteria:

(1) Is the relationship of the knob to the problem clear?
(2) Is it clear how to investigate the knob?

The first criterion helps eliminate the inconsequential. For instance, one team member's special expertise relative to a knob may lead the group to seriously consider an irrelevant knob. Consequently, if the originator of an idea cannot explain why a knob merits investigation, it is dropped from the list. As for the second criterion, the originator of an idea may be unable to think of a way to try the knob. The other team members might then suggest how the knob can be acted upon during the investigation.

Both **screening criteria** work to insure that knobs suggested during the brainstorming session are worthy of further discussion. SPS teams must keep the objective of the listing step in focus: a concise list of knobs that can and should be investigated.

All team members must feel comfortable about contributing whatever ideas they have about the problem. On the other hand, the SPS rules of selection (discussed later in this chapter) assure that SPS goals are observed during the listing process. To nurture a genuine flow of ideas while producing a feasible list, the facilitator must enforce *both* brainstorming guidelines and rules of selection during listing. Experienced facilitators may be able to apply both simultaneously. For instructional purposes, however, we are presenting them as consecutive procedures during the listing step.

The Cause-and-Effect Diagram

This problem-analysis tool originated with Professor Kaoru Ishikawa in 1943. It gained widespread acceptance throughout Japanese industry before being introduced in the U.S. and other countries.[2] The cause-and-effect (CE) diagram is also referred to as the Ishikawa diagram or—due to its appearance—the fishbone diagram. It visually depicts the variables that impact a problem, usually according to the common categories of people, materials, methods, and equipment.

> Cause-and-effect diagrams are drawn to clearly illustrate the various causes affecting product quality by sorting out and relating the causes. Therefore a good cause-and-effect diagram is one that fits the purpose, and there is no one definite form.[2]

Like brainstorming, CE diagrams are best developed in group settings that encourage a free flow of ideas. Unlike brainstorming, all ideas are suggested to fit major categories on the diagram. Using this structured approach improves the likelihood that all important knobs are listed. Figures 5.2, 5.3, and 5.4 show examples of CE diagrams for manufacturing, design, and administrative problems.

Another advantage of the CE analysis is its distinct separation of primary knobs from subknobs. For example, Figure 5.5 is a section from a CE diagram identifying two primary equipment knobs, pressure and tool condition. Each is affected by several subknobs. In brainstorming, tool condition might be listed as three separate variables: tool condition, tool change interval, and tool condition before tool replacement versus after. The CE

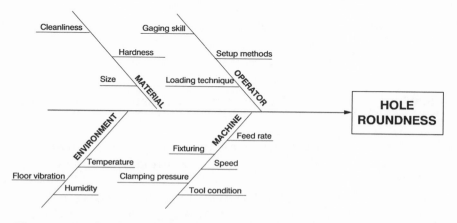

Figure 5.2   Cause-and-effect diagram for a manufacturing problem

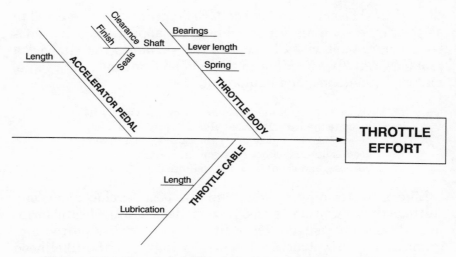

Figure 5.3   Cause-and-effect diagram for a design problem

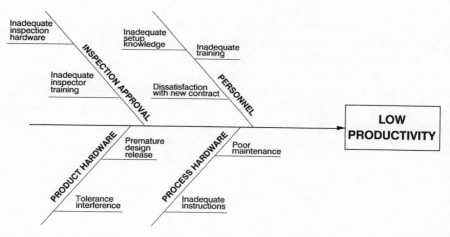

Figure 5.4   Cause-and-effect diagram for an administrative problem

diagram organizes the relationships among these tool-related variables, displaying them as a single primary knob with several subknobs.

Practically speaking, the CE analysis distinguishes a possible investigative trial from the different ways to conduct that trial. Tool condition becomes the knob to investigate, while its sub-

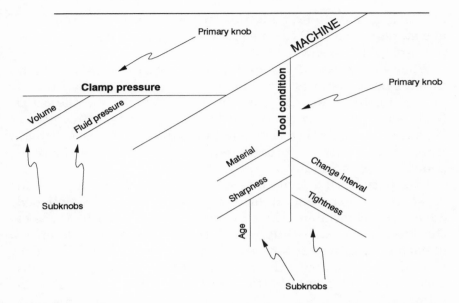

Figure 5.5   Detail of a CE diagram showing the relationship of knobs to subknobs

knobs become the means to create change. There are thus several ways to try how the tool affects the problem. A trial requires observing process output under more than one condition. With many production factors affecting the tool, SPS favors the subknob that is most easily used to change the tool's condition.

The net result of the CE analysis is an organized list of knobs with corresponding investigative actions. It might be considered "focused brainstorming." As such, the CE diagram helps to capitalize on the expertise of team members. For example, material variables would be listed most logically by a metallurgist, chemist, or ceramist. Operating variables, on the other hand, are identified most easily by an operator or supervisor.

The Process Flow Diagram

The process flow diagram (PFD) is a common industrial engineering tool for planning purposes. Using standard symbols, it graphically depicts the steps in a process. When applied to manufacturing, it includes activities such as inspection, transport, and storage. The PFD can also represent schematically the components in an assembly.

When process variables and output characteristics are added to a PFD, it becomes a valuable method for identifying and listing knobs. Like the cause-and-effect diagram, the PFD framework *organizes* the knobs suggested by team members. Essentially, the PFD structure requires that variables are physically located within a process sequence or within specific components of an assembly.

This disciplined activity might follow a brainstorming session or—with an experienced facilitator—might be accomplished during brainstorming. The PFD provides teams with a type of checklist to systematically review their ideas for completeness at each process step or for each component in an assembly. The PFD also helps manage the variables list by isolating the knobs pertinent at the point of attack identified during problem definition.

All processes can be represented by one of the three types of process flow diagrams: series, parallel, and complex (combined series and parallel). Figures 5.6, 5.7, and 5.8 illustrate each of the PFD types.

The rationale for determining which knobs to list is different for series and parallel processes. In the series PFD, the list should include the knobs identified for the step immediately upstream from the point at which the problem occurs. In Figure 5.6, for example, the knobs for Operation 2 (E, F, G, H, I) are important, in addition to its input material—a total of six knobs.

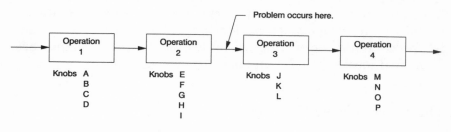

Figure 5.6   Process flow diagram for a series process

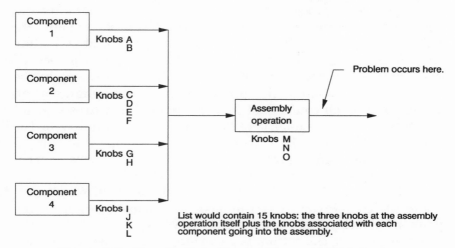

Figure 5.7   Process flow diagram for a parallel process

Input material is included on the variables list for practical reasons. First, as the input material for Operation 2 varies, it reflects variation occurring in Knobs A through D of Operation 1. By investigating only the input material, the list is kept manageable. If input material turns out to be important, then the investigation moves upstream to evaluate how Knobs A, B, C, and D affect Operation 1 *output*—the *input* material for Operation 2.

Including input material on the variables list also offers opportunities to apply the forgiving principle. If the material varies a great deal, there may be settings of Knobs E through I that desensitize Operation 2 to the quality of the incoming material. How forgiving knobs are applied will be discussed further in Chapter 7 on evaluating variables.

The effect of input material can be investigated by contrasting two material samples selected at random (referred to as "basket checks" in Chapter 4). If any particular characteristic of the input material is suspected, however, samples showing differences in that characteristic can be carefully selected. For example, with a problem of non-cleanup at a honing operation, the roundness of the incoming material was suspected to especially affect the problem. The samples selected for investigation had different degrees of roundness.

In the parallel process, as in the series process, knobs affecting the operation immediately upstream from the problem point are listed. In Figure 5.7, those knobs would be M, N and O. Unlike the series process, however, the parallel process is presented with several streams of input material. These are usually the components of an assembled product such as an appliance or an automobile. Each component has one or more features that affect either the assembly operation or the final quality of the assembled product. The features of each component should be listed, as shown in Figure 5.7, in addition to the knobs governing the assembly operation. For the process in Figure 5.7, therefore, the list would include a total of 15 knobs, A through O.

For the complex process, the basis for listing depends on the point of attack. If that point is within a series portion of the complex process, the rationale governing a simple series process should be used. If the attack begins downstream from a parallel portion of the process, the parallel process rationale should be used. Using the PFD with the complex process is most impor-

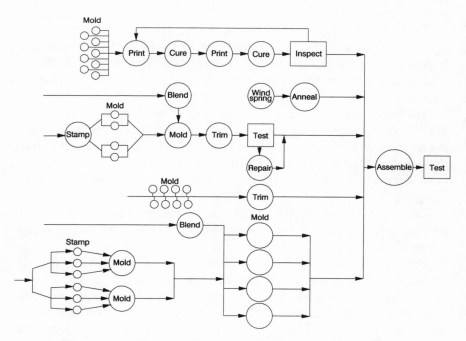

Figure 5.8   Process flow diagram for a complex process

tant, both to focus the point of attack and to keep the variables list manageable. Even the most complex problem can be broken down into series and parallel components, allowing a fairly straightforward listing of knobs.

It may be helpful to combine the process flow and cause-and-effect diagrams in certain situations. Ishikawa, who classifies CE diagrams by types, calls such a combination the "production process classification" type.[2] A small CE diagram is drawn for each operation in the PFD. This arrangement of suspect knobs not only pinpoints where to attack the problem, but also helps identify the knob/subknob relationships at each process step.

Use of the process flow diagram offers an additional, unique benefit that is realized beyond the listing step. Distinguishing five steps (define, list, prioritize, evaluate, optimize) may give the impression SPS is neatly followed to a successful conclusion. But in the real world of solving messy problems, the team may have to return to earlier steps. The PFD is especially useful for investigating very complex problems since it facilitates the pinpointing of which knobs to try *first*. Later, as knowledge about the process is gained, the PFD also guides the team in locating *additional* sources of variation to investigate.

Other Methods of Identification

In addition to the CE diagram and the process flow chart, other systematic techniques can be used to generate ideas for the variables list. The SPS team is encouraged to use its creativity by trying whatever methods are helpful in particular problem solving situations.

For a problem encountered during product design and development, basic techniques used by mechanical engineers may help generate the list. A free body diagram, for example, shows all the various forces acting on a component. Sketching one for a problem with an assembly will help insure the list is complete. Failure mode and effects analysis (FMEA) and fault tree analysis (FTA) can also suggest suspect knobs for problems in design or complex systems.

Basic engineering formulas may be helpful in creating the variables list. For instance, if an engineering equation includes the diameter of an orifice, perhaps the size of the orifice should be investigated. Any variable appearing in an engineering equation should be considered for the variables list.

Summary: Methods of Identification

The common objective of all methods for identifying variables is to "storm" the problem. A thorough list of knobs possibly affecting the problem should be the end result. Brainstorming per se is unstructured or free form, and thus important ideas may be overlooked. The cause-and-effect or process flow diagrams offer a more organized approach to listing. Each provides a distinctive and unmistakable structure. Some teams may prefer working with a predetermined structure in listing their ideas about the problem.

It might also be desirable to use brainstorming along with one of the other methods. The knobs listed during brainstorming could be fit into the structure of a CE diagram or a process flow diagram as a secondary step. Each team must decide which of the methods, or combination of methods, suits their particular problem. Figure 5.9 suggests how the various methods of iden-

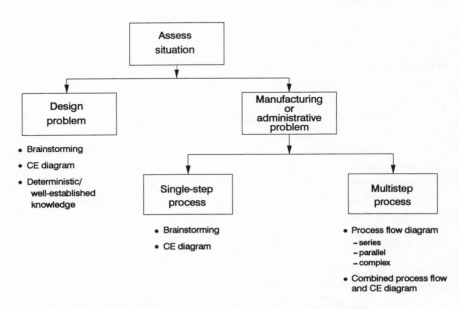

Figure 5.9   Selecting a method of variables identification

tification might be used. Regardless of method, the listing step should be marked by the spirit of openness and trust necessary for successful brainstorming.

Applying SPS Rules of Selection

After dissecting the problem to uncover all possible suspect knobs, the next goal is to reduce the list to a manageable number. SPS teams apply three rules of selection. The first rule is concerned with economy:

> **Rule 1: Knobs first selected for investigation must be inexpensively turnable.**

This first rule of selection is also the first SPS execution principle. It stresses that easily turnable knobs should always be investigated first (Table 5.1). This principle is founded on the belief that experimentation should be practical, efficient and productive.

SPS aims to conduct investigations at virtually zero cost, and only easily turnable knobs can be tested for free. Further, when a solution requires a permanent hardware change, the team must consider the feasibility of the change. If, in fact, the solution cannot be implemented due to technical or financial limi-

Table 5.1 Hierarchy of knob "turnability"

Turnability	Example	Cost to Business
Easily turnable	Furnace temperature	$
Less easy to turn	Modify fixture	$$
Difficult to turn	Rebuild furnace	$$$
Very difficult to turn	Buy a new furnace	$$$$
Extremely difficult to turn	Develop new furnace technology	$$$$$
Impossible to turn	Let somebody else do it: subcontract or purchase	$$$$$$
Problem avoidance	*Give up business to the competition!*	*$$$$$$$$$$$$$$*

tations, then the preceding investigation was a waste of time and resources. In following Rule 1, only easily turnable knobs are investigated in the first place. The odds are then in the team's favor that their solution will be both technically and financially feasible to implement.

Because of these economic concerns, the SPS team first exhausts the potential benefits from easily turnable knobs before considering expensive-to-turn knobs. If a solution is not found at the end of the investigation, the SPS team backtracks to try progressively more difficult-to-turn knobs. The trials continue until the problem is solved, or until it's decided it would be too costly to solve the problem. SPS might also reveal the upper limit of the current process, indicating that only new technology will solve the problem. The evaluation chapter will discuss these possibilities in more detail.

The concern for ease of turnability is most important during investigation. Investigators should be able to turn knobs from one setting to another and back again; that is, knobs to be tried should be easily reversible. Some knobs may be easy to turn permanently in implementing a change, but very difficult to change *temporarily* for the sake of experimentation.

For example, if the important knobs are the dimensions on a molded part, it would be extremely difficult to remove and then replace material in the mold to get different dimensions. "Turning" the dimension knobs thus takes more ingenuity. Investigators would have to observe naturally occurring changes, providing those changes occur over a wide enough range.

It might be found that parts from a different cavity have different dimensions. The effect of those differences could be analyzed without any expense to *create* the differences. If they are found to be important, a solution could be implemented by permanently changing the mold. With SPS, a permanent change occurs only after an investigation indicates it is workable and economically justified.

Rule 2: Only primary knobs should be retained on the variables list. Subknobs should be considered only to manipulate the primary knob.

The goal of the SPS team is to produce a variables list that is complete yet manageable. The list must be exhaustive, including all knobs that could possibly help to solve the problem. Nevertheless, if subknobs are added, the list can quickly become unmanageable. Including subknobs can lead to loss of focus and confusion.

In injection molding, for example, mold temperature is a primary knob affected by many subknobs. These include the setting of the heating element, the temperature of the material, the amount of time the mold is open between cycles, and any interruptions during production. Most problem solvers would groan, "There are too many variables." Mold temperature itself, however, adds a single knob to the variables list. If it turns out to be one of the "vital few," investigating its subknobs will help discover how to maintain the temperature at its preferred setting.

Although subknobs should not be retained on the variables list, they are extremely important in problem solving, both during the investigation and especially during implementation. If several subknobs affect a key knob, problem solvers have more than one option for changing that knob during investigation. They can select the subknob that is least expensive or most convenient to manipulate.

> **Rule 3: Only those knobs that reflect new, fundamental knowledge of the process should be retained on the variables list. If the effect of certain variables is already understood or if variables reflect only business options, they generally do not warrant investigation.**

Problem solvers often sidetrack their efforts to learn more about the process under scrutiny. Any investigative effort that does not lead to *new* knowledge relative to the process is not only a waste of resources but will delay reaching a solution. Following Rule 3 will eliminate two common time-wasters initiated during listing.

First, investigators should not reinvent the wheel by listing variables they already have well-established knowledge about. In a forging operation, for instance, heated parts must be processed in an inert nitrogen atmosphere to prevent rapid oxidation. While brainstorming a metallurgical problem, it was suggested that leaks allowing oxygen to enter the nitrogen atmosphere could be investigated. In their follow-up discussion, the team discovered there were numerous cracks in the material surrounding the nitrogen atmosphere. The cracks had not been repaired due to inadequate maintenance. No investigation was warranted, just the good sense to improve maintenance practices.

Second, problem solvers should confine their attention to knobs representing technical considerations. In attempting to isolate causes, they should not examine knobs reflecting business decisions. Business knobs include different operators, different shifts, different suppliers, and different machines. *Comparisons* of these do little to increase knowledge of the process to be improved.

For instance, it is not uncommon for quality control personnel to study Machine A versus Machine B or Supplier X versus Supplier Y. Even when differences are found in contrasting such business options, process understanding has not been improved. Further, what if Machine A is not operating at its optimum, and thus Machine B is declared to be the better machine? What has been learned about the process itself? In fact, if Machine A's knobs were at their preferred combination of settings, it might show up to be far better than Machine B. Instead of making such simple comparisons between the machines themselves, the technical aspects of knobs that affect the output of Machines A and B should be identified and studied.

There may be exceptions to Rule 3. If it is known that only one supplier is actually a contributor to the problem, property differences among suppliers' products could indeed shed light on the problem. Suppose the higher material hardness of one supplier's product is connected to the problem. Then hardness may be an important factor in causing the problem.

Nevertheless, purchased or incoming material should not be listed alone. Rather, it should always be listed along with other process knobs. The reason is simple: If only incoming material is listed, it will be assumed guilty. If it is listed along with other knobs, it is then just one of many suspects.

Rule 3 prevents incoming material from overshadowing those knobs that reflect fundamental knowledge of the process. Investigative discoveries about temperature, pressure, speed, cure time, and operator skill represent improved manufacturing process knowledge. If the deficiencies of incoming material are included on the list with other process variables, opportunities to forgive such deficiencies may be discovered. A slower speed or increased cure time, for instance, may make the process more tolerant of differences in a supplier's material.

As already explained, it can be important to investigate differences among the *properties* of supplied materials. Finding differences among suppliers, however, is secondary. In general, problem solving will be most successful when its primary aim is to understand the knobs in the investigators' own processes.

Summary: Rules of Selection

Using these guidelines, only primary knobs that are technically important to the problem and economically feasible to investigate remain on the list. Rule 1 insists that easily, inexpensively turnable knobs be given first consideration in all problem investigations. Rule 2 aids in keeping the list manageable by restricting it to primary knobs only. Rule 3 reminds problem solvers that their efforts should increase their understanding of the process needing improvement. Each of these rules reflects the philosophical thrust of SPS towards productive, financially responsible investigations. Table 5.2 shows how the rules of selection would narrow a list of knobs.

The Forgiving Principle in Practice

As introduced in Chapter 4, the forgiving principle contrasts two approaches to solving a problem. The "control upstream" approach views the problem as due to variables already present in the input materials. With this way of thinking, those working on the problem typically conclude the problem is beyond their control. They believe if quality characteristics from the supplier and environmental factors were controlled, they would not have a problem.

In the "forgive downstream" approach, problem solvers seek to understand the many naturally varying situations affecting their process. Working with the knobs within their control, they determine to find a workable solution despite incoming and external variables beyond their immediate control. By forgiving downstream, the condition of the process output is essentially unaffected by the condition of the process input.

Table 5.2   A list of variables for a thermal deburr operation: the
deliverable item at the end of SPS Step 2

Initial list as generated by any of the methods of identification	Knobs retained on the list	Reason for exclusion
1. Amount of charge	■	
2. Natural gas line pressure	■	
3. Cleanliness of mixing block		Established knowledge
4. Ambient temperature		Unturnable
5. Dwell time	■	
6. Ambient humidity		Unturnable
7. Part configuration		Customer requirement
8. Oxygen line pressure	■	
9. Total mass in basket	■	
10. Extent of burrs		Unturnable
11. Number of parts	■	
12. Cycle time		Business variable

**The problem solving process for any situation can be
described as learning to understand variables.** Sooner or
later—somewhere, somehow—successful problem solvers must
learn to deal with variables.

The simple example in Chapter 4 of the driver encountering a
rough stretch of road illustrates two practical ramifications of the
forgiving principle. First, despite our desire to drive only on
smooth roads, it is unrealistic to expect we will never encounter
a rough road. Learning to forgive rough roads means slowing
down. Such action forces understanding of the variables affecting
our own machines. Practically speaking, the most advantageous
place to start understanding variables is with our own processes,
moving upstream only if forgiving knobs cannot be found.

The second aspect of the forgiving principle's usefulness is
highlighted by this question: If those who have a problem look
upstream for a solution, where do their upstream suppliers look?
Further upstream? Upstream control thinking can create a

chain reaction, circulating the problem among all upstream parties associated with the process. This reaction results in a very costly problem solution.

Looking for opportunities to forgive downstream is an economical alternative to controlling upstream. Why? Because the inexpensive, easily turnable knobs are considered *first*. The first SPS rule of selection is based on this thinking.

Unfortunately, upstream control thinking is ingrained throughout industry. Incoming variables are frequently assumed to be guilty without any evidence to prove their guilt. Variables within the control of those managing the problematic process, however, are frequently ignored.

With the forgiving principle, just the opposite emphasis is true. Knobs that can improve understanding of fundamental process knowledge are the ones investigated most vigorously. The bias of upstream control thinking is thus countered by the third rule of selection. Upstream control may need to be pursued for the long term. Realistically, however, the forgive downstream principle should be mastered as a productive approach to problem solving.

The Teamwork Factor

POINT ONE: A valid and complete list of variables is difficult to generate without teamwork. Left alone to solve problems, individuals are likely to follow their hunches. Individual bias can be especially counterproductive during listing. Through a variety of perspectives, however, team interaction is more likely to uncover the many possible variables that affect a problem.

Only in an uncritical, impartial setting will team members productively share their knowledge. The facilitator must thus be alert to maintaining an atmosphere that is open and blamefree. The facilitator may have to remind the team that their objective is to identify guilty knobs, not guilty people!

POINT TWO: There must be no suggestion that the individuals with the top ideas will be rewarded. If any rewards are given, they should be equally shared by all team members. The primary objective of teamwork—working together toward a common goal—must be reinforced.

POINT THREE: Because facilitators are central to the SPS process, they should be carefully selected. The ideal SPS facilitator is a well-rounded, flexible person. A generalist's perspective enables the facilitator to appreciate and incorporate all the viewpoints involved with complex problems. Flexibility is indispensable in dealing with the diversity of people, problems, and situations that facilitators encounter.

The facilitator's adaptability should also extend to the use of statistics. SPS facilitators cannot be biased in their use of statistical techniques, favoring one or two to the exclusion of all others. Instead, they must be ready to use a variety of statistical tools. The utilitarian approach of SPS selects "the right tool for the job."

SPS uses the most expedient tools yet follows a disciplined path. A profile of the ideal facilitator thus includes these traits: self-starting, resourceful, and thorough. In short, a hands-on results-getter.

People skills are essential. Anyone who's ever been involved in small groups will agree that the facilitator can make or break a group's effectiveness. The facilitator's knowledge of how people work together in groups keeps the team on track and moving forward. A certain amount of savvy is necessary to recognize and handle behaviors that detract from the group's progress. Someone who can relate to different personalities will possess a distinct advantage in facilitating teamwork.

As helpful as a congenial personality is, well-developed communication skills are certainly the primary requirement for successful SPS facilitators. Among these skills are active listening, timely restatement and summarization, and clarification of facts and ideas. These same communication abilities are also necessary for the teaching that the facilitator does. Whether introducing statistical methods or guiding the SPS process, the facilitator must use language clearly, keep focused on the topic, and respond to feedback from team members.

Conclusion

Listing variables helps to create order in the problem solving process. Without this step, problem solvers randomly investigate factors they think are affecting the problem. Such a disorganized approach only results in more confusion while wasting limited problem solving resources.

Because SPS cautions against assuming any particular variable is guilty, the term *suspect* is applied to variables during the listing step. In addition, variables are described as **knobs to be turned** in evaluating their effect on the problem. The knob terminology helps to fulfill SPS goals by emphasizing the important distinctions between *primary knobs* and *subknobs* and *turnable* versus *unturnable* knobs.

The list of knobs that results from SPS Step 2 must be both complete and manageable. First, all bases must be covered in identifying knobs that might affect the problem. Prominent techniques to insure thoroughness are brainstorming, the cause-and-effect diagram, and the process flow diagram. The nonjudgmental atmosphere fostered by classical brainstorming should mark the listing activity, whichever technique or combination of techniques is used. Next, SPS applies three rules of selection in narrowing the list down to only those knobs that would be technically and financially feasible to investigate.

SPS operates from the premise that problems can only be permanently solved when the variables affecting them are objectively identified and understood. With its insistence on economical investigations, SPS advocates first increasing fundamental process knowledge before looking upstream for solutions. A basic aim of Statistical Problem Solving might be summed up in this behavioral goal:

> When you can look at any problem situation as a collection of knobs, you're almost there.

References

1. Alex F. Osborn, "Creative Collaboration by Groups" in *Applied Imagination: Principles and Procedures of Creative Problem Solving*, 3rd rev. ed., New York: Charles Scribner's Sons, 1963.

2. Kaoru Ishikawa, *Guide to Quality Control*, Tokyo: Asian Productivity Organization, 1976, Chapter 3.

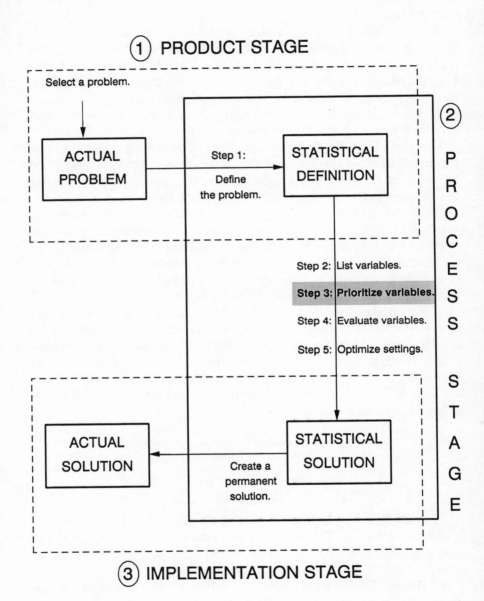

① PRODUCT STAGE

Select a problem.

ACTUAL PROBLEM

Step 1: Define the problem.

STATISTICAL DEFINITION

② PROCESS STAGE

Step 2: List variables.

Step 3: Prioritize variables.

Step 4: Evaluate variables.

Step 5: Optimize settings.

ACTUAL SOLUTION

Create a permanent solution.

STATISTICAL SOLUTION

③ IMPLEMENTATION STAGE

Chapter 6

Prioritizing
Variables
(SPS Step 3)

Issue:	Effective problem resolution demands an in-depth investigation of all important variables. For cost-effective investigation, the list of suspect variables must be reduced to a workable number.
SPS Response:	SPS prioritization takes a least-cost approach. The methods used fall into three categories, identified in order of their increasing cost and execution difficulty.

1. **Existing data.** Information that can be compiled at very little expense is readily available in logs and other records. Correlation analysis and contingency tables are the specific methods used to extract needed information from existing data.
2. **Subjective methods.** Variables on the list are prioritized based upon the accumulated experience of team members. Consensus decision-making through discussion or rating and ranking is used to capitalize on existing knowledge.
3. **Planned data collection.** If existing data or team knowledge is insufficient, new data are needed. Either screening experiments or planned observational studies are used to obtain new data.

SPS Result:	Identification of the top few variables to be fully evaluated.

Why Prioritization Is Necessary

A full evaluation of how variables and their combined effects cause undesirable variation is essential to problem solving. Whenever there are more than a few knobs (variables) on the list, prioritizing them singles out the top candidates for evaluation. Understanding how much effort goes into a full evaluation of variables underscores the need for prioritization. In addition, evaluation can become unmanageable as the number of variables—plus any interactions among them—increases. Successful problem solvers understand what interactions are, why they are important to investigate, and exactly how they affect the manageability of problem investigations.

The Importance of Understanding Variable Interactions

Problem solvers can understand a knob by observing its effect at different settings. Consider an engineer, whom we will call Barb, trying to understand how the various knobs in a grinding operation affect part roundness.

Barb has had some training in designing experiments. Although it's possible to try many settings, she knows it's preferable to try each knob initially at only two settings. Barb also knows that to understand two knobs it is not sufficient to observe each knob independently at two different settings. The possible combinations of the knobs' settings should also be observed. If the knobs are feed rate and spindle speed, the effect of the feed rate may be different depending on the spindle speed, and vice versa. Figure 6.1a depicts the experiment Barb set up with the four combinations needed to evaluate feed rate and spindle speed. Each square contains the average out-of-roundness for the possible combinations.

The results of Barb's experiment illustrate how variables can interact, as shown in the graph of Figure 6.1b. At the slow feed rate, as spindle speed increases, out-of-round increases. The relationship changes at the fast feed rate, so as spindle speed *increases*, out-of-round *decreases*.

If Barb had studied the spindle speed at the slow feed rate only, she would have concluded the process should run at the slower speed. If she had studied the spindle speed at the fast feed rate only, she would have concluded the opposite. To understand interaction, remember that we can't make a statement about Knob A's effect without knowing where Knob B is set. Likewise, we can't make a statement about Knob B's effect without knowing where Knob A is set. Thus, it makes no sense to discuss what the spindle speed should be unless the feed rate is known, and vice versa.

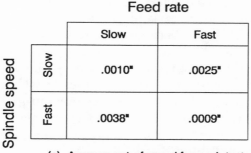

(a) Average out-of-round for each test

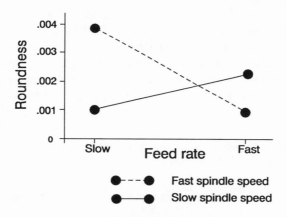

(b) Graph showing feed x speed interaction

Figure 6.1   Results of a test evaluating the effect of spindle speed and feed rate on part roundness

Interactions among variables not only complicate the interpretation of experimental results, but can also create confusion during production. An operator may have discovered, for instance, that feed rate affects roundness. When encountering a roundness problem, the operator would consequently adjust the feed rate. Usually this adjustment was made while running at the slow spindle speed. But what if the machine is running at the fast spindle speed? When the operator slows down the feed rate expecting to improve roundness, the problem will actually worsen (see Figure 6.1b). The situation contradicts the operator's previous experience.

The confusion caused when variables interact makes problems difficult or even impossible to solve. Many problems become chronic precisely because a one-variable-at-a-time approach will not be successful when interactions are present.

Returning to Barb's roundness problem, a colleague suggested trying a different material for the grinding wheel. So she decided to compare one alternative to the current grinding wheel. She also wondered about the effect of clamping pressure. Settling on an experiment for four knobs, Barb ended up with 16 tests, as shown in Table 6.1.

She was about to begin when her boss said, "You should look at the frequency of dressing the grinding wheel. I'm sure that affects roundness. Besides, we could double wheel life if we cut the amount or frequency of the dress in half!" To please her boss, she'd have to duplicate her 16-combination experiment for each amount of wheel dressing. Suddenly Barb's experiment contained 32 test combinations to fully evaluate all five variables at

Table 6.1 Combinations to evaluate feed rate, spindle speed, grinding wheel material, and clamping pressure

			Low clamping pressure		High clamping pressure	
			Fast feed rate	Slow feed rate	Fast feed rate	Slow feed rate
Current wheel material	Slow spindle speed		Test 1	Test 2	Test 3	Test 4
	Fast spindle speed		Test 5	Test 6	Test 7	Test 8
New wheel material	Slow spindle speed		Test 9	Test 10	Test 11	Test 12
	Fast spindle speed		Test 13	Test 14	Test 15	Test 16

two levels each. A *full evaluation* aims to understand all the possible variable interactions.

Barb was again ready to begin when she learned another engineer was looking at a different coolant for their plant. If Barb wanted to evaluate the effect of the new coolant versus the current coolant, her experiment would double again, rising to 64 test combinations.

Still another engineer asked if a potential change to the part under study on a previous operation would affect the grinding operation. Now up to 128 possible combinations, Barb thought, "There must be a better way!" There is: Precede evaluation with prioritization of the knobs suspected to affect the problem.

Barb's quandary is not uncommon. Virtually all problems are affected by more than one variable. In fact, for a typical problem, the variables list (SPS Step 2) may contain as many as 15 to 25 suspect variables. Barb's evaluation experiment became unmanageable with only seven variables, each at two settings. If 20 variables are examined, each at a current setting and one alternative setting, the possible combinations number 1,048,576. And what about examining each of the 20 at three settings? It would require about three and a half billion tests!

Obviously, no sane problem solver would attempt such a ridiculous experiment. The complexity of dealing with variables, however, provokes careful consideration of which are in fact essential to problem solving success.

According to the Pareto principle (also called the 80/20 rule), only a few of the variables on a typical suspect list will prove to be important. If there were 20 suspect knobs, for example, 80% of potential improvement could result from understanding only four of those knobs. Only a few knobs, therefore, require full evaluation to solve the problem. The challenge to problem solvers is to place the odds strongly in their favor that they correctly pick the "top few" knobs. SPS relies on prioritization methods that economically select those top few.

In Barb's case, a colleague who knew something about statistically designed experiments suggested she try a screening experiment. She could study all seven knobs in 16 experiments using a type of experiment called a fractional factorial design. He explained that such experiments are mathematically very efficient; you get a lot of information with very little data. What would Barb be giving up, however, by looking at only 16 of the possible 128 combinations of her seven-knob experiment? She would give up knowledge about variable interactions, such as the feed rate/spindle speed interaction discussed above.

Confounding: The Unavoidable Nuisance

If Barb sacrifices knowledge about variable interactions, where does that information go? It becomes confounded, confused, mixed up with the effects of the knobs under study and any other interactions.

A simple example illustrates the problem of confounding. Imagine you own two cats named Hustle and Bustle. Frequently, when returning home from work, you find a mess made of your house plants. You don't know, however, if the mess was made by Hustle, Bustle, or both. The individual behavior of the cats is confounded by their equal opportunity to be mischievous.

To find the culprit, you would have to confine each cat in a different part of the house for a sufficient period, say one week each. After the two-week test, you might find when Hustle had the chance to make a mess, the house remained clean. When Bustle had the same opportunity, your house plants were attacked. You would conclude that Hustle is innocent and Bustle is guilty. Your conclusion is reliable because you eliminated the ambiguity in the data.

To understand confounding in a technical sense, consider an experiment with three knobs (A, B, and C), each at two settings. The first three columns in Table 6.2 indicate the settings of each knob for the eight combinations in the experiment. The eight tests are all the possible combinations of A, B, and C. The remaining four columns are used to analyze variable interactions. For example, the fourth column—interaction AB—is generated by multiplying the pluses and minuses from columns A and B. The other columns are defined in the same manner, with the last column assigned to the three-factor interaction ABC. Once the data are collected, the effect of each knob and each interaction can be calculated using an algorithm developed by Yates.[1]

A fourth knob, D, can be added to the experiment without increasing the number of tests. D's settings can be assigned to any column already representing one of the interactions. As-

Table 6.2 Experimental layout for 3 or 4 knobs in 8 tests

Column number →	1	2	3	4	5	6	7
Test number ↓	A	B	C	AB	AC	BC	ABC or D
1	−	−	−	+	+	+	−
2	+	−	−	−	−	+	+
3	−	+	−	−	+	−	+
4	+	+	−	+	−	−	−
5	−	−	+	+	−	−	+
6	+	−	+	−	+	−	−
7	−	+	+	−	−	+	−
8	+	+	+	+	+	+	+

A,B,C, and D are knobs.
AB, AC, BC, and ABC indicate knob interactions.
− indicates knob set at low level.
+ indicates knob set at high level.

signing additional knobs to columns representing interactions—in Table 6.2, the last four—is the most common method used to create screening experiment designs. The probability of three knobs (A, B, C) interacting is typically less than that of any two (AB, AC, BC) interacting. Hence, most experimenters would choose the ABC column for D.

Suppose in running the experiment of Table 6.2 we find that the column to which we assigned D has a strong effect. Now what? Is it D that is actually having the effect? Is the ABC interaction having the effect? Or are both D and ABC in some proportion together having the effect?

The calculations for D and ABC are mathematically identical. Thus, the data and analysis from an eight-test experiment cannot separate their effects. The effects are inseparably mixed, or confounded. The only way to clear up any confusion definitively is to run more experimental tests representing new combinations. The objective is to get data that are not confounded, as was possible when Hustle and Bustle were separated.

Confounding + Interactions = Double Trouble

Because interactions among variables are common, careful experimental planning and analysis is crucial. Interactions will confuse attempts to solve a problem when a one-variable-at-a-time approach is followed. Even if screening experiments are used to investigate several variables at a time, the confounding of variables and interactions can still create confusion. The feed/speed interaction of Barb's grinding problem illustrates a two-factor interaction. Interactions can and do occur for three or more variables as well. In our experience, the solutions to many chronic problems require understanding the interactions of two, three, and even four variables.

Variable interactions can only be fully understood through evaluation (SPS Step 4); there are no magic methods or shortcuts that eliminate confounding. SPS prioritization, however, does streamline the total problem solving effort. By identifying the top few knobs for evaluation, prioritization helps to conserve experimental resources. SPS evaluation then goes into sufficient depth to allow full understanding of each variable, plus any interactions among the variables.

Because SPS seeks to minimize the impact of a problem investigation on day-to-day business operations, the number of tests must be manageable. Table 6.3 shows the number of combinations necessary to evaluate from two to nine knobs, all at either two or three settings. The table indicates that the number of experiments for three to five variables—the top few—is usually manageable.

Summarizing the Case for Prioritization

In virtually all cases, dealing with problems means dealing with more than one variable, plus the likely interactions between those variables. The presence of interactions means that not

Table 6.3   Number of test combinations
required to evaluate several knobs,
with the manageable numbers
indicated within the bold border

		Number of settings	
		2	3
Number of knobs	2	4	9
	3	8	27
	4	16	81
	5	32	243
	6	64	729
	7	128	2,187
	8	256	6,561
	9	512	19,683

only variables but their combinations as well must be evaluated. The reality of confounding requires a careful and planned approach to problem investigation.

Because evaluating more than a few variables is a complicated and expensive task, prioritization of the variables list is essential. Few, in fact, would argue against prioritizing. What is lacking in most problem solving approaches is a set of tools to accomplish efficient and unbiased prioritization for a variety of problem situations.

SPS Prioritization

Before beginning prioritization, the team should again consider selection of a problem solving tactic (as introduced in Chapter 2). If a tactic could not be decided on before the listing step, it often becomes clear after listing. For example, an SPS team was considering how to extend the useful life of a sensor. In reviewing their variables list, it was apparent they were looking at a mix of process control knobs, system redesign knobs, and investigative knobs. To help them decide on a problem solving tactic, they classified the knobs on their list according to the four tactics, as illustrated in Table 6.4.

A discussion of the five process control knobs led the team to conclude that all five were stable. Next they realized that investigating the knobs to optimize the system might result in a

Table 6.4   Classification of knobs by their relationship to problem solving tactics

Knobs in a sensor problem	Tactic 1: process control	Tactic 2: system optimization	Tactic 3: system redesign	Tactic 4: new system
1. Film thickness		X		
2. Film hardness			X	
3. Film density			X	
4. Cure temperature	X			
5. Cure time		X		
6. Cure atmosphere			X	
7. Contact hardness			X	
8. Contact end condition	X			
9. Contact length			X	
10. Contact finger configuration			X	
11. Shaft end play		X		
12. Substrate flatness	X			
13. Substrate material			X	
14. Eliminate contacts				X

quick and inexpensive solution. Since they were also aware that redesigning the system would mean a longer investigation, they decided to pursue it only if the optimization route proved unsuccessful. By settling on the system optimization tactic, they were able to reduce their list to five knobs before beginning the prioritization step.

Opinions vary on strategies for prioritizing many variables. All academic disputes fade into the background, however, when discussing an actual problem and deciding on the method *for that particular situation*. Faced with real problems in real time, problem solvers become very pragmatic. The "correct" method is the one that gets the job done, not necessarily the one that is academically preferred.

As a results-oriented approach, SPS relies on a repertoire of prioritization methods. The SPS facilitator must understand and be ready to use all of them. The facilitator's guidance in selecting the most productive method is important to the success of SPS prioritization.

In the statistical quality control field, screening experiments are often considered to be the only method for identifying key variables. For SPS practitioners, they are one of several prioritization tools. The particular use of three other methods to rank variables is characteristic of SPS: (1) correlation analysis, (2) contingency tables, and (3) subjective rating and ranking. Correlation analysis and contingency tables are commonly used statistical methods, but using them to prioritize variables is an SPS innovation, as is the subjective method.

The selection of the most appropriate method for a given situation is integral to SPS Step 3. To prioritize the variables from the listing step, the team is guided by three questions:

1. Does existing data include information about the variables on the list?
2. How much knowledge do team members have about the problem?
3. How difficult will it be to collect new data on the variables?

In preparing to prioritize, the team should first consider whether or not available data can help in the task. Data may be found in many places, including process logs, setup sheets, inspection records, or inspection and test results from prototypes. When pertinent data exists, it is usually the primary source of information for the prioritization step. Existing data may be in the form of variables data, attributes data, or a combination of both. For variables data, correlation analysis should be used. With attributes data, or a combination of attributes and variables data, the contingency table method of prioritization should be used.

When data is not available, an attempt should be made to prioritize the variables on the list using the team's collective knowledge. With the subjective method, suspect knobs are first individually rated by team members, and then rank-ordered based on the ratings. Although a potentially effective method, in some instances teams may not have the knowledge or experience to successfully prioritize knobs. It therefore becomes necessary to collect new data.

The team's third consideration has to do with the ease with which variables on the list can be investigated. If the knobs can be easily turned, screening experiments are preferred. If the knobs are relatively difficult to turn, the planned collection of observational data is relied on.

Figure 6.2 summarizes the logic used by SPS for selecting a prioritization method. No single method should be considered better than the others. The objective of the prioritization step is to arrive quickly and economically at a valid ranking of the variables list. Favoring one method over the others would hinder that goal. The remainder of this chapter takes a close look at each of the methods used in the three major SPS routes for prioritizing variables.

SPS Route 1: Using Existing Data

Analysis of existing data is accomplished with scatterplots or contingency tables. Which tool applies depends on the type of data being analyzed. Variables data are expressed as numbers along a scale; correlation analysis applies. Attributes data take the form of words in discrete categories, such as *yes* or *no*; contingency table analysis applies.

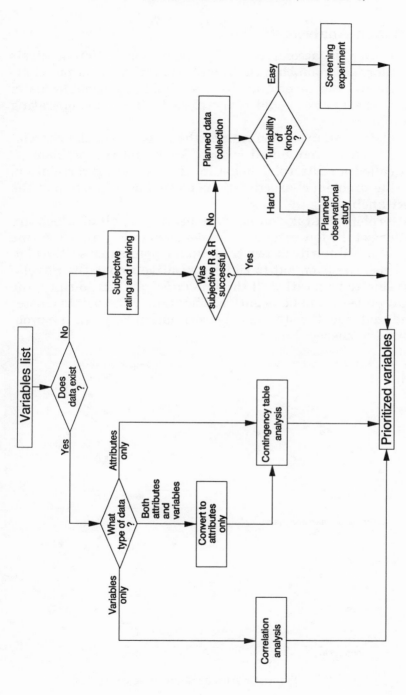

Figure 6.2   Logic for selecting a prioritization method

Correlation Analysis

Prioritization is accomplished by using correlation analysis when information on both the troublesome process output characteristic and the suspect knobs is available as variables data. Data on the knobs should cover close to their full operating ranges.

Correlation analysis determines the strength of the association between an individual suspect knob and the problem. A graph called a scatterplot helps in understanding correlation. On it, the problem characteristic is plotted as a function of the suspect knob.

Scatterplots can take on many appearances, all of which are variations of the few general cases depicted in Figure 6.3. A line of best fit is ordinarily drawn through the points in a scatterplot. If the line *rises* from left to right (a positive slope), the correlation is said to be positive. If the line *falls* from left to right, the correlation is said to be negative. The tighter the points cluster around that line, the stronger the correlation between the problem and the suspect knob.

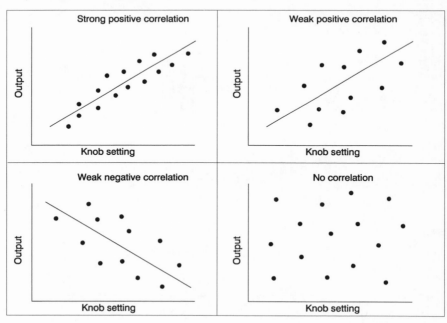

Figure 6.3   Typical patterns seen in scatterplots

Correlation is measured by a statistic called the correlation coefficient. It ranges in value from −1, denoting a strong negative correlation, to +1, indicating a strong positive correlation; 0 denotes no correlation. The correlation coefficient can be easily calculated on scientific calculators or on personal computers with spreadsheet or statistics software. Reference 2 suggests sources for the correlation coefficient formula.

Using correlation analysis to prioritize variables is very straightforward. Consider an injection molding operation in which a dimension must be better controlled. First, compile data from the process log or other source. Make a column for the problem condition and a column for each suspect knob, as illustrated in Table 6.5. Second, set up a scatterplot for each knob versus the problem condition. Graphical displays of data often

Table 6.5   Process log data for an injection molding problem

No.	Suspect knob settings							
	Barrel temperature			Mold temp	Pack pressure	Pack time	Cool time	Problem dimension
	Zone 1	Zone 2	Nozzle					
1	495	500	490	172	530	8.0	24	9.37
2	535	545	480	176	490	7.7	16	9.42
3	500	510	490	172	490	8.0	22	9.35
4	520	540	485	180	530	7.5	22	9.39
5	500	505	520	178	530	8.0	16	9.32
6	535	545	480	188	550	7.5	20	9.49
7	510	515	520	178	480	7.5	20	9.30
8	530	545	480	182	490	8.5	20	9.47
9	525	545	495	176	540	6.6	18	9.35
10	485	495	520	178	530	7.8	18	9.28
11	490	495	480	182	480	8.0	18	9.46
12	505	515	520	180	470	6.6	16	9.33
13	500	505	490	174	510	7.0	16	9.37
14	475	475	520	186	510	7.5	26	9.34
15	490	495	510	174	470	7.7	22	9.30
16	510	515	520	176	490	6.6	18	9.30
17	490	495	510	176	540	7.7	18	9.34
18	495	505	480	188	550	7.2	18	9.49
19	515	525	480	182	550	7.5	16	9.42
20	505	505	520	178	510	7.5	18	9.33

reveal relationships that are missed when the analysis relies heavily on "number crunching." Figure 6.4 shows scatterplots for two of the knobs in our injection molding example. Third, using the raw data, calculate the correlation coefficient for each knob. Finally, rank the knobs according to the absolute value of the correlation coefficients, as done in Table 6.6. The ranking isolates the top few suspects. Usually the cutoff point for the top few is decided by looking for a wide gap between the higher and lower correlation coefficients.

Problem solvers should avoid four common pitfalls when using correlation analysis. The first is forming invalid conclusions about the nature of the relationship between a suspect knob and

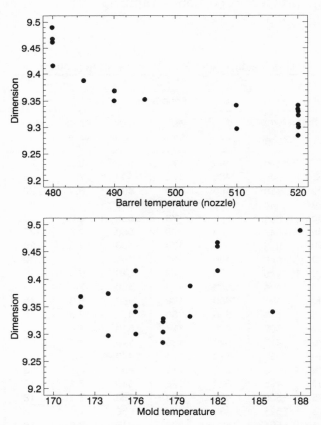

Figure 6.4   Scatterplots for an injection molding problem

Table 6.6   Prioritized ranking based on correlation
analysis

Knob	Correlation coefficient	Ranking
Barrel temperature:		
Zone 1	.43	3
Zone 2	.43	4
Nozzle	-.86	1 *
Mold temperature	.72	2 *
Pack pressure	.29	5
Pack time	.23	6
Cool time	-.07	7

*Indicates top two knobs for evaluation.

the problem. The correlation coefficient measures the degree of association between a knob and the process output condition. This association should not be assumed to be a cause-effect relationship. Two things occurring simultaneously or under similar conditions do not necessarily mean that one causes the other. Investigators finding a strong correlation are tempted to conclude they have discovered a cause of the problem, but there is always a chance that conclusion is false.

For example, Bob's boss was very strict about punctuality. When Bob was confronted about his tardiness, he reached into his desk drawer and pulled out a scatterplot. Figure 6.5 shows Bob's arrival times along the vertical axis and the arrival times of John, his colleague, along the horizontal axis. Then Bob claimed, "It's obvious John makes me late." His boss gave him the benefit of the doubt by asking, "Oh, do you and John carpool?" With "no" for an answer, what would his boss think about Bob's correlation?

In fact, there *was* a causal explanation for Bob's data. Both Bob and John drive the same route to work. If the traffic slows down on one particular stretch of freeway, both Bob and John are

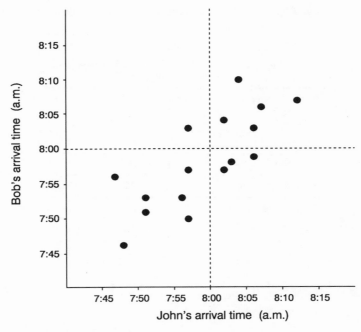

Figure 6.5   Scatterplot of arrival times illustrating a nonsense correlation

delayed. The arrival times of both men are consequently influenced by the same set of conditions. Scatterplots of traffic flow versus either John's or Bob's arrival times would show a positive correlation, in this case from a true cause-effect relationship.

Correlation analysis cannot pass final judgment. It can only rank variables by degree of suspicion—the goal of prioritization. Because correlation analysis cannot establish causal relationships, a full evaluation of the top few suspected knobs must be performed, as directed by SPS Step 4.

Another common pitfall in using correlation analysis is the drawing of mathematically correct conclusions from possibly invalid or biased data. Existing data should thus be viewed with a healthy skepticism by asking questions about its origin. When and how was it collected? Are any data excluded? Are there any pressures on the operating personnel to hide or fudge data? Only if accurate data are supplied to the team can the correlation analysis be meaningful.

A third pitfall is possible when dealing with two sets of information. Even though data might exist on both the problem condition and the condition of the suspect knobs, it may not be possible to match the data. In the injection molding example above, the inspection data taken at one point in time are recorded simultaneously with the process settings. What if the inspection data are recorded by an inspector and the process conditions are independently recorded by the operator? The SPS team could not connect the inspection results with corresponding process conditions and thus would be unable to perform correlation analysis.

The fourth pitfall with correlation analysis is using data that do not cover a knob's full operating range occurring under normal conditions. In our injection molding example, the barrel temperature may vary from 470 to 545 degrees. If the process log contains temperatures ranging only from 490 to 525, then the full effect of barrel temperature may not be realized. It may consequently be ranked lower than it should be. To avoid this pitfall, records should be reviewed to see that they cover the full operating range for each knob.

Physical knowledge of the process may sometimes override the concern that a knob vary over its full operating range. For example, barrel temperature might not vary over a wide range for a good reason. Knowing a wide temperature variation causes undesirable changes in the process output, the operator may tightly control the temperature.

In summary, observe these four cautions:

- First, remember that a strong correlation does not prove a causal relationship exists between a knob and a problem. It only heightens suspicion.
- Second, know the origin of existing data. Ask questions about it and understand the conditions under which it was collected.
- Third, be sure that data on the knobs and information on the problem condition can be matched up one to one.
- Finally, check that data for each suspect knob cover the full operating range under normal conditions.

The value of correlation analysis is limited since it cannot deal with variable interactions. However, the strength of correlation between each suspect and the problem can be used to rank knobs according to their likelihood of contributing to the problem.

Contingency Table Analysis

Because correlation analysis is more precise, its use is preferred over contingency tables. Correlation analysis, however, only applies when both the problem output condition and all the suspect knob settings are expressed as variables data. It cannot handle attributes data. Contingency table analysis (CTA) applies when information on either the process output condition and/or one or more of its suspect knobs must be expressed as attributes data. CTA also works for attributes and variables data mixed.

Like correlation analysis, contingency table analysis determines the strength of the association between a suspect knob and the problem. That association is understood by creating a cell for each possible combination of the problem condition and suspect knob status. Contingency tables deal with only one variable at a time. Nevertheless, when each knob is compared to the problem condition, the relative strength of each association helps rank-order the knobs for investigation in SPS Step 4.

Prioritizing through CTA begins by setting up a table for each suspect knob to depict its relationship to the problem. Horizontal rows identify the different output conditions, while columns represent the status of the suspect variables. As correlation analysis uses the correlation coefficient, CTA uses a measure of association called the chi-square statistic. For each table, calculations yield a value for the chi-square statistic. In general, the larger the chi-square value, the stronger the association between the suspect knob and the problem.

A probability number (significance level) is derived from a table of chi-square values. This number represents the chance a given result could occur by coincidence. The smaller the probability number, the greater the chance the knob is having a real effect on the output condition. Sources on the calculations used to perform contingency table analysis are cited in Reference 3. For quicker, more accurate results, CTA can be performed on personal computers with a general statistics package.

Contingency table analysis for prioritizing suspect knobs follows this general procedure:

130

1. Set up a contingency table for each knob:
   (a) Create categories of the problem situation for the rows.
   (b) Describe discrete conditions of the knob in the columns.
2. Convert any variables data to attributes data.
3. Tally the data for each cell in each table.
4. Perform the calculations to obtain a chi-square value and a probability number for each table.
5. Rank the knobs by their probability numbers to determine the top few.

A problem with valve leakage illustrates CTA. Measured in drops per minute at a final test, failing valves were found in every lot. The SPS team listed six suspect knobs, identified in the column headings of Table 6.7.

To perform CTA, a contingency table was set up for each suspect knob to depict its association with the leakage condition. The team decided on three categories for valve conditions: no leaks, one drop per minute, two or more drops per minute. These problem categories became the three horizontal rows in each contingency table.

Discrete conditions for each knob were also decided on. For instance, the data on scratches were already in attributes form. Each sample was simply described as having (yes) or not having (no) scratches. Another knob, roundness, was originally in variables data form and was converted to attributes data; both data forms for roundness are identified in Table 6.7. For contingency table analysis, the roundness condition is described in discrete terms as acceptable, marginal, or unacceptable for each sample. Table 6.7 shows data for all the suspect conditions along with the leakage condition.

Table 6.8 is the contingency table for roundness, later found to be the number one suspect. After the data in each table were tallied, chi-square values and their corresponding probability factors were calculated. Finally, the suspect knobs were ranked by their probability factors, as shown in Table 6.9.

The four cautions for correlation analysis apply to contingency table analysis as well. First, contingency table analysis does not establish causal relationships, but only raises or lowers the degree of suspicion about a knob. Second, the origin of the data should be well understood. Third, the knob data and the

Table 6.7   Database for prioritizing knobs using contingency table analysis

Sample number	Surface finish	Visible scratches	Pits	Contamination	Roundness Variables	Roundness Attributes	Eccentricity	Leakage
1	unacceptable	no	no	none	0.0008	acceptable	bad	0
2	acceptable	yes	yes	moderate	0.0007	acceptable	bad	1
3	acceptable	yes	yes	none	0.0015	marginal	good	0
4	unacceptable	no	no	heavy	0.0004	acceptable	good	0
5	acceptable	no	yes	none	0.0021	unacceptable	good	1
6	acceptable	yes	no	moderate	0.0021	unacceptable	bad	1
7	acceptable	no	no	heavy	0.0005	acceptable	good	0
8	acceptable	yes	no	none	0.0004	acceptable	good	1
9	acceptable	yes	no	none	0.0008	acceptable	good	1
10	acceptable	yes	no	none	0.0009	acceptable	good	1
11	unacceptable	no	yes	moderate	0.0005	acceptable	bad	0
12	unacceptable	yes	yes	none	0.0024	unacceptable	good	1
13	acceptable	no	no	moderate	0.0023	unacceptable	good	1
14	acceptable	no	yes	moderate	0.0028	unacceptable	good	2
15	acceptable	yes	yes	moderate	0.0022	unacceptable	good	0
16	acceptable	no	yes	moderate	0.0008	acceptable	good	0
17	acceptable	yes	yes	none	0.0010	marginal	good	0
...								
55	unacceptable	yes	yes	heavy	0.0017	marginal	good	1
56	acceptable	yes	yes	moderate	0.0010	marginal	good	0
57	acceptable	yes	yes	heavy	0.0024	unacceptable	good	1
58	acceptable	no	no	moderate	0.0022	unacceptable	bad	1
59	acceptable	no	yes	heavy	0.0011	marginal	good	0
60	unacceptable	yes	yes	heavy	0.0022	unacceptable	good	1
61	acceptable	no	yes	none	0.0003	acceptable	good	2

Table 6.8 A contingency table showing the relationship of roundness to leakage

		Roundness			
		Acceptable	Marginal	Unacceptable	Totals
Leakage	0 drops	17 [12.8]	6 [6.4]	3 [6.8]	26
	1 drop	9 [11.3]	6 [5.6]	8 [6.0]	23
	2 drops	4 [5.9]	3 [3.0]	5 [3.1]	12
	Totals	30	15	16	Grand total 61

Numbers in cells indicate the number of occurrences for a set of conditions. Numbers in small boxes within cells are expected values for the cell.

Table 6.9 Ranking of knobs based on contingency table analysis

Knob	Chi-square (X^2)	Probability factor (P)	Ranking
Visible scratches	5.5	.06	1 *
Eccentricity	4.4	.11	2 *
Roundness	6.4	.17	3 *
Pits	2.5	.28	4
Surface finish	2.4	.29	5
Contamination	3.1	.55	6

*Indicates top few knobs.

data on the problem condition must be matched one to one. Finally, the data for each suspect knob should cover the knob's full normal operating range.

In the search for root causes, it is a common practice to focus on the product that exhibits a problem condition. Rarely is good product also considered in conventional problem solving. Typically, only failed parts are examined to find what is "wrong." As might be expected, any unusual condition found in the problem product is automatically assumed guilty of causing the problem.

For instance, contamination was suspected of causing the valve leakage in the above example. Referring to Table 6.10, if only leaking parts were examined, 33 (sum of parts that both leak and show contamination, or 7 + 14 + 4 + 8) of 35 (23 + 12) pieces would have shown some level of contamination. It might then be concluded that contamination was the problem cause. Yet, 24 (4 + 20) out of the 26 good parts also showed contamination. If contamination was really the root cause, then the 24 good parts showing contamination should also have leaked. Although contamination might be a contributing cause, contingency table analysis—by looking at both good and bad

Table 6.10   A contingency table showing the relationship of contamination to leakage

		Contamination			
		Heavy	Moderate	None	Totals
Leakage	0 drops	4 [6.4]	20 [8.5]	2 [.9]	26
	1 drop	7 [5.7]	14 [15.8]	2 [.8]	23
	2 drops	4 [2.9]	8 [8.3]	0 [.8]	12
	Totals	15	42	4	Grand total 61

Numbers in cells indicate the number of occurrences for a set of conditions. Numbers in small boxes within cells are expected values for the cell.

product—shows it is not the major cause. Other knobs actually warrant a higher degree of suspicion, a fact that conventional problem solving would have missed completely.

SPS Route 2: Tapping Existing Knowledge

Data may not be readily available to perform correlation or contingency table analysis. If sufficient knowledge about the problem exists among team members, subjective methods are preferred over collecting new data.

Sometimes simple discussion can result in a consensus—general agreement—about which knobs should be included in the top few for evaluation. Typically, discussion alone is successful when problems are not too complex and are confined to just one or two departments. Discussion can also succeed frequently in the product/process development environment where lists of variables tend to be shorter and team knowledge is high.

When discussion alone does not lead to consensus on the top few knobs, the team should use the **subjective rating and ranking** method. This unique SPS approach for prioritizing variables is effective in a wide variety of situations and costs virtually nothing to execute. The only cost is the hour or so spent by the team and a few sheets of paper.

Team members independently assess each suspect knob on a scale of one to ten according to their interest in investigating the knob. The median rating for each knob is then used to rank-order the list of knobs. In short, a consensus on the top few knobs is reached through a voting-like procedure that protects against individual bias swaying the group.

Presented here as a step-by-step procedure, subjective rating and ranking may actually vary in form. The sessions can be either freewheeling or highly structured, depending on the style of the group. The team must only progress towards its goal—sound individual ratings of the suspect knobs. The facilitator's role is to keep the discussion on track, yet not stifle productive interchange among team members.

Subjective rating and ranking may begin as a continuation of the listing discussion (SPS Step 2), or the team may prefer to take it up at a new meeting. The procedure includes these tasks:

1. Each knob is discussed so all team members better understand why it is on the list. Team members instruct each other by sharing their knowledge on the problem. For example, an engineer explains underlying physical or design principles, while an operator describes what happens during production or, specifically, when a certain knob is adjusted.
2. Each team member individually rates the suspect knobs in response to these directions: "Rate each knob on a scale of one to ten. If you have a strong interest to experiment with a knob, give it a rating of ten; if you have no interest, give it a rating of one." The team should also be cautioned not to base their ratings on the ease of execution. Ratings are anonymously entered on a form like that shown in Figure 6.6.
3. The facilitator collects the ratings and tabulates them, as shown in Figure 6.7.
4. The facilitator scrutinizes the ratings and leads any further discussion that may be needed. (Criteria for reviewing the ratings are explained below.)

Rate each knob on a scale of 1 to 10. 10 = Very Interested in investigating 1 = Not at all Interested in investigating	
Knobs	**Ratings**
Amount of charge	9
Natural gas line pressure	6
Dwell time	7
Oxygen line pressure	6
Total mass in basket	5
Number of parts	3

Reference for knobs: See Table 5.2 in Chapter 5.

Figure 6.6   Sample form for the subjective rating

Knob	Team member ratings									Median	Notes	Priority Ranking
	1	2	3	4	5	6	7	8	9			
A	2	4	4	6	2	3	2			3		10
B	4	5	4	2	5	3	5			4		9
C	10	10	10	10	10	10	10			10	u	1
D	9	10	7	8	9	9	8			9		3
E	1	1	1	1	1	1	1			1	u	12
F	3	3	5	4	6	9*	6			5	o*	6
G	7	9	10	9	9	8	9			9		2
H	8	9	9	6	8	7	5			8		4
I	5	8	8	2	4	9	2			5	s	7
J	7	6	4	5	3	5	4			5		8
K	2	2	4	1	3	2	3			2		11
L	7	6	5	7	4	6	5			6		5

Notes: s = split   o = outlier   u = unanimous high (10) or low (1)

Figure 6.7   Summary sheet for tabulating subjective ratings

5. The median rating for each suspect knob is found. Knobs are then rank-ordered according to their median ratings.

Important to the success of the subjective method is the facilitator's review of the ratings before using them to rank the knobs. The first concern is the overall range of the team's ratings. If they are limited to a very narrow range, then the team did not discriminate well among the knobs.

Likewise, the rating ranges of individual team members should be reviewed. A person who rates all knobs "1" must believe the solution does not lie among the knobs on the list. At the other extreme, the person assigning all "10s" is willing to try anything. All "5s" reflect too little analysis. All these individuals need a better understanding of the problem solving process. The facilitator may have to further explain the rating procedure and then ask the team to reconsider their ratings.

Next the facilitator should check for *outliers* and *splits*. Outliers are one or two individual ratings that stand out from the rest of the group. One way to handle outliers is to ignore them when calculating the median rating. However, an outlier may have resulted from someone's genuine misunderstanding about a knob. Or, one team member may have some special knowledge about the knob that was not disclosed in the pre-rating stage. Team members sometimes take their own knowledge for granted and assume everyone shares it. On the other hand, resistance to group work can lead to the deliberate withholding of information. Facilitators must be alert to such possible sabotage of the group effort.

Splits suggest a polarized group. About half the ratings are low and half high, although there may also be one or two ratings in the middle. Too many split ratings may make the subjective method ineffective for finding the top knobs.

Knobs causing either split or outlier ratings should receive additional discussion. Explicit questions from the facilitator will clarify misunderstandings or add important information about the knob. Afterwards, the team should have a chance to change their ratings.

The facilitator should also be alert for any knobs given team ratings of all tens or all ones. A knob with all tens is definitely important to the team. Usually such a unanimously high rating is assigned when it is already understood how the knob affects the process output. Recalling the third rule of selection for listing (SPS Step 2), the knob should have never been listed or should have been dropped from the list before prioritization. Nevertheless, if rules are meant to be broken, then SPS teams may list knobs that need no investigation.

This point demands emphasis: When they know the knob's preferred condition, the team should not waste resources on an investigation. They should simply take action to assure the knob is permanently at its proper setting. If, however, that setting is unknown, then the knob must be evaluated as part of SPS Step 4.

At the other ratings' extreme, any knob that receives all ones should be dropped from the list and forgotten. How did such a knob get on the list in the first place? Simple. Team members may initially suspect a knob is affecting the problem, but they change their minds after the group thoroughly discusses the knob. Without team analysis, a solitary problem solver might waste valuable time by investigating such knobs. This situation highlights how teamwork and group discussion benefit the problem solving process.

After the ratings have been reviewed, clarified, and possibly changed, the facilitator finds the median rating for each knob. Only then are the suspect knobs ranked based on these median ratings. When the team must choose between two knobs with the same median rating, a graphical representation of the individual ratings can help make the choice. Figure 6.8 depicts such a case. Knob A would be chosen over Knob B because it has more higher individual ratings.

How subjective rating and ranking is conducted is crucial to its success as a prioritization method. To start with, allowing sufficient time for thorough discussion of all suspect knobs is essential. The experience of each team member should be used to scrutinize the knob that the member thinks important. This exchange of information raises everyone's understanding of the problem, helping to assure sound ratings.

As open as the discussion should be, the ratings should be done privately. Everyone is subject to personal bias due to a combination of experience, influence by others, and specific technical knowledge or the lack of it. For instance, a metallurgist will be sensitive to how material condition can affect problems and thus

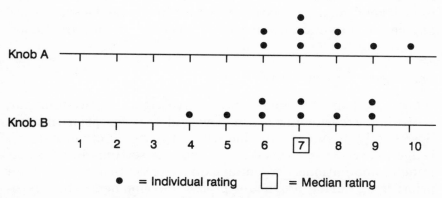

Figure 6.8   A graphical representation of ratings for two knobs, each with a median rating of 7

may be very suspicious of it. Material condition may not seem as important, however, to other members of the team. Only private ratings can prevent personal bias from swaying team members in their individual judgments of knob importance. *Private ratings help assure the overall group rating is the composite of several separate ratings, and not the result of "groupthink."*

After the subjective rating and ranking session, all team members should have a chance to agree or disagree with the top few knobs. It is not uncommon for entire groups to lose their perspective or miss the obvious. If time permits, it is therefore advisable to adjourn and have the team mull over the results of the subjective method. The facilitator can then check with team members to see if everyone is satisfied with the outcome. If not, appropriate discussion and re-ranking may be in order. The key success factor is never allowing a sense of urgency to prevent thorough consideration of all knobs.

SPS Route 3: Collecting New Data

When existing data are not available and the subjective method fails to identify the top few knobs, new data must be collected. Problem solvers must choose between two distinct methods. First is the carefully planned and carefully executed collection of data known as a screening experiment. Second is the observation and notation of naturally occurring changes in the process, referred to as a planned observational study.[4] The method used depends upon the ease with which knobs can be turned and any potentially undesirable consequences of turning the knobs.

Screening Experiments

When used in an appropriate investigation environment, screening experiments are a powerful tool for prioritization. Specifically, they are valuable when it is relatively easy to arrange many suspect variables at extreme settings in predetermined combinations. Screening experiments are also helpful for prioritizing during product or process development when existing knowledge is limited and new knobs are being created.

Table 6.11 shows the layout of an experiment involving 14

Table 6.11   Layout for a Plackett-Burman experiment for a molding blister problem

Test number	Etching	Phosohate	Adhesive	Adhesive dilution	Drying temperature	Stock scorch	Stock weight	Stock load	Lube concentration	Lube flow rate	Cure time	Cure temperature	Closure rate	Pressure	Number of blisters
1	+1	−1	−1	+1	+1	+1	+1	−1	+1	−1	+1	−1	−1	−1	28
2	−1	+1	−1	−1	−1	−1	+1	+1	−1	+1	+1	−1	−1	+1	11
3	−1	+1	+1	−1	+1	+1	−1	−1	+1	+1	+1	+1	−1	+1	40
4	+1	+1	−1	−1	+1	+1	+1	+1	−1	+1	−1	+1	−1	−1	108
5	−1	−1	+1	+1	+1	+1	−1	+1	−1	+1	−1	−1	−1	−1	22
6	+1	−1	+1	+1	−1	−1	+1	+1	+1	+1	−1	+1	−1	+1	10
7	−1	−1	−1	−1	−1	−1	−1	−1	−1	−1	−1	−1	−1	−1	44
8	+1	+1	+1	−1	+1	−1	+1	−1	−1	−1	−1	+1	+1	−1	108
9	−1	−1	+1	+1	−1	+1	+1	−1	−1	+1	+1	+1	+1	−1	13
10	−1	+1	+1	+1	+1	−1	+1	−1	+1	−1	−1	−1	−1	+1	4
11	+1	+1	−1	+1	+1	−1	−1	+1	+1	+1	+1	−1	+1	−1	54
12	+1	−1	−1	−1	−1	+1	+1	−1	+1	+1	−1	−1	+1	+1	68
13	+1	−1	+1	+1	−1	+1	−1	+1	−1	−1	−1	−1	+1	+1	15
14	−1	+1	+1	−1	−1	−1	−1	+1	+1	−1	−1	+1	−1	−1	14
15	+1	+1	−1	−1	+1	+1	−1	+1	+1	−1	+1	+1	+1	+1	73
16	−1	−1	−1	+1	−1	+1	−1	−1	−1	−1	+1	+1	−1	+1	3
17	+1	+1	+1	−1	−1	+1	+1	+1	+1	−1	+1	−1	+1	−1	1
18	−1	−1	+1	−1	+1	−1	−1	−1	−1	+1	+1	−1	+1	+1	95
19	−1	+1	−1	+1	−1	−1	−1	−1	+1	+1	−1	+1	+1	−1	0
20	−1	−1	−1	+1	+1	−1	+1	+1	−1	−1	+1	+1	+1	+1	14

+ 1 indicates high setting.
− 1 indicates low setting.

variables. The first 14 columns show the high (1) and low settings (−1) of the variables. The last column contains the resulting process output under a given row's conditions. This particular arrangement was developed by Plackett and Burman.[5]
Similar designs include Taguchi's orthogonal arrays[6] and fractional factorial designs.[7] All these designs have an important
common feature: they are orthogonal.

Orthogonality insures that no variable in an experiment exerts
unfair influence on any other variable. To illustrate this fairness
concept, listen to a conversation between two operators at shift
change:

Joe: How'd it go today?

Bob: Great. I didn't crack even one rivet.

Joe: Really? I must have broken 15 or more last night.
What's your secret?

Bob: Well, I reduced the cycle time setting from 45 to 35.

Joe: I don't think that makes any difference. Besides, I was
working with those Acme rivets yesterday. You had
the Superior rivets today. That made the difference,
not cycle time.

Bob: Okay, let's do a test. We'll get rivets from both suppliers. Then we'll each run the process at both speeds,
with both brands of rivets. Then we can tell if it's the
rivets or the cycle time.

Bob set up a schedule like that shown in Table 6.12. It allows
a fair comparison of the effect of supplier influence independent
of cycle time. Acme rivets are run at both 35 and 45 cycles per
minute; likewise, the Superior rivets are run at the 35 and 45
settings. The same fair arrangement is true for cycle time. For a
cycle time of 35, both Acme and Superior rivets are tried; for the
cycle time of 45, both Acme and Superior products are also run.
Thus, when contrasting the effect of the two rivet suppliers, the
effect of cycle time is neutralized. And when contrasting the
effect of 35 versus 45 in cycle times, the effect of rivet suppliers
is neutralized. The orthogonal arrangement allows examination
of both rivet supplier and cycle time simultaneously.

When contrasting the output for the high and low settings of

Table 6.12   Data collection sheet for cracked rivet problem

	Rivet supplier	Cycle time	Number of cracked rivets
First 2 hours	Superior	35	
Second 2 hours	Acme	45	
Third 2 hours	Acme	35	
Fourth 2 hours	Superior	45	

a particular variable within an orthogonal design, all the remaining variables must have an equal number of high and low settings. This arrangement cancels the individual effect of each variable. It is assumed that any interaction between knobs is negligible compared to the independent effects of the knobs. By definition, orthogonal comparisons are independent of each other. Table 6.11 has the same orthogonal property as the simple example of Table 6.12, except the orthogonality is maintained for 14 variables—in only 20 tests.

When conducting a screening experiment, the chosen settings should represent the operational extremes of the possible settings for each knob being studied. Knobs are prioritized by how much each influences the process output as it is turned from one extreme setting to the other. As each knob is tried, it is simultaneously being "tested" by the other knobs in the experiment.

For the particular Plackett-Burman experiment shown in Table 6.11, up to 19 knobs can test each other. Knobs of key importance will withstand this scrutiny by showing an obvious effect on the process output, even as the remaining knobs continuously change combinations. As illustrated in Figure 6.9, adhesive dilution, drying temperature, and etching proved to be the top knobs in the molding blister problem of Table 6.11. Their effects on the process were not diminished by the changing conditions of the 13 other knobs.

The Difficulty of Conducting Screening Experiments

From a mathematical perspective, screening experiments are very efficient. They provide the widest possible coverage of the

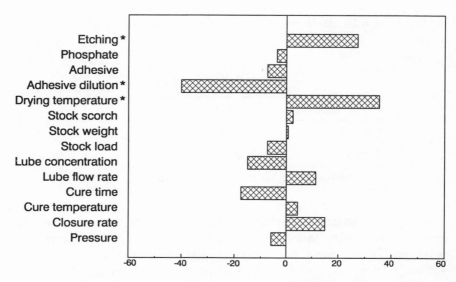

Figure 6.9 Graphical representation of strength of effect for each knob in the screening experiment. * Indicates the top few knobs.

experimental space with very few tests. Consequently, when the conditions described in the following paragraphs can be met, screening experiments are valuable for prioritizing.

In fact, however, the range of problems for which screening experiments are feasible is very narrow compared to the wide variety of problems facing industry. The cost and difficulty involved in conducting these experiments are rarely discussed in statistical literature. To successfully and economically conduct a screening experiment, two conditions must be met.

Primarily, each knob must not only be easy to alter but must be altered *independently* of all the other knobs in the experiment. If the knobs are different dimensions on the same component produced in a "WHAM" process, experimentation will be difficult. In WHAM operations such as screw machining, injection molding, casting, and stamping, or on transfer lines, many product characteristics are simultaneously produced. It is thus difficult to impossible to get specific combinations of dimensions on a part. To get the needed experimental combinations from a WHAM process, extensive sorting and inspecting must be done, or the tooling hardware must be permanently altered. The reversibility of settings required in a screening experiment is therefore impossible to achieve.

Extraordinary means such as prototype fabrication to produce experimental hardware would be very costly. Under such conditions, screening experiment results may not even be valid. Objections by anxious operating personnel are another potential difficulty with screening experiments. It may be feared that certain experimental combinations of knob settings will wreak havoc with either the equipment or the product.

The second condition for a successful screening experiment recognizes the complexity of the experimental matrix, such as in Table 6.11. Problem solvers must understand precisely what activity is required for each combination of knobs in the matrix. Meticulous planning and strict execution are necessary. There are many ways in which the experiment can be botched, including turning one or more knobs to the wrong setting or mislabeling results.

Even in a controlled laboratory setting, keeping track of an experiment involving 10, 12, or 14 variables is extremely challenging and requires much care. In a real-time production environment, conducting a screening experiment can become impossibly confusing, even for the experienced experimenter.

The expectations an experimenter has for a screening experiment must be in line with its limitations. Some practitioners want to use screening experiments to *evaluate* variables because of their mathematical efficiency. Screening experiments, however, confound variable effects with variable interactions. Results may be interpreted in more than one way, and it is impossible—without including additional combinations—to sort out which interpretation is correct. To rationalize the confounding, proponents of screening experiments make assumptions on mathematical grounds about the relatively minor role of interactions. Such mathematical assumptions may or may not fit the actual problem situation faced by the SPS team.

Real physical interactions may be present and may even be the primary source of variation. By ignoring interactions, screening experiments simply do not provide the full evaluation required to solve a problem. They should be used mainly as a prioritization tool, therefore, and only when economically and practically feasible.

The Planned Collection of Observational Data

When it is not possible or practical to carry out a screening experiment, prioritization can be accomplished with a planned observational study. As its name suggests, this method plans the observation and recording of naturally occurring changes in the process variables and output. As an economical source of information, it is most effective when data are plentiful and the problem magnitude is small to medium. This combination results in a mixture of acceptable and unacceptable process output.

Using observational data for prioritizing variables requires *careful* planning. To begin with, the recording of information must be accurate and consistent. Care in documentation is especially critical when data collection spans more than one shift, involving more than one individual.

Both the status of each suspect knob and the corresponding condition of the process output are recorded in real-time. When possible, it is desirable to display the output condition on an SPC chart with the status of the suspect knobs recorded below each plotted data point. This is a use of investigative SPC (ISPC), introduced in Chapter 4. It serves to both define the problem and prioritize the variables list.

Before beginning the analysis of observational data, the SPS team must decide if there is adequate data. Data adequacy is defined as output variation that is large enough to consider problematic. That is, the data must include both acceptable and unacceptable output. If no samples of unacceptable output are present, not enough knob changes have occurred to create the problem.

It may take some time before the natural changes in the process necessary to see excessive variation occur. This delay in obtaining complete data is a potential drawback in using observational data.

Once all the necessary data are collected, either correlation analysis or contingency table analysis is used to determine the top few knobs for full evaluation.

The Teamwork Factor

POINT ONE: The team must include everyone who has knowledge of the problem. If key people are missing from the team, a leading suspect knob could be neglected, making problem solution unlikely. For example, a design engineer's understanding of a certain physical principle might cast suspicion on one particular knob. That knob might not seem important to others on the team with less knowledge of physics. Similarly, insignificant knobs may be included in the top few due to a lack of sufficient knowledge within the group. Problem solving resources will then be wasted.

As presented in Chapter 3, the SPS team's membership is dynamic. For successful use of the subjective prioritization method, it may be necessary to add persons with special knowledge. Their temporary participation helps insure accurate selection of the top knobs.

POINT TWO: From a basic understanding of group dynamics, the facilitator should take precautions to prevent strong personalities from dominating the team. For example, a metallurgist could steer the group toward considering material condition a top knob. This possibility emphasizes the importance of having team members rate the knobs privately. Each team member then considers the metallurgist's views objectively, free from any pressure to agree or disagree.

Besides subject matter experts, managers can also pressure a group. Therefore, the opinions of managers should not be allowed to intimidate or sway the team's investigation of the problem. The SPS process succeeds only if all team members have an equal influence on the outcome of the investigation. Once again, anonymous ratings protect the team from political concerns that can bias prioritization.

POINT THREE: The facilitator must be alert for possibly biased or invalid data. Only if existing data are complete and sound can the team successfully base prioritization on the data. The facilitator's role in questioning the when and how of data collection is therefore essential. In time, all SPS team members should be able to pose those questions.

POINT FOUR: SPS prioritization emphasizes the most practicable method, from the preferred use of easily accessible information to the carefully planned collection of new data. With any of the methods, team consensus on the results should be achieved. The facilitator should confirm that everyone is satisfied with the top knobs before moving on to evaluation of those knobs. Evaluation requires too much effort to attempt it without the consent and support of the full team.

POINT FIVE: The SPS facilitator is an active participant in the SPS process, not just an observer. Just how much facilitators contribute to each SPS step, however, depends on their familiarity with the problem situation. If their knowledge of the problem justifies their input, for example, they should rate the knobs. On the other hand, if they have had no contact with the problem, they should abstain from rating the knobs.

Conclusion

Understanding the complexity created by not just variables but also their interactions is the only way to solve chronic problems permanently. Precisely because variables and their interactions can cause considerable confusion, identifying the most important variables is crucial to efficient problem solving. The prioritization step paves the way to productive evaluation of just the top few knobs contributing to the problem. This systematic approach to "too many variables!" is at the basis of our Chapter 2 claim that SPS can handle the unmanageable.

Initially, all knobs listed during SPS Step 2 are considered equally suspect of causing the problem. Step 3 refines the degree of suspicion by ranking the knobs according to their departure from innocence. As is true for all SPS steps, the most economical methods are used to prioritize suspect knobs. In selecting the appropriate method, one of three routes is followed: (1) use existing data, (2) use subjective knowledge, or (3) collect new data.

If sound, complete data exists, SPS capitalizes on its availability. Correlation analysis is the preferred tool for revealing how strongly an individual suspect knob relates to the problem. Only variables data, however, can be handled by correlation analysis. When information is in the form of attributes data or a combination of attributes and variables data, contingency table analysis is used. Problem solvers must remember that neither of these methods can establish causal relationships between knobs and problems. Correlation analysis and contingency table analysis are used only to rank-order knobs for scrutiny in the next SPS step.

When usable data are not available, knobs can be prioritized through the subjective rating and ranking method. A characteristic SPS tool, the subjective method is more expedient than collecting new data. It relies totally on the team's combined experience with the knobs on the list. A thorough, open discussion of all suspect knobs is crucial to this method's success. Afterwards, team members individually rate the knobs according to which they think most suspicious of causing the problem. The ratings are then used to rank-order the knobs, thereby identifying the top few knobs for evaluation.

As effective as the subjective method can be, team members may find they do not possess adequate knowledge to identify the key knobs. The third route for prioritizing knobs is then necessary, requiring the collection of new data. As always, economy is a deciding factor in selecting the specific method. If the suspect knobs can be easily turned independently of one another, screening experiments can provide important information for prioritization. Frequently, however, the specific combinations of suspect knob settings required by a screening experiment can only be achieved through extraordinary arrangements. In addition, their complexity demands that problem solvers are experienced with the planning and execution details of screening experiments.

When screening experiments are impractical, the team can plan to collect new data by observing and recording changes occurring naturally in the process. This method involves the systematic monitoring of both the suspect knobs and the process output. The investigative use of statistical process control (ISPC), described in Chapter 4, is applicable to the collection of observational data.

As with all the prioritization techniques, the use of observational data should be approached cautiously. It must represent the full range of process output—acceptable to unacceptable. To collect adequate data may therefore take a considerable amount of time. Once the observational data set is complete, either correlation analysis or contingency table analysis is applied as discussed above.

Selecting the method for prioritizing knobs is a situational decision. With SPS, that decision is based on economy, efficiency, and—not least of all—the adequacy of available information. The results of the prioritization step will only be as good as the data or subjective judgments used to identify the key knobs. By observing the cautions described in this chapter, the SPS team can begin in-depth evaluation confident that they are focusing their efforts on the top few knobs.

References

1. George E. P. Box, William G. Hunter, and J. Stuart Hunter, *Statistics for Experimenters*, New York: John Wiley & Sons, Inc., 1978.

2. Acheson J. Duncan, *Quality Control and Industrial Statistics*, 4th ed.; Homewood, IL: Richard D. Irwin, Inc., 1974. Also, John Neter, William Wasserman, and Michael H. Kutner, *Applied Linear Regression Models*; Homewood, IL: Richard D. Irwin, Inc., 1983.

3. Box, Hunter, and Hunter. Also, Duncan.

4. William G. Cochran, *Planning and Analysis of Observational Studies*, edited by Lincoln E. Moses and Frederick Mosteller, New York: John Wiley & Sons, 1983.

5. Samuel Kotz, Norman L. Johnson, and Campbell B. Read, editors, *Encyclopedia of Statistical Sciences*, Vol. 6, New York: John Wiley & Sons, 1985. Also, Douglas C. Montgomery, *Design and Analysis of Experiments*, 2nd ed., New York: John Wiley & Sons, 1984.

6. Genichi Taguchi, *System of Experimental Design*; White Plains, NY: Kraus International Publications and Dearborn, MI: ASI Press, 1987.

7. Robert A. McLean and Virgil L. Anderson, *Applied Factorial and Fractional Designs*, New York: Marcel Dekker, Inc., 1984. Also, Box, Hunter, and Hunter.

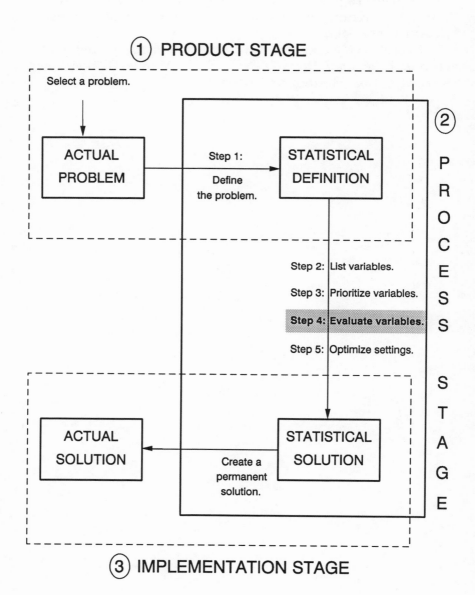

Chapter 7

Evaluating the Top
Few Variables
(SPS Step 4)

Issue:	Without a thorough understanding of the top few variables, no problem will be permanently solved.
SPS Response:	Variables are evaluated in one of three ways, with emphasis on selecting the least expensive:
	1. Actively change variable settings.
	2. Combine changing some variable settings with observing random changes within variables not easily changed.
	3. Observe random changes only when it is not possible to manipulate any variable settings.
	The statistical methods used are the analysis of variance and multiple regression analysis.
SPS Results:	1. An understanding of how the important variables and their combinations affect output variation.
	2. Knowledge of the required setting for each key variable to improve performance.
	3. An estimate of potential improvement with key variables at their proper settings.

The Purpose of Evaluation

Evaluating the top few variables is at the heart of the SPS process. In Chapter 2, good quality was equated with consistency in the operation of a product or the delivery of a service. Quality problems occur when excessive variation causes us to miss our target or objective. To control variation, those knobs causing the variation must be identified and understood.

The first three SPS steps are aimed at *identifying* the potentially important knobs. First, problem definition describes the undesirable variation causing the problem. Second, the listing of

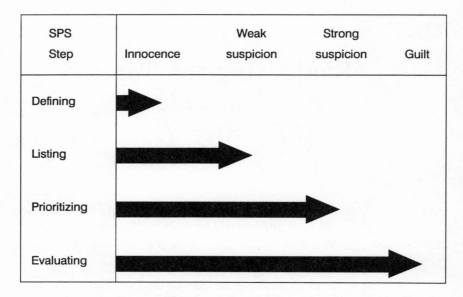

Figure 7.1 Each successive SPS step further separates the guilty knobs from the innocent knobs, as illustrated in this continuum.

knobs suspected to affect the problem is guided by the problem definition. Third, prioritizing the list reveals which knobs should receive in-depth evaluation.

The essential task of *understanding* the top knobs and their combinations is accomplished during the evaluation step. Sometimes a solution is discovered before reaching the evaluation stage, but in most cases evaluating variables is essential to solving the problem. Evaluation is often so successful that optimization (SPS Step 5) is unnecessary. Continuous improvement efforts can then be focused on the next problem.

During the evaluation step, the investigation moves from the level of *suspicion* to the level of *guilt*. Figure 7.1 depicts how SPS Steps 1–4 carry suspect knobs along a continuum of innocence to guilt. In-depth evaluation confirms which knobs and combinations of knob settings are in fact causing the problem.

Issues and Challenges Faced During Evaluation

The subject of evaluating many variables simultaneously is popularly known as *design of experiments* (DOE). The DOE concept has basically the same objectives as the SPS evaluation step. Both attempt to confirm which variables and their combinations are guilty of creating the undesirable variation in the process. SPS evaluation has broader application than DOE, however, because it can deal with a wider variety of problem situations and execution challenges.

The versatility of SPS is due to its **problem-driven orientation**. After looking at a problem as well as its execution requirements, the SPS team selects the most effective, economical tools and tactics for that investigation.

When quality improvement efforts are method driven, problem solvers naturally debate which tool to use. There is little value, however, in debating the effectiveness of statistical techniques apart from the specific context in which they are applied. Which is better, a screw driver or a hammer? It depends on the situation. Am I driving screws or nails? If nails, the hammer is better; if screws, the screwdriver. It is the same with technical issues surrounding statistical methods. The debate over methods is resolved when faced with a specific problem. The best method is the one that results in a timely, economical solution.

Mathematical Efficiency Versus Total Efficiency

The challenge to problem solvers is to complete the evaluation at the least possible cost and in the shortest possible time. Evaluation requires data, and collecting data costs time and money. The total cost of an investigation is determined by the amount of data collected times the cost-per-unit of data. The two parts of this formula represent the major factors affecting the cost of an evaluation: mathematical efficiency and execution difficulty.

Difficulty in conducting an investigation depends on the cost to change a knob from its original setting to an alternate setting and back again. Mathematical efficiency refers to how much useful information can be extracted from a given amount of data. The most mathematically efficient method of evaluation is the full factorial experiment. With relatively little data, the effect of each knob and all the possible interactions among the knobs can be discovered.

Table 7.1 depicts a three-knob experiment with two-knob interactions (AB, AC, and BC) and a three-knob interaction

Table 7.1   A designed experiment layout showing columns to calculate 7 effects from 8 tests

Test	Knobs							Data
	A	B	C	AB	BC	AC	ABC	
1	−	−	−	+	+	+	−	29.6
2	+	−	−	−	+	−	+	16.8
3	−	+	−	−	−	+	+	10.4
4	+	+	−	+	−	−	−	10.6
5	−	−	+	+	−	−	+	11.8
6	+	−	+	−	−	+	−	16.4
7	−	+	+	−	+	−	−	5.0
8	+	+	+	+	+	+	+	12.6

(ABC). Analysis of this experiment yields a total of seven units of information from only eight tests. Consider a four-knob experiment requiring 16 tests. From the four knobs, six two-knob interactions, four three-knob interactions, and one four-knob interaction, 15 units of information result.

Most experts recommend repeating each test at least once. If repeated, the three-knob experiment would require 16 samples (2 × 8 tests) and the four-knob experiment would require 32 samples (2 × 16 tests). All these tests still represent a very efficient source of information. Compare these tests with a typical short-term capability study in manufacturing where 30 to 50 samples are collected. Yet, only three units of information are extracted: the location (average), dispersion (standard deviation), and shape of the process output distribution (histogram).

Although full factorial experiments are efficient mathematically, they can be extremely difficult and expensive to perform. As the number of knobs under study increases, the complexity of the experiment rises exponentially. (See Table 6.3 in Chapter 6.)

Experimental hardware can be costly, and conducting the experiment can be time consuming and confusing for all but the most experienced experimenters. In addition, certain experimental combinations could produce bad parts or damage equipment.

The cost of an evaluation may be less using a less mathematically efficient scheme, even though more data points will be collected. In particular, a planned observational study for evaluation may be more efficient overall. Problems requiring the evaluation of parts from a "WHAM" process—in which many product traits are simultaneously produced—illustrate this point.

Because individual part characteristics cannot be independently controlled, parts from a WHAM process are especially difficult to evaluate using a factorial experiment. For example, in one case, over half the output was failing a final test, requiring product repair and rebuild. A major component in the product came from a WHAM process, screw machining.

The troubleshooters working on this case decided on a factorial experiment to find which dimensions on the component were causing the problem. They first requested eight experimental components from the screw machine department. However, they learned the combinations of dimensions desired could not be created without major tooling changes and excessive downtime. They ended up waiting several weeks and paying several thousand dollars to order the special components from a prototype shop.

Meanwhile, the SPS approach was also taken on the same problem. Twenty completed units were used, ten that passed and ten that failed the final test. The units were disassembled and suspected key dimensions were measured—the same dimensions that were varied in the factorial experiment. Multiple regression analysis was used to evaluate the relationship between the final test results and the suspected key dimensions. The analysis showed which dimensions were important and suggested that better target values were needed on the blueprints. The screw machine setup was altered to reflect the new target values, and the pass rate at the final test went up to almost 100%.

Several weeks later the experimental components were ready

Table 7.2   Comparison of costs for two approaches to evaluating a problem

	Designed Experiment (Sample size = 8)		Planned Observational Study (Sample size = 20)	
	Per unit	Total	Per unit	Total
Fabrication cost	$800	$6400	$0	$0
Inspection cost	$12	$96	$12	$240
Final test cost	$1	$8	$1	$20
Total	$813	$6504	$13	$260

for the factorial experiment. Results essentially matched those from the SPS evaluation, which used planned observational data from existing production components. Both methods gave the same answer, but one at considerably less time and cost.

Table 7.2 summarizes the cost of investigation for each approach to this screw machine example. Although using observational data required that more samples be collected and analyzed, the cost of each observation was small compared with the cost for experimental components. In addition, the planned observational study gave a faster answer—a few days compared with over a month—because it was selected to match the execution challenges.

The Element of Surprise

Statistical Problem Solving relies heavily on existing knowledge based on both theory and experience. Still, the results of the evaluation step are often surprising to the SPS team. A knob thought to be important may be found to have very little effect on the problem. Interactions among the important knobs may have been unanticipated. The amount of potential improvement may be far above or far below the team's expectations. It is this element of surprise so common in chronic problems that makes evaluation necessary. Surprises like these also convince the most reluctant team member of the usefulness of SPS techniques.

Chapter 6 stressed the prioritizing of suspect knobs as a prelude to evaluating knobs. Some teachers of the Taguchi approach to DOE recommend that problem solvers predict what interactions may be present and make them a part of the experiment. By so doing, the size of the experiment can be reduced. Yet even when interaction is understood, correctly predicting interactions *within the operating ranges* of the top few knobs is highly unlikely. Incorrect predictions about interactions will prevent valid evaluations. In contrast, SPS evaluation makes no assumptions about the presence or absence of interactions.

Operating Ranges Versus Operating Relationships

Many problem solutions emerge only when interactions among important knobs are understood. Thus, it is not sufficient to specify operating ranges for the important knobs. Operating *relationships* among the important knobs must also be specified. For example, the grinding problem discussed in Chapter 6 showed an interaction between the feed rate and spindle speed. Figure 7.2 illustrates how the operating relationship between the feed and speed must be specified to minimize the out-of-round condition. It is not sufficient to say that a slower spindle speed or a faster feed rate is needed. Both knob settings must be specified in relation to each other. For improved roundness, if the spindle speed is set to fast, the feed rate must also be set to fast. If the spindle speed is slow, the feed rate must be slow.

SPS Versus One Knob at a Time

Problem solvers who have succeeded with a one-knob-at-a-time approach do not see any need for a multiknob approach. The latter approach is more efficient, however, and has a higher

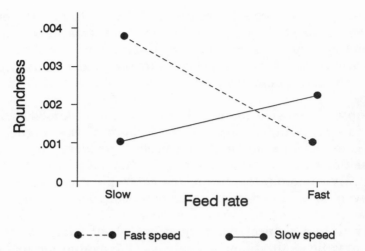

Figure 7.2   For improved roundness, if spindle speed is set on fast, then feed rate must also be fast. If spindle speed is set on slow, feed rate must be slow.

overall success rate. A one-knob-at-a-time approach can only be totally successful if there are no interactions present, as shown in Table 7.3.

The single-knob approach has limited success primarily because it assumes interactions are absent. Whether or not interactions are contributing to the problem cannot be known until after the knobs have been evaluated. To ensure problem solving

Table 7.3   SPS will be successful in all problem situations.

	No interactions present	Interactions present
One-knob-at-a-time approach	Successful	Not successful
SPS approach	Successful	Successful

success, therefore, the presence of interactions must be anticipated. If the evaluation finds there are no important interactions, nothing will be lost. The multiknob approach is still the
most efficient and successful approach overall.

How often do knob interactions play an important role in finding a problem solution? Are interactions among more than two
variables common? When considering *all* problems, interactions
may not play a major role. But for *chronic* problems, the presence of interactions is a major reason the one-knob-at-a-time
approach fails.

The use of screening experiments for evaluation purposes assumes that knob interactions—especially among more than two
knobs—rarely play an important role in causing problems. In
our experience using SPS, however, interactions among two or
more knobs are a real and common occurrence. Because we deal
primarily with chronic problems, the high proportion of interactions we see may not be representative of all problems. Nevertheless, assumptions made during the evaluation step should
neither preclude the presence of interactions nor favor some
interactions over others.

Knob Reversibility

A full evaluation of the top few knobs cannot occur if all their
possible combinations are not tried. Often problem solvers recognize that more than one knob may be important, but their
investigation is hit and miss. For example, a team of engineers
inspected sample parts for flatness and surface finish. The team
arbitrarily selected processing combinations of fabricating,
grinding, lapping, and heat treating for their investigation. Instead, they could have viewed the various process steps as knobs
in an experiment.

Table 7.4 shows an experimental layout of all the possible
combinations for a complete evaluation of this problem. Asterisks indicate the combinations actually tested by the engineers.
Since they missed so many combinations, they gained no fundamental knowledge about the independent effect of each knob.
They could determine neither the relative importance of each
knob nor the presence of interactions among the knobs. The
point is, all combinations must be tried for an evaluation to be
successful.

Table 7.4 Asterisks indicate the trial-and-error combinations, shown as a subset of the total possible combinations.

| | | Grind | | No grind | |
		Lap	No lap	Lap	No lap
Heat treat method 1	Stamp	1	2	3	4 ★
	Machine	5 ★	6 ★	7 ★	8
Heat treat method 2	Stamp	9	10 ★	11 ★	12
	Machine	13 ★	14	15	16

All possible combinations can be tried only if changes in the important knobs are *reversible*. Experimenters often change the existing setting of a knob, expecting improvement. If none occurs, the knob may remain at the new setting either because it cannot be changed back or because changing it back is an admission of failure. During SPS evaluation, however, the ability to turn knobs in either direction is essential. Ideally, the changing of a knob should resemble the simple flicking of a switch, easily moving from one setting to another and back again.

One-direction changes are not investigation, but implementation. For example, if an injection molding problem is being investigated, removing steel from the die is not a reversible change. Changing the machine settings, however, is relatively easy and temporary. SPS would look first at whether an injection molding problem could be corrected by adjusting machine or process parameters. Only if using easily turnable, reversible knobs failed would cutting the steel in the die be considered.

Irreversible changes can also result for political reasons. Problem solvers may have to defend an unnecessary expenditure if a knob is restored to its original setting. When an implemented change does not yield the hoped-for improvement, problem solvers may rationalize that the change was "directionally correct."

In the one-knob-at-a-time approach, it is common for problem solvers to change direction in the middle of an investigation. At the root of hit-and-miss investigations are poorly defined problems and the failure to list and prioritize knobs before beginning. It is not surprising then that new knobs are introduced once an experiment is under way. Such zigzagging creates confusion and prevents reliable analysis of whatever data are collected.

The SPS evaluation is the result of careful planning. Ideally, once started, the evaluation should be completed without straying from the plan. When SPS steps leading up to evaluation are carefully executed, there is rarely the need to change a planned evaluation. If new knowledge is gained during the evaluation, however, the team should consider whether to complete the evaluation, stop and replan the evaluation, or possibly return to earlier SPS steps.

The Evaluation Procedure

The procedure for performing the SPS evaluation step can be summarized as follows:

1. Review the problem definition.
2. Select performance characteristics.
3. Review each of the top few knobs.
    (a) Describe the behavior, control, and operating range of the knob.
    (b) Decide how the knob will change.
    (c) Indicate the settings at which the knob will be evaluated.
4. Plan the data collection.
    (a) Decide where, when, and how the samples will be collected.
    (b) Determine how the samples will be measured.
    (c) Create forms to record the data.
    (d) Assign responsibilities.
5. Collect the data according to the plan.
6. Check the data for sufficiency and stability.

7. Analyze the data.
8. Describe the statistical solution to the problem.
   (a) Which knobs and their interactions are creating the variation in the process output?
   (b) For each guilty knob, what is the correct setting to improve output performance?
   (c) What is the expected improvement if the knob settings are implemented?

Each aspect of this procedure will be detailed in the following pages.

Review Problem Definition

If the problem is due to process instability, investigative SPC should be used first. Only after SPC techniques are exhausted should SPS be used to evaluate problems of instability. SPS deals effectively with complex problems, whether or not instability persists.

When the process output can be described using variables data, there are three possible classes of problems, as shown in Table 7.5. For Class 1 problems, evaluation should seek to understand which knobs affect ability to hit the target. For Class 2 problems, the evaluation should be planned to reveal which

Table 7.5 Possible problem situations faced under stable conditions

		Process location	
		On target	Off target
Process spread	Capable	O. K.	Class 1 problem
	Incapable	Class 2 problem	Class 3 problem

knobs improve the capability or spread of the process output. For Class 3 problems, knobs that affect the location and knobs that affect the spread must both be understood. (Problems involving attributes data constitute a separate category of problems.) The type of problem affects how the data collection is planned and how the data are analyzed.

Select a Performance Characteristic

The SPS team must first select an appropriate performance characteristic—the criterion by which the knobs are evaluated. Selection is based on the problem definition, the nature of the process output, and the class of problem as described above.

Class 1 problems are typically evaluated using measures of process location such as the average, mathematical transformations of the average,[1] or the median. Class 2 problems can be evaluated using measures of process spread such as the range or the standard deviation.[2] Class 3 problems can be evaluated looking at location and dispersion effects separately or using measures that combine them, such as Taguchi's signal-to-noise ratios.[3]

Qualitative problems (those using attributes data) make up a separate category of problems. When a quality attribute either passes or fails, the problem is evaluated using proportion defective or defects per unit as the performance characteristic. Administrative problems are evaluated by the team ranking possible improvement actions along a scale, say from 1 to 10. Ordinal numbers are used also for technical problems requiring subjective judgment of qualitative characteristics, such as blemishes on a molded part.

The SPS facilitator must guide the team in selecting a performance characteristic. In many problems, more than one characteristic representing more than one type of problem will be evaluated. For instance, the evaluation of a valve may include data on the performance of flow rate, leakage, and response time.

Review the Top Few Knobs

Knob Knowledge. Knobs exhibit a variety of behaviors. To decide how knobs can be manipulated, the team must review what they know about each knob, as follows:

1. Natural *knob behavior* should be understood. Inherently stable knobs will hold their settings indefinitely. Other knobs change with time by drifting, cycling, or shifting to new levels.
2. *Knob control* should be reviewed. Some knobs are easy to control, while others are difficult or nearly impossible to control. For instance, a spindle speed can be easily changed by moving a belt to a different pulley. Material thickness in a stamping operation, however, may be uncontrollable from coil to coil of steel.
3. The *operating range* of each knob should be determined and explicitly stated.

Knob Turnability. In deciding how each knob should be changed for evaluation, the SPS team is faced with three possibilities. **First, an easily turnable knob whose effect is understood can be turned from one extreme of its operating range to the other.** Factorial experiments require such quick setting changes.

Second, knobs of uncertain effect should be turned only over a limited range, expressed as "turned with comfort." The team may be unsure about a knob's effect when it is turned over its full operating range while other knobs are also turned over their ranges. One of the SPS execution principles addresses the range over which knobs should be evaluated. **Knobs should be turned as far as possible during the evaluation without damaging equipment or exceeding the historical level of defects.** Involving operating personnel in determining ranges can guard against their violating this principle. (SPS execution principles are also discussed under planning the data collection in this chapter.)

Extreme settings could be explored before the actual evaluation is under way. To illustrate, during SPS on an injection molding problem, team members expressed doubts that planned combinations of knob settings would even work. The extreme setting combinations were consequently tried on a small scale before the full-scale evaluation began. The extreme combinations worked and the evaluation proceeded as planned.

Third, some knobs are impossible to turn due to the expense involved. For instance, controlling the temperature in a factory may require prohibitively expensive air conditioning. Or process complexity might mean turning knobs for the sake of experimentation would totally disrupt production. In such cases, SPS watches natural changes in the knobs during normal running of the process.

Naturally changing data are used in planned observational studies, as introduced in Chapter 6. Data collection would stop once all knobs had naturally varied across the desired ranges. Observing naturally occurring changes is an expedient compromise in which many observations of inexpensive data are collected over a relatively long period. The alternative is the execution of an expensive designed experiment over a short time with fewer samples. Risks associated with the interpretation of observational data are addressed later in this chapter. (Cautions to take in the use of observational data were also considered in Chapter 6.)

Knob Settings. Finally, the team must decide on the specific settings or—if natural changes are observed—range of settings to study for each knob. For actively turned knobs, discrete settings must be selected. For instance, if the knob in question is temperature, the settings might be 1550 degrees and 1750 degrees.

Knobs should be evaluated at just two settings, unless there are compelling reasons to look at more than two. As the number of settings for each knob increases, the number of possible combinations in the experiment rises rapidly. Table 7.6 shows the number of test combinations that must be studied for two to four knobs, each at two or three settings. Some of the combinations, as identified by asterisks, may be too large for economical evaluation.

There are cases when it is justified to look at more than two settings during the evaluation step. Figure 7.3 plots three possible relationships between knobs and process output. Just as interactions cannot usually be anticipated, so it is difficult to predict accurately how knobs might be related to output. A simple relationship that would be discovered easily at only two settings is depicted in Figure 7.3a.

Figure 7.3b is troublesome to interpret due to the curvature in the relationship between the knob and the process output. If

Table 7.6 The number of tests required based on the number of knobs and the number of settings for each knob

Number of settings				Minimum test combinations required
First knob	Second knob	Third knob	Fourth knob	
2	2	—	—	4
3	2	—	—	6
3	3	—	—	9
2	2	2	—	8
2	2	3	—	12
2	3	3	—	18
3	3	3	—	27 *
2	2	2	2	16
3	2	2	2	24
3	3	2	2	36 *
3	3	3	2	54 *
3	3	3	3	81 *

*Required number of tests typically exceeds a manageable number.

only settings 1 and 3 are studied, the interpolation along the dotted line would be inaccurate. The practical consequences of such an error must be weighed against the expense of adding a third setting.

Studying three levels for the knob in Figure 7.3c is certainly justified. If only settings 1 and 3 are studied, the team might conclude that the knob has no effect. If only settings 1 and 2 are studied, the team might conclude that going beyond setting 2

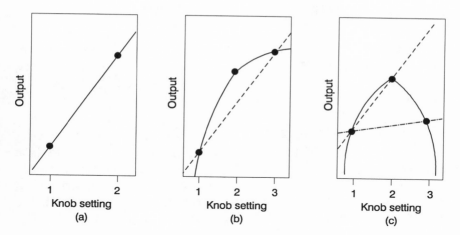

Figure 7.3 Three possible relationships between knob settings and process output

would yield further improvement. Such extrapolation, however, should be avoided.

It is a common experience for team members to be uncomfortable with only two settings in evaluating a knob. They wonder what effect the knob has between the two settings or just beyond the settings. We have observed many trial-and-error problem solvers who decide a particular knob is most important and test it at many levels, six or more. They explain they are attempting to map the effect of the knob or discover an operating window. Often, however, they have prematurely concluded that the knob is the top knob. They then commit their resources to understanding it. Their results may not be accurate, however, if the knob is interacting with other knobs. Detailed studies of a single knob or the most important knobs as revealed by the evaluation step are more appropriate to the optimization step.

Once the team agrees on the number of settings for the actively turned knobs, the actual values of the settings are selected. Per SPS execution principles, the settings should be over as wide a range as possible without creating defects or damaging equipment. For those knobs whose natural changes will be observed, the team must decide on the range of values they need to observe. Based on that range, data collection continues until the desired changes occur.

Plan the Data Collection

Planning the data collection to evaluate the top few knobs requires a sound understanding of statistical design of experiments. As essential as the facilitator's guidance is, the knowledge of the team members is equally essential.

SPS Execution Principles. Intimate knowledge of the process is needed to fulfill two SPS execution principles during data collection. First, with existing processes, data collection should occur during normal production operations **without affecting operating efficiency**. The SPS team must use their knowledge of the process to create sampling methods that will not disrupt operations.

Second, when changing knob settings, **the historical level of defects should not be exceeded**. If a given combination of knob settings produces too many defects, the team should quickly move on to the next combination. With an ultrasonic welding problem, the plan called for running 15 parts after changing knob settings to allow the process to stabilize, then five pieces were collected. The knobs were changed to a new combination, 15 parts run to stabilize the process, five pieces collected—and so on. With one combination, the operator noticed that the first two pieces did not fuse. Should the run have been continued to complete the sample size? Of course not.

The output characteristic under evaluation was the force required to break the weld. If welding was successful, the two-piece sample would have provided enough data. Since the two pieces did not weld at all, no force data were available for that combination. With most of the data in the range of 35 to 40 pounds, a very low value—say 5 pounds—could be substituted for the missing data. Another approach to missing data is to use computer programs that can handle missing values or unbalanced data sets. The analyst, however, should heed software warnings and check the documentation regarding missing or unbalanced data.

For problems in research and development, the SPS facilitator should seek help in designing an experiment that efficiently uses laboratory time and equipment. One very efficient way to reduce costs is to build experimental hardware as part of a customer prototype order. If the experimental hardware meets the requirements, it can become part of the prototype order, reducing the cost of the experiment.

Table 7.5 earlier identified three classes of problems. SPS evaluation seeks to discover how knobs affect output location, dispersion, or both. The effect of each knob cannot be known before data are collected and analyzed. With variables data, therefore, information to discover both location and dispersion effects should be collected during the evaluation.

Data Collection Logistics.   Where, when, and how the data will be collected must be decided. Every detail about the data collection should be explicitly discussed by the team and carefully documented. Nothing should be assumed. If three machines all perform the same operation, which one of the three will be used? Decide and document. If only eight tests can be performed during a shift and 16 are needed, when will the tests be done? On one shift two days in a row? On two consecutive shifts? Decide and document. How will samples be taken? Is special stock or material required? Will items be serialized or measured on the spot and returned to the process flow? It may be advisable to discuss a possible procedure, then try it once to see how it works.

Sample Measurement.   Next, determine how the samples will be measured. If there is an accepted measurement technique already in use, discuss its appropriateness for the SPS evaluation study. A common concern is the adequacy of available measurement methods. Our experience indicates if a measurement method is adequate to run the process, then it is adequate to solve the problem. The exception, of course, is when the measurement method *is* the problem. As with all other data collection issues, nothing should be assumed about how the parts will be measured.

Data Collection Forms.   When collecting data during operations, many things happen at once. Forms that include instructions, a place to record all the data, and room for comments should be prepared in advance. A "runs sheet" similar to that in Figure 7.4 is a helpful aid. One is prepared for each test and

```
┌─────────────────────────────────────────────────────────┐
│          EXPERIMENTAL RUNS SHEET : DIP SOLDER TEST        │
│                                                           │
│  ○                                                        │
│        Date: _____   Time: _____   Test #:__12__ │
│                                                           │
│     1.  Allow minimum of 10 minutes stabilization after making settings. │
│     2.  Adjust process to following settings.             │
│                                                           │
│          A.  Preheat temperature:      500°F              │
│          B.  Solder temperature:       600°F              │
│          C.  Solder time:              1.5 secs.          │
│  ○       D.  Solder depth :            2.0 mm             │
│                                                           │
│     3.  Remove 10 parts to tray # 12.                     │
│                                                           │
│     4.  Record Data:  Splatter?  (Yes = Y, No = N)        │
│              1. Y  N        6. Y  N                        │
│              2. Y  N        7. Y  N                        │
│              3. Y  N        8. Y  N                        │
│              4. Y  N        9. Y  N                        │
│              5. Y  N       10. Y  N                        │
│                                                           │
│     5.  Comments/Notes:                                   │
│  ○                                                        │
│                                                           │
└─────────────────────────────────────────────────────────┘
```

Figure 7.4 A runs sheet provides the information required to conduct a test, plus record data and notes.

placed sequentially in a three-ring binder. As each test is completed, the experimenter simply turns the page.

As an outline of the test procedure, the runs sheet doubles as a checklist to verify that all steps in the procedure have been followed. All data plus any pertinent notes are recorded on the runs sheet. It is advisable to use the sheet for a small-scale dry run to be sure it is clear and complete. Good documentation is crucial to the success of the evaluation data collection.

Data Collection Assignments. Once the SPS facilitator has designed the experiment and developed the various logistics,

172

team members are assigned specific tasks in preparing for and conducting the experiment. Responsibilities encompass gathering needed materials and equipment, managing the experiment, making measurements, recording data, and storing samples for possible further analysis. A realistic timetable for task completion should be agreed to by the team.

Collect the Data

After a successful dry run, the evaluation begins. All specifics of the plan, as detailed above, must be faithfully and carefully carried out. However, those assigned to collecting the data should stop if they have any questions about how things are progressing. They should not hesitate to call a team meeting to discuss any concerns.

Check the Data

Data Sufficiency Requirements with Designed Experiments. The listing and prioritizing steps assess the likelihood of any knob's contributing to the troublesome problem variation. They deal with *degrees of suspicion*. The evaluation step moves to the level of *guilt*. For a sound determination of which knobs are actually guilty of causing unwanted variation, the evaluation data must satisfy four requirements:

1. It must be derived from an adequate sample size.
2. It must have been collected using a range of settings that represents the full operating range of each knob.
3. It must assure the statistical independence, or orthogonality, of the knobs.
4. It must represent the full range of process output seen under normal operating conditions.

Consider a straightforward case where there are three important knobs to evaluate and each can be actively turned between two levels. There are eight possible combinations of knob settings, as shown in Figure 7.5. In this factorial experiment, all eight combinations will be studied. If each knob is viewed as falling along the axis of a cube, samples are taken at each corner. This type of experiment yields an ideal data set since the changes in each knob occur totally independent of changes in all

	B-		B+	
	A-	A+	A-	A+
C-	Test 1	Test 2	Test 3	Test 4
C+	Test 5	Test 6	Test 7	Test 8

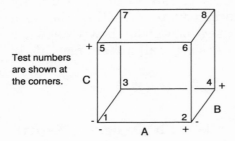

Test numbers are shown at the corners.

Test Number	Knob settings		
	A	B	C
1	-	-	-
2	+	-	-
3	-	+	-
4	+	+	-
5	-	-	+
6	+	-	+
7	-	+	+
8	+	+	+

Figure 7.5   Three ways to represent a designed experiment with three knobs, each at two settings

the other knobs. The experiment is orthogonal, as discussed in Chapter 6.

When a designed experiment is performed to obtain the evaluation data, checking the data for sufficiency is straightforward. Together, the designed experiment and data collection plan explicitly make provisions for the first three requirements.

The sample size is decided upon before the data collection begins and is thus sufficient by design. In a factorial experiment with three knobs, each set at two levels, eight combinations of knob settings are investigated. Each combination is run a *minimum* of two times, in effect conducting the entire experiment twice. The practice of repeating experimental runs, called *replication*, provides an estimate of experimental noise, also known as error variation. Table 7.7 lays out an experimental plan in which runs 9 through 16 replicate runs 1 through 8. Each set of runs is conducted in a random order.

It is often both easy and economical to take several samples in a row for a given combination of knobs. Repeats *within* a given

Table 7.7   Eight combinations are required to evaluate three knobs, each at two settings. Replication yields sixteen total tests, with three repetitions each.

Standard order	Test order (random)	Knob A setting	Knob B setting	Knob C setting	Data
1	2	Low	Low	Low	67, 70, 70
1	13	Low	Low	Low	71, 73, 69
2	3	High	Low	Low	52, 49, 53
2	15	High	Low	Low	55, 57, 51
3	7	Low	High	Low	28, 23, 30
3	10	Low	High	Low	24, 25, 23
4	5	High	High	Low	42, 42, 45
4	16	High	High	Low	43, 49, 39
5	6	Low	Low	High	78, 74, 77
5	12	Low	Low	High	79, 73, 78
6	1	High	Low	High	45, 47, 42
6	14	High	Low	High	49, 48, 49
7	8	Low	High	High	72, 75, 69
7	11	Low	High	High	80, 76, 79
8	4	High	High	High	40, 37, 36
8	9	High	High	High	41, 41, 38

experimental run, called *repetitions*, also provide a measure of experimental error variation. Further, repetitions provide valuable data for evaluating dispersion effects. In Table 7.7 the repetitions are shown in the last column.

In some cases, each experimental run is extremely expensive to conduct. This is especially true during product development, where knobs are being created. It is possible in these cases to run an *unreplicated* factorial experiment in which the sample size equals the number of knob combinations.

Running experiments without replication should be done only when the cost of execution is very high. Repeated or replicated tests provide the most accurate estimate of experimental error. Two tests of each knob combination is the minimum number to yield repeated data. Consequently, the minimum adequate sample size is twice the number of knob combinations.

Because knob settings are specified as part of an experimental plan, their range will usually be adequate, fulfilling the second data sufficiency requirement. In addition, a designed experiment is orthogonal by design, satisfying the requirement for knob independence.

The last requirement for evaluation data is that the range of output variation during the experiment is essentially equal to the variation during normal operations. If the troublesome problem variation is not seen during the experiment, the data is not likely to lead to a problem solution. If the output variation is too small, the team should evaluate whether the knobs were turned far enough. They should also consider the possibility that an important knob was overlooked in the listing and prioritization steps.

In an ideal problem solving environment, all evaluations would be based upon factorial experiments because of their perfect orthogonality and mathematical efficiency. In many cases, however, one or more knobs cannot be turned over their full range or in all possible combinations. The team must then be satisfied with observing naturally occurring changes.

Observational Data Sufficiency. With planned observational studies, the data must be more carefully scrutinized for sufficiency. The same four requirements described above apply.

The minimum sample size for observational data is modeled after the factorial experiment. When each knob is investigated at two levels, as in Table 7.7, the number of combinations is 2^k, with k representing the number of knobs. Allowing for replication, that sample size is doubled to yield a minimum sample formula:

$$n = 2^{(k+1)},$$

where n = minimum sample size,
       k = number of knobs being evaluated.

This minimum is based on the other three sufficiency conditions being satisfied as well. If getting data is relatively inexpensive, additional data should be collected to increase the precision of the analysis.

To satisfy the second requirement for data sufficiency with observational data, each knob should show variation over the full range expected in regular operations. If any knob does not vary sufficiently, data collection must continue until that knob changes over its full operating range.

In meeting the third requirement, statistical independence of knobs can be checked in two ways. A correlation matrix like that in Table 7.8 can be set up to show all the possible pairwise matchings of the knobs being evaluated. The correlation coefficient should be low, showing weak correlation and lack of dependence. Statistical independence can also be checked graphically by drawing a scatterplot—also called a scatter diagram—for all possible pairs of knobs being evaluated. Figure 7.6 shows a scatterplot in which the knobs are highly correlated. Two knobs that are not correlated change independently, as depicted in Figure 7.7.

If the correlation coefficients or scatterplots indicate some of the knobs are not changing independently, then the team must consider the reason. In Figure 7.6 there are only points with Knobs A and B both at their low settings or both at their high settings. If this pattern of plots is due simply to the luck of the draw, then more data should be collected until the plot resem-

Table 7.8   Table of correlation coefficients among the four knobs in a planned observational study

Knobs	A	B	C	D
A	1 .00	.32	- .17	.21
B	.32	1 .00	.03	.23
C	- .17	.03	1 .00	- .13
D	.21	.23	- .13	1 .00

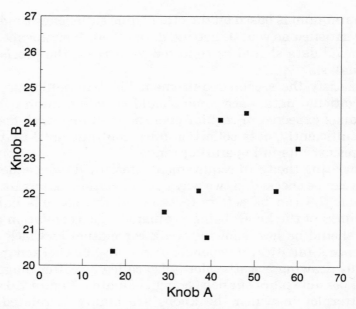

Figure 7.6 Knobs A and B tend to change together and are highly correlated.

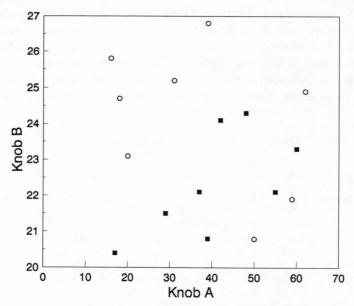

Figure 7.7 After more data are collected (represented by the dots), A and B are no longer highly correlated.

bles Figure 7.7. If the team is comfortable with changing A and B, the knobs can be turned to get their missing combinations of settings. Figure 7.7 shows the independence of A and B after additional data were collected.

Operating the process may require that if one knob is changed, a corresponding change in another knob must be made. Therefore, it may be impossible to collect orthogonal data, and the facilitator must judge whether or not to evaluate the data with some qualifications about the interpretation. When statistical independence of the knobs is not possible, observational data are most vulnerable to misuse. Conclusions and implementation plans must be made very carefully.

To satisfy the fourth requirement, a range of process output variation comparable to that found in normal operations must be present in the observational data set. The team must continue to collect data until they see the necessary range of variation.

Data Stability. Once the data set is found to be sufficient, it should also be checked for stability. After plotting the data on an appropriate control chart, any out-of-control points or trends should be evaluated. Often an out-of-control pattern reflects how the knobs were turned for the experiment. If knob changes account for the out-of-control conditions, the analysis can proceed. However, if there are strong trends over time or out-of-control points that do not correspond with knob changes, data evaluation will not be valid.

The team should consider what is creating the instability. The cause may be an important knob that was overlooked previously in the SPS process. If instabilities in the data cannot be explained, any conclusions based on it would be very misleading. The data should therefore *not* be used for evaluation.

How can instability first appear during the evaluation step? Even when the first four SPS steps are carefully followed, unanticipated instabilities can occur. For example, an evaluation included temperature as one of the knobs. Before beginning the evaluation, a check of the actual temperature revealed that it was off location. A hardware problem with the temperature control system was discovered and corrected. If it had not been corrected, the evaluation would have been invalid.

Instability can even nullify the results of an evaluation after the solution is implemented. In a problem with a heat-treating operation, for instance, SPS was used through the evaluation step and a solution was successfully implemented. After two months, the problem reappeared even with all the important knobs maintained at their correct settings. Using investigative SPC, the team monitored several knobs, including one difficult-to-turn knob not included as part of the original evaluation. They discovered the additional knob was varying surprisingly far beyond its normal operating range, causing the instability in the process output. A hardware malfunction allowing the knob to change in an uncontrolled manner was corrected. Then the heat-treating process ran trouble-free once again.

Analyze the Data

Understanding Variation. The objective of SPS is to learn how to reduce the undesirable variation causing the problem. Analysis recognizes variation in the process output that can be understood and variation that cannot be understood. The latter is the variation inherent to the product or process, no matter how well the product is made or the process controlled.

The understood variation leads to a problem solution. It is the *new or better understanding* of how the top few knobs affect the understood variation that we refer to as the statistical solution to the problem. The team must then use their creativity to develop an implementation plan for translating the statistical solution into an actual solution, as discussed in Chapter 9. This plan changes the product or process hardware to fix the important knobs at their proper settings permanently.

Through their new understanding of the top knobs, the team can predict the improvement when the guilty knobs are at their proper settings. They can then decide if their proposed actual solution is economically feasible *before* implementation dollars are spent.

The specific methods of analysis used for evaluation depend on the problem definition, how the knobs are turned, and the nature of the data available. Initially, specific methods determine which knobs are guilty of contributing to the problem by separating the understood variation from the variation that cannot be understood. Next, a wide variety of techniques—primarily graphical—are used to further describe how each guilty knob affects the process output.

For the sake of example, we'll work through a problem of too much warping while laminating a film coating to a fibrous substrate. The problem was defined as a stable, off-target condition. Through the listing and prioritizing steps, three knobs were identified for evaluation, each at two settings.

The three top knobs were preheater contact, film tension, and lamination speed. The performance characteristic selected was the average warpage for the five coated substrates produced under various experimental conditions. Table 7.9 shows the average warpage for each test. Since the ideal condition would be no warping, the target value was zero.

The raw data for the warpage problem had five replicates for each cell in Table 7.9. Even though the five samples for each test were produced with identical knob settings, the five samples resulted in different warpage measurements. Differences in sample measurements may be very small or quite large. Such variation in the results of experimentation is called experimental error or *noise*. The magnitude of noise is equal to the magnitude of variation that cannot be understood.

Noise can influence experimental conclusions in two ways. First, we might conclude that an observed difference is the result of a changing knob, when, in fact, it is just the noise. Second, experimental noise can mask the effect of knobs under investigation.

Table 7.9   Average warpage for each test

	Edge tension tight		Edge tension loose	
	Preheater wrap 75%	Preheater wrap 25%	Preheater wrap 75%	Preheater wrap 25%
Speed 460	Test 1 31.4	Test 2 26.8	Test 4 27.6	Test 3 30.0
Speed 380	Test 8 31.8	Test 7 44.6	Test 5 25.6	Test 6 25.4

As already stated, the initial objective of analysis is to separate the variation we understand from the noise. Analysis of variance (ANOVA) accomplishes the goal of separating understood variation from noise. For the warpage problem, results are shown in the standard ANOVA table of Table 7.10. We recommend a personal computer to perform ANOVA, although the calculations can be done by hand using the Yates algorithm.[4] The following paragraphs highlight the ANOVA method of analysis. Interested readers are directed to any standard statistics textbook for a more detailed discussion of ANOVA.

The ANOVA Table. Sources of variation are identified in the first column of the ANOVA table. There are two main categories, variation *between* groups and variation *within* groups. By turning knobs, the differences between groups are purposely created for the experiment. The variation between groups can thus be understood. The between-group variation consists of sources of variation attributable to both individual knobs and knob interactions. In Table 7.10, the between-group sources of variation are the three knobs, the three two-factor interactions, and the one three-factor interaction.

Table 7.10   Standard ANOVA table for warpage evaluation

Source of variation	Sum of squares	Degrees of freedom	Mean square	F-ratio	Significance level
Knob A: Preheater wrap	0.1	1	0.1	.00	.948
Knob B: Edge tension	810.0	1	810.0	35.53	.000
Knob C: Speed	291.6	1	291.6	12.79	.001
Knob interaction AB	160.0	1	160.0	7.02	.012
Knob interaction AC	384.4	1	384.4	16.86	.000
Knob interaction BC	136.9	1	136.9	6.00	.020
Knob interaction ABC	62.5	1	62.5	2.74	.108
Residual	729.6	32	22.8		
Total	2575.1	39			

Variation within groups is not attributable to changes made during experimentation and thus remains to be explained. Usually referred to as *residual* variation, it is the variation that cannot be understood.

The sources of variation are quantified in the second column, headed *sum of squares* (SS). The larger the SS, the greater the contribution a given knob or interaction makes to the variation in process output. We find the information in the ANOVA table very useful for predicting the expected improvement in output variation.

The degrees of freedom for each knob or interaction appear in the third column of the ANOVA table. Degrees of freedom can be thought of as opportunities to learn. They depend on the number of knobs and knob settings, and the amount of data collected. Although in Table 7.10 the degrees of freedom for each knob and interaction is equal, this is not always true. Each sum of squares is therefore divided by the degrees of freedom to yield a *mean square*, listed in the table's fourth column. The mean or *average* square enables fair comparisons among the effects of the knobs and their interactions.

The F-ratio statistic in the fifth column is used to see how confident we are that a knob or knob combination departs from innocence. The F-ratio is calculated by dividing the mean square for each knob by the mean square of the residual. It is the ratio of the variation we do understand to the variation we don't understand. As the F-ratio increases, our confidence increases and improves our opportunity to solve the problem.

The last column in the ANOVA table is a probability factor that quantifies the statistical *significance* of the F-ratio. It describes how far a particular F-ratio departs from what could be expected to happen by chance alone. The smaller the significance level, the greater the departure from both chance and innocence.

Significance. With SPS, practical significance prevails over statistical significance. The proof of statistically significant results is not as important as a major business improvement. The opportunity to reduce the unwanted variation revealed by the sum of squares is emphasized over the F-ratio or the significance level. A practical result combined with subject matter knowledge and experience often provides sufficient evidence to move forward with implementation, even though the result is not statistically significant. In cases of product or process development when knowledge is limited, however, a statistically significant result is generally a prerequisite for claiming a practical result.

Whether or not a result is statistically significant depends in part upon the sample size. If a result is not statistically significant or is marginally significant, increasing the sample size leads to a more precise estimate of a knob's effect.

Shouldn't any statistically significant result be implemented? For instance, a weld strength must improve from 10 to 85 pounds to solve a problem. Changing the setting of a particular knob creates a statistically significant result, moving the weld strength from 10 to 14. Isn't that significant? If we must travel from New York to Los Angeles, will we celebrate when we reach Philadelphia? Insufficient progress, but directionally correct!

On the other hand, a statistically significant result may not seem practical initially. In one case, turning knobs to improved settings was proven significant and could raise the yield from an average of 92% to 93%. Although the improvement was proportionally small, when scaled up to production volumes it represented a real financial savings. Further, by using SPS, the cost of investigating and implementing the improvement was virtually zero.

Guilty Knobs. Table 7.10 indicates the most important knob affecting warpage was edge tension. Based on its sum of squares, changes in the tension knob accounted for about 31% ($100 \times 810/2571.1$) of the total variation seen in the experiment. The remaining two knobs—preheater wrap and speed—had a strong interacting effect on each other. Their combined effect accounted for an additional 15% of the variation.

The ANOVA table will reveal which knobs and knob combinations are most important. It does not explain, however, the *why* of knob guilt. Further analysis is needed to understand how knobs are affecting variation. Graphics help in this effort, especially with readily available computer programs. Figure 7.8 plots warpage at the loose and tight settings of the edge tension knob, showing which setting would yield the least warpage. The interaction plot of preheater wrap and speed in Figure 7.9 indicates the combined settings that would yield the least warpage.

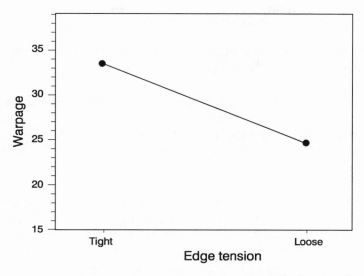

Figure 7.8   Average warpage as a function of edge tension

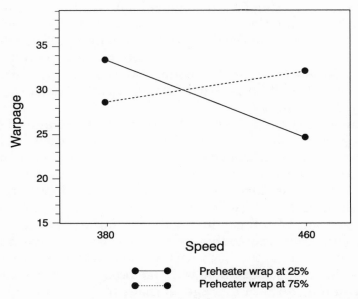

Figure 7.9   Interaction plot to depict combined effect of speed and preheater wrap on warpage

Describe the Statistical Solution

The evaluation step yields a statistical solution to the problem that answers these three questions:

1. Which knobs and their interactions are guilty of causing the process output variation?
2. How should each guilty knob be set to improve the output?
3. What improvement can be expected at the new knob settings?

How were these questions answered to create a statistical solution for our problem of warping during lamination? Analysis of variance identified edge tension as most important in affecting warpage. Next in importance was the interaction of preheater wrap and speed. Least guilty was speed alone. Evaluation found the settings for all three knobs important to solving the warpage problem. In many other evaluations, however, one or more of the top few knobs have no real effect on the output, despite how suspicious they appeared.

The correct setting for the tension knob was the loose setting used in the evaluation. We sometimes speak of the correct setting as **approximate best**, suggesting it may be refined during the optimization step. For instance, the operator may further loosen the tension in small increments. By so doing, additional improvement may be realized beyond those settings explored during the evaluation.

As previously cited, Figure 7.9 illustrates the combined effect that preheater wrap and speed would have on warpage. It is not sufficient to indicate a correct setting for one knob without also indicating how the other should be set. The interaction plot reveals that the combined settings should be preheater wrap at 25 with speed at 460. As with the setting for edge tension, these settings might be refined during the optimization step.

The data from the evaluation can be used to estimate the improved process capability with the knobs at their approximate best settings. In our example warpage problem, the process had been running with an average warpage of 29 with a standard deviation of 8. Using standard methods of prediction, we could expect some product with warpage as high as 63. About 10% of the product exceeded the limit of 40 maximum warpage, as illustrated in the *before* distribution of Figure 7.10.

With all the knobs at their proper settings, the average warpage would drop to about 20 (see Test 3 in Table 7.9), with a standard deviation of about 5 (the square root of the mean square residual in Table 7.10). We would not expect any product with warpage above 35, which is well within the required limit. In production, almost all the product had less warpage with the knobs at their new settings than before the evaluation. Not only

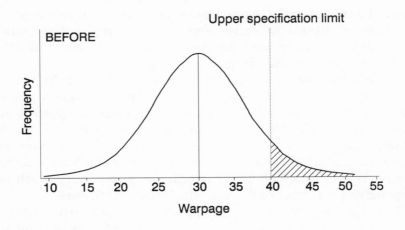

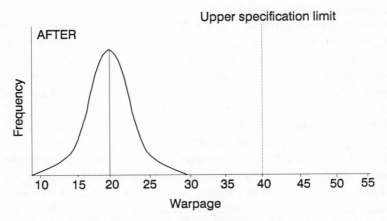

Figure 7.10   Comparison of process capability of warpage before and after fixing knobs at their correct settings

was there no longer any product exceeding the specification limit, but much more product was closer to the desired condition of zero warpage. Actual production performance thus confirmed the expected results of the SPS evaluation.

Refining the Statistical Solution Using Models

The relationship between the process output and important process variables may be expressed as a mathematical equation, usually referred to as a model. Models developed from experimental data are called *empirical* models, while models based on the laws of physics are called *deterministic*. In situations where modeling may be helpful, problem solvers can seek assistance from an expert on modeling.

Models are useful in three basic situations. First, refined product or process knowledge can help to calibrate quickly a product function or process output to a new level. Consider process output averaging 150 for an important characteristic, and the customer wants a new target of 200. A model of the process can simulate changing key knob settings to discover which will yield an average of 200. The use of simulation is typically much less expensive than trial and error with actual hardware.

Modeling a process can also accurately predict the improvement if new costs are incurred to better control a given knob. For example, a problem with a potentiometer included a purchased component as one of the top few knobs. The evaluation revealed the purchased component contributed to the problem variation. A model showed the cost of improving the component, however, would be more than the savings from the improvement. The implementation of the problem solution consequently focused on knobs that were cost effective to control.

A third reason for developing a process model is to exploit the forgiving principle, to be discussed later in the chapter.

Would a model have been useful for our warpage problem? Results of the evaluation indicated the problem could be solved without any new process hardware. Proper knob settings alone would achieve the desired performance objective. In fact, the better setting for speed was the faster one. Thus, not only would the quality losses be eliminated, but productivity would increase. In this case, using a model would have added nothing to the solution.

The usefulness of a model is one issue. Feasibility is another. Because a two-knob interaction between speed and preheater wrap contributed to the output variation, several different models could fit the data. Without more data, the most appropriate model could not be selected. Typically, data to develop a model including interactions are collected during the optimization step when knobs are tried at many more settings.

Selecting a Method of Analysis

All things being equal, a three or four-knob designed experiment provides evaluation data that are the most straightforward to analyze. However, only a portion of real problems are so neat and simple that they can be evaluated with a designed experiment. Due to execution considerations, performing a designed experiment may not be economically feasible or even physically possible. With some problems the evaluation must be performed using a planned observational study, as described earlier in the chapter.

For the variety of situations confronting problem solvers, there are other methods for evaluating the effects of knobs and their interactions. Prominent are the analysis of covariance (ANCOVA)[5] and multiple regression analysis. There are also many simpler approaches to ANOVA. These include the analysis of means,[6] the analysis of ranges,[7] the Yates algorithm, and the normal probability plot of knob effects.[8]

The use of statistical methods should always be problem driven, not method driven. Method-driven strategies often result in unnecessarily expensive investigations. With SPS, the particular method used depends upon the execution challenges for the problem circumstances. Table 7.11 identifies the method of analysis to use based on knob turnability.

When the top knobs are easy and inexpensive to turn, they should be turned over their full range and in all possible combinations. Hard or impossible-to-turn knobs are observed as they naturally change through a planned observational study. In the intermediate case are easy-to-turn knobs that are turned "with comfort" over a limited range of settings because their

Table 7.11 Method of analysis to use based on how knobs are turned

Easy to Turn		Hard to Turn	Impossible to Turn	Method of analysis
Knobs turned over full range (plus all combinations)	Knobs turned over limited range	Knobs observed	Knobs observed	
■	■	■	■	MR
■	■	■		MR
■	■		■	MR
■	■			MR
■		■	■	MR
■		■		MR
■			■	ANCOVA
■				ANOVA
	■	■	■	MR
	■	■		MR
	■		■	MR
	■			MR
		■	■	MR
		■		MR
			■	MR

MR = multiple regression analysis
ANOVA = analysis of variance
ANCOVA = analysis of covariance

natural changes are not occurring fast enough. In many experiments the three types of knobs are evaluated together.

The interest in how knobs are turned for an evaluation is driven by SPS execution principles, highlighted earlier. One is concerned with maintaining operating efficiency. Another cautions against turning knobs so far that product or process equipment is destroyed.

The SPS facilitator guides the group in selecting and using the most appropriate method for a given evaluation. Problem analysis has been greatly simplified by the personal computer and the many statistical software packages available for it. Techniques that would have taken weeks just to make the calculations can now be completed in minutes on the personal computer.

Characterizing How Knobs Affect the Output

The evaluation step creates an appreciation of the specific relationship between each important knob and the process output. Analysis of evaluation data leads to improved knob settings, which can be explored for further improvement during the optimization step. The data coupled with subject matter knowledge suggest clues in understanding how a given knob and the output are related. Graphics effectively highlight this relationship.

Figures 7.11 and 7.12 illustrate some of the more commonly observed knob-output relationships. Evaluation data do not always allow the detailed characterization of a knob's effect as depicted in these figures. Additional data or knowledge of the underlying physics of the product and process is usually necessary to develop the depth of understanding implied by the figures. The discussion that follows explains how the knob-output relationship might be exploited to reduce variation.

Coarse and Fine Knobs

When a small change in a knob setting creates a big change in the process output, the knob is called a *coarse* knob. Conversely, when a big change in a knob setting creates a small change in

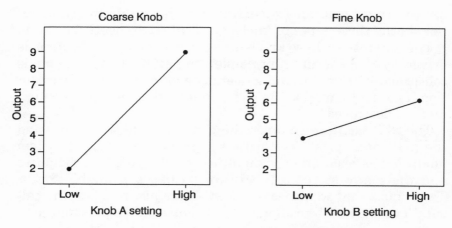

Figure 7.11   Coarse and fine knobs contrasted

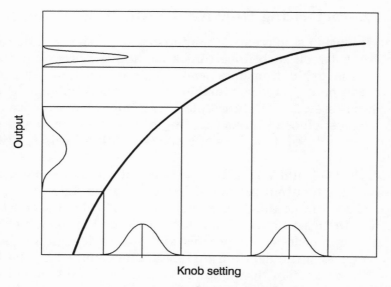

Figure 7.12   Reducing output variation by exploiting nonlinear relationships

the process output, the knob is called a *fine* knob. Coarse and fine knobs are contrasted in Figure 7.11. Any movement in a coarse knob can create big changes and thus big problems with the process output. Coarse knobs should thus be locked in at their correct settings. Fine knobs can then be used for small adjustments in centering the process. The identification of coarse and fine knobs is especially important when solving problems due to off-target conditions.

Reducing Transmitted Variation

Figure 7.11 implies that changes in the knob cause variation in the output. The nature of the physical relationship between a knob and the output influences how knob variation is transmitted to output variation. Not all knobs have the kind of straight-line relationship between knob and output depicted in Figure 7.11. Often the relationship is better depicted by a curve, as shown in Figure 7.12. Curvature can be discovered only when knobs are evaluated at more than two settings. Since most evaluations involve only two settings, further exploration of curvature usually happens during optimization (SPS Step 5).

When curvature exists, it often presents opportunities to reduce variation at virtually no expense. The knob along the horizontal axis in Figure 7.12 can be thought of as a component in a product, a process parameter, or an environmental factor. The figure illustrates the variation transmitted from a knob to the output at different points on the curve. By setting the knob to the flat part of the curve, the output becomes much less variable. In fact, the variation reduction occurs even though the range of variation in the knob has increased.

Since the early 1980s more and more emphasis has been placed on improving products by reducing variation in product function. Credit must be given to Dr. Genichi Taguchi for his contributions to making products *robust*. A robust product is insensitive to variation in components, to variations in process parameters, and to environmental influences. Although Dr. Taguchi offers parameter design as the principal means to achieving robustness, there are other effective and economical strategies. The sources cited in Reference 9 discuss various strategies for achieving robustness, also referred to as *ruggedness* in product or process design.[10]

The Forgiving Principle in Practice

Creating a robust product is one effective way to compensate for variation in component or process parameters. Robustness can only be achieved, however, if the necessary physics exist in the product or process. In many cases such opportunities simply do not exist. From the SPS perspective, the forgiving principle suggests three other ways to compensate for unwanted variation:

- Exploit knob interactions so the product or process is insensitive to difficult-to-control knobs.
- Use a feed-forward mode for one knob to compensate for deficiencies in a second knob.
- Use a feedback loop for one knob to compensate for deficiencies in a second knob.

Knob deficiencies may be forgiven by exploiting knob interactions. In the interaction of Figure 7.13, at the lower setting of Knob B, Knob A is a coarse knob. At the higher setting of Knob B, Knob A becomes a fine knob. With Knob B at its higher

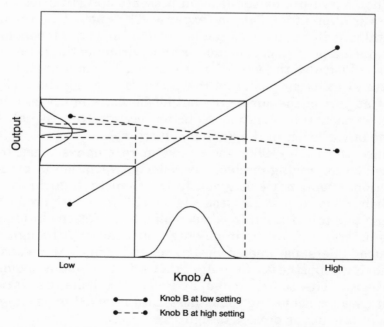

Figure 7.13   Using knob interactions to exploit the forgiving principle

setting, Knob A can vary over a wide range and still have little effect on the process output variation.

Still another way to forgive knob deficiencies is through a feed-forward mode. After a difficult-to-control knob is measured, an appropriate change is made in a forgiving knob to prevent unwanted changes in the output. Figure 7.14 depicts a feed-forward system. Before or during processing, Knob B is measured. If necessary, Knob A is then adjusted to compensate for Knob B's condition.

The forgiving adjustment can be manual or automated. Machine setup is an example of manual feed-forward. After checking material thickness, the operator adjusts the settings to forgive any deviation from the specified thickness. An assembly operation provides an automated feed-forward example. After a difficult-to-control dimension is automatically gauged, a robot selects a matching component from a rack of presorted components.

A feedback system offers a third way to achieve forgiveness in a process. Feedback loops are nothing new. The SPS evaluation, however, helps select which knobs will be most effective in making the compensating adjustments. Figure 7.15 shows a typical

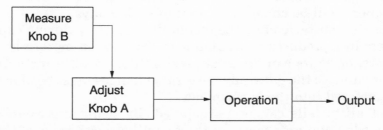

Figure 7.14   A feed-forward system where Knob A is adjusted to compensate for Knob B's variation

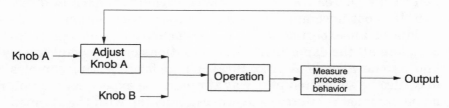

Figure 7.15   A feedback system to keep output on target. Knob A is adjusted after measuring process behavior.

feedback loop. Feedback systems often measure the process output itself. Some feedback systems, called adaptive control, monitor process symptoms such as current draw on a motor.

The difference between the feed-forward and feedback systems lies in when measurements are taken. With feed-forward, the knobs are measured *before* the operation; forgiving adjustments are then made so the target is hit more consistently. With feedback, process behavior is measured immediately *after* output is produced; a knob is then adjusted to return the process to target.

The Teamwork Factor

POINT ONE: Potential pitfalls await those performing an evaluation experiment. A careful verbal rehearsal of the experiment goes a long way toward recognizing many of them.

One potential difficulty is a delay in changing knobs. Even easy-to-turn knobs can present an execution challenge if changing a setting does not result in an immediate effect. For example, in a sintering evaluation the time-temperature profile was one of the knobs. Every time it was changed, the furnace took almost an hour to assume the set value. To avoid adversely affecting production efficiency, the team must plan in detail how the knobs will be changed in light of such delays.

Another obstacle might be instability occurring during experiments in a production environment. Changes in materials, operators, or shifts can all create instability. Because instability can invalidate the data, any necessary changes must be planned and factored into the experiment.

Not all pitfalls can be anticipated. By using the combined knowledge and experience of the team, however, most of these traps can be anticipated and avoided.

POINT TWO: Teamwork prevents capricious changes in direction. It is not uncommon for someone to suggest changes in the middle of an experiment. That person may see no reason to complete all the experimental combinations or may want to set knobs to new levels. A procedural change for collecting samples may also be suggested part way through the experiment. Team members must reinforce each other in sticking with the planned evaluation despite forceful arguments by individuals wanting to change course.

POINT THREE: Contributions from the entire team are important to interpret and understand the results of the evaluation. Results can fall anywhere along a continuum. At one end the evaluation simply confirms the team's suspicions about the knobs under study. No insights are gained, but knob settings may be refined. At the other end of the continuum is the discovery of something new, something that contradicts conventional wisdom about the knobs. A fresh appreciation of the process emerges as the team wrestles with the analysis. The synergy of several minds working together is highly effective in creating new understanding from new information.

Conclusion

Not all problems require strict execution of all SPS steps, as brought out in Chapter 2. The problem may be solved before reaching the evaluation step. Ordinarily, however, a complete understanding of the top few knobs is crucial to problem solution. The SPS evaluation step zeroes in on those knobs and knob combinations guilty of creating the troublesome variation at the root of the problem.

Methods chosen for SPS evaluation depend on time and cost. The evaluation is problem dependent, not method dependent. As with the entire SPS process, the team makes evaluation decisions based on ease of execution and economy. For instance, although factorial experiments are mathematically efficient, the practical efficiency of planned observational studies may better fulfill SPS goals. Observing changes as they naturally occur in the process may also be better if knobs cannot be turned over their full range or in all their combinations.

If a knob doesn't turn, you don't learn. Consequently, knob turnability is a basic concern during the evaluation step. Because easily turnable knobs can be examined over a wide range of settings, they are ideal for problem investigation. Knobs that can be explored over only a limited range must be turned cautiously. Difficult or impossible-to-turn knobs require the most problem solving creativity through the use of observational data. SPS execution principles guide all decisions on knob turnability.

The SPS evaluation procedure begins with the selection of performance characteristics—the criteria used for knob evaluation. The team then reviews what they know about the knobs to be evaluated, including typical knob behavior and control. Next they carefully plan and carry out data collection. SPS execution principles guide how the data will be gathered. Finally, the data is analyzed after it is checked for sufficiency and stability. The outcome is knowledge of how the top few knobs contribute to the problem variation.

A statistical solution is the end product of the evaluation step. It describes which knobs and knob interactions are in fact guilty and how they should be set to reduce the undesirable variation. In addition, SPS evaluation suggests what improvement can be expected if the new settings are implemented.

The evaluation step is the culmination of the previous SPS steps and often successfully ends the investigation. Five specific outcomes of the evaluation step are possible.

The *desired* outcome is a genuine problem solution. In the warpage during lamination problem used in this chapter, regulating edge tension emerged as an effective and economical solution. The SPS team then moved on to plan implementation, the subject of Chapter 9. Later, after a solution is implemented, the SPS optimization step may help squeeze out remaining improvement in the existing process by fine tuning knob settings.

A second outcome is a statistical solution that would cost more to translate into an actual solution than would be gained by eliminating the problem. When SPS execution principles are carefully followed, however, this outcome rarely occurs. It is almost always cheaper to fix a problem than to live with it.

A third possibility is the realization of *some* immediate improvement. The final solution is found using the tools of the SPS optimization step, the subject of the next chapter.

A fourth possible outcome is that no solution is found by investigating the easiest-to-turn knobs first. The team would then return to the listing and prioritizing steps and reconsider knobs that are more expensive to investigate and implement.

Finally, there is always the possibility that a solution will not be discovered using existing technology. Recall that the first three problem solving tactics—as introduced in Chapter 2—work with the existing system. If none of those tactics are adequate for solving the problem, the team is justified in considering new technology, the fourth and most costly problem solving tactic. Since all the options available in the existing design or process are investigated first, however, SPS arrives at the *need* for new technology objectively and definitively.

References

1. George E. P. Box, William G. Hunter, and J. Stuart Hunter, *Statistics for Experimenters*, New York: John Wiley & Sons, Inc., 1978.

2. George E. P. Box and R. Daniel Meyer, "Dispersion Effects from Fractional Designs," *Technometrics*, Vol. 28, pages 19–27, 1986.

3. Raghu N. Kackar, "Off-Line Quality Control, Parameter Design, and the Taguchi Method," *Journal of Quality Technology*, American Society for Quality Control, Vol. 17, No. 4, October 1985. Also, George E. P. Box, "Signal to Noise Ratios, Performance Criteria and Transformations," *Technometrics*, Vol. 30, pages 1–40, 1988.

4. Box, Hunter, and Hunter, page 407.

5. Acheson J. Duncan, *Quality Control and Industrial Statistics*, 4th ed.; Homewood, IL: Richard D. Irwin, Inc., 1974.

6. Ellis R. Ott, *Process Quality Control: Troubleshooting and Interpretation of Data*, New York: McGraw-Hill Book Co., 1975.

7. Neil R. Ullman, "The Analysis of Means (ANOM) for Signal and Noise," *Journal of Quality Technology*, American Society for Quality Control, Vol. 21, No. 2, April 1989.

8. C. Daniel, "Use of Half Normal Plots in Interpreting Factorial Two Level Experiments," *Technometrics*, Vol. 1, pages 311–341, 1959. Also, Box, Hunter, and Hunter, pages 329–334.

9. George E. P. Box, Soren Bisgaard, and Conrad A. Fung, "An Explanation and Critique of Taguchi's Contributions to Quality Engineering," *Quality and Reliability Engineering International*, Vol. 4, pages 123–131, 1988. Also, Box and Fung, *Studies in Quality Improvement: Minimizing Transmitted Variation by Parameter Design*, Report No. 8, Center for Quality and Productivity Improvement, University of Wisconsin—Madison, February 1986. Also, Kackar, *Journal of Quality Technology*, October 1985.

10. Ronald D. Snee, "Statistical Thinking and Its Contribution to Total Quality," *The American Statistician*, American Statistical Association, Vol. 44, No. 2, May 1990.

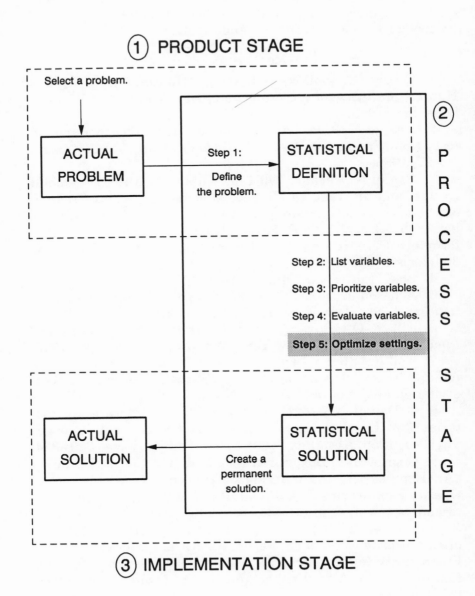

Chapter 8

Optimizing
Variable Settings
(SPS Step 5)

Issue:	For ongoing process improvement, the relationship between important variables and the process output must be fully understood.
SPS Response:	The approximate best settings discovered during SPS evaluation are refined. Optimization of knob settings is achieved through common sense experimentation, Monte Carlo simulation, or planned experimentation.
SPS Result:	Improved knowledge of the target and range of process knobs to achieve the desired target and range of process output.

An Extension of the Evaluation Step

After SPS evaluation, the problem solving team knows which knobs or knob interactions cause the undesirable variation in the process output. The team has also discovered which knob settings will create the desired process performance. Successful completion of the evaluation step can be compared to the golfer who lands the ball on the green. The next logical step in problem solving *or* golf is optimization. For problem solvers, optimizing means further investigation of the important knobs to maximize process performance. For golfers, it's putting the ball in the hole.

Optimization methods depend on the outcome of the evaluation step and cover a wide range of effort and complexity. Figure 8.1 illustrates the relative effort required to accomplish optimization.

The simplest way to optimize a process is through **common sense experimentation**. For example, the student driver iden-

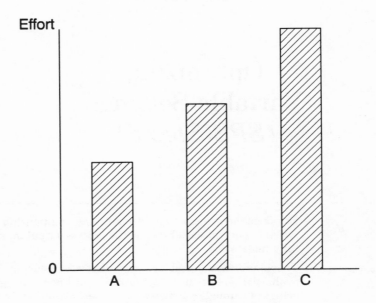

A = Common-sense experimentation
B = Monte Carlo simulation
C = Planned experimentation

Figure 8.1   Relative effort required to accomplish process optimization

tifies two important knobs—the accelerator to go and the brake
to stop. At first, the novice's driving is often erratic, characterized
by rough starts and abrupt stops. By experimenting, the student
learns how to use the knobs to both accelerate and stop smoothly.
Optimized driving results from simply operating the knobs after
learning their basic functions. Common sense experimentation is
successful if limited to one or two guilty knobs that have an
easy-to-understand relationship with the process output.

A more complex route to optimization models the process
through multiple regression analysis first and then uses the
model for **Monte Carlo simulation**. This route applies to situations with several guilty knobs and knob interactions. Models
of production processes can be economically developed by carefully monitoring the top few knobs and the process output. Once
the knobs-output relationship is known, Monte Carlo simulation

is a fast and inexpensive way to find the combination of knob settings that optimizes the output. The Monte Carlo procedure for variables data is straightforward. With some extra effort and special techniques, it is also a useful procedure for attributes data or a mixture of variables and attributes data.

The most complex and difficult means of optimization is **planned experimentation**. Knob settings are slightly and systematically changed to explore fully how the important knobs relate to the output. Successive tests are guided by the results of preceding tests.

The distinction between variables data and attributes data has been made in earlier chapters. Knob settings can also be expressed by two similar categories—*continuous* or *discrete*. Continuous is analogous to the variables category, while discrete is analogous to attributes.

Knobs such as speed, pressure, temperature, and feed rate can be described as **continuous knobs**; their settings can take any value along a scale. Type of material, order of operations, workholding method, and the presence or absence of a design feature exemplify **discrete knobs**. Their settings are confined to a finite number of distinct values.

Setting choices for discrete knobs may be many or as few as two. When the choices are few, all possible settings can be evaluated during SPS Step 4; optimization of discrete knobs is then not required. On the other hand, if many discrete settings are possible, optimization is required to select among the options. The following example illustrates how a discrete knob is treated during the optimization step.

SPS evaluation of one problem found fixturing to be the top knob. When the current fixture was evaluated against an alternate one, the new fixture made the problem worse. The team concluded they already had the best possible fixture. It was suggested, however, that by understanding the difference between the current and new fixtures, a third fixture might solve the problem. Additional fixture designs were tried with varying effects on the problem. By selecting among several discrete designs, the fixture knob was optimized and the problem was solved.

Continuous knobs almost always require refinement of settings discovered during the evaluation step. For example, in an ultrasonic welding operation a higher amplitude was evaluated as the better setting. Perhaps the weld could be even better if the correct amplitude were adjusted a little higher or lower. Optimization methods will reveal if additional improvement is possible. Because optimization is necessary more often for continuous knobs than for discrete knobs, the methods described in this chapter apply to knobs adjustable along a scale.

What if *both* continuous and discrete knobs are found to be guilty? In such hybrid cases, the discrete knobs are held at their correct settings discovered during evaluation while the continuous knobs are optimized. If the discrete knobs have many setting choices, however, both the discrete and continuous knobs are optimized.

Table 8.1 summarizes the SPS approaches to optimization based upon the specifics of the situation.

Common Sense Experimentation

When there are only one or two guilty knobs and their effect on the process output is easy to understand, common sense experimentation can optimize their settings. In nearly all such cases, there are no knob interactions to complicate an understanding of the problem situation.

Common sense experimentation is consistent with the human tendency to tinker, explore, and experiment. Typically, however, tinkering is impulsive and ignores scientific principles. SPS facilitates a scientific approach to tinkering.

To illustrate effective common sense optimization, consider an automotive component that malfunctioned intermittently. Evaluation factors included the load of two springs, the presence or absence of a hydraulic bleed path, changing an electronic parameter, and different clearances between moving parts. The hydraulic bleed path proved to be the top knob, but the exact bleed size required to solve the problem was not determined during evaluation. Using common sense experimentation to try several increments of sizes in the design, a final bleed size was easily decided. This case also shows how a knob treated as a discrete knob during the evaluation step can be treated as a continuous knob during the optimization step, when additional setting choices become feasible.

Table 8.1   Determining the SPS approach to optimization

Categories of important knobs	Types of knobs	Number of possible settings	Necessity of optimization	Type of effort
Single knob	Discrete	Few	Not necessary	—
		Many	Necessary	A
	Continuous	Unlimited	Necessary	A
Multiple independent knobs	Discrete	Few	Not necessary	—
		Many	Necessary	A
	Continuous	Unlimited	Necessary	A
Multiple interacting knobs	Discrete	Few	Not necessary	—
		Many	Necessary	C
	Continuous and easily turnable	Unlimited	Necessary	C
	Continuous but not easily turnable	Unlimited	Necessary	B

A = Common sense experimentation
B = Monte Carlo simulation
C = Planned experimentation

This example is typical of SPS optimization. The SPS evaluation step reveals the one or two guilty knobs out of the ten or twenty knobs initially listed. Correct settings for those guilty knobs, however, may not be immediately obvious. Common sense exploration of knob settings will result in a full understanding of their effects on the process.

Common sense experimentation will not always be effective. If evaluation reveals more than two important knobs or interacting knobs, optimization will require a more disciplined approach.

Monte Carlo Simulation

Authors' Note: By its nature, the material in this section is highly technical. Our aim was to explain it as

> *simply as possible without oversimplifying it. We have two suggestions as you read this section: (1) Only a small percentage of all your problems will benefit from Monte Carlo simulation, so don't be discouraged if the material seems too complex for your needs. (2) If you think you could use Monte Carlo for any of your problems, find expert help to assist you with it.*

The goal of Monte Carlo simulation is to understand how fluctuations in the knobs affect variation in the process output. Specifically, this technique uses a computer to explore how changes in the target and range of the important knobs affect the target and range of the process output.

Monte Carlo simulation is most effectively applied in an actual production environment, where observational data are readily available. Monte Carlo simulation can be used when there is incapability due to excessive dispersion, an off-target condition, or a combination of an off-target condition and excessive dispersion.

Monte Carlo simulation is a multistep technique requiring mathematical and engineering skills.[1] The description that follows is very general. Tasks for performing Monte Carlo simulation are:

1. Collect sufficient data.
2. Use multiple regression analysis to generate a mathematical model of the process.
3. Characterize the knob fluctuations.
4. Confirm the model.
5. Use the model to explore (simulate) how the knobs affect the output.
6. Assess the results of the simulation.
7. Perform additional simulate/assess cycles as required.

A problem with a gas valve illustrates most of the tasks in performing Monte Carlo simulation. In order to meter gas properly, the needle in the valve must open between 22 and 28 mm from its seat. If it does not open far enough, an insufficient flow will cause a system shutdown. If it opens too far, there is danger of fire or explosion.

SPS evaluation concluded that three design parameters—Knobs K1, K3, and K4—affected the needle valve displacement. Specifications for these parameters were:

K1: 2.00 ±0.30
K3: 4.80 ±1.05
K4: 3.00 ±0.30

All three parameters were being produced within their specifications, yet at times the displacement requirement of 22–28 mm was not met. We will follow this example throughout the explanation of the Monte Carlo simulation tasks.

Monte Carlo Task 1: Collect Data

First, enough data must be available to generate a mathematical equation—a *model*—that depicts the relationship between the knobs and the output. Data from the evaluation step is sufficient to show which knobs are guilty of causing the problem. Sometimes it is also adequate for modeling the process. Usually, however, additional data must be collected to develop a valid and useful model.

Observational data are collected as the guilty knobs change. Some knobs change naturally. Some change due to adjustments by automated feedback systems. Others are changed by curious operators thinking they might improve the output. Whatever the cause, as the knobs change, their settings are recorded along with the corresponding process output. For our gas valve problem, Table 8.2 shows that 20 samples were collected with values for K1, K3, K4, and the output—needle displacement.

Monte Carlo Task 2: Build a Model

With sufficient data, multiple regression analysis is used to develop a mathematical model of the process. The form the model takes depends on the nature of the relationship between the knobs and the output. A description of how models are built is well beyond the scope of this book. Because considerable mathematical skill is required, problem solvers should seek the help

Table 8.2 Raw data for Monte Carlo simulation model

Observation number	Knob K1 value	Knob K3 value	Knob K4 value	Needle displacement
1	2.1	4.6	2.8	24.4
2	2.1	4.8	3.1	25.9
3	1.8	4.3	2.9	21.9
4	2.1	4.6	2.9	24.3
5	2.0	5.1	3.0	25.1
20	2.1	5.6	3.0	28.7

of an experienced engineer or statistician. Knob-output relationships can be simple or complex, as the formulas below illustrate.

The first formula depicts a simple relationship—free of interactions—between three knobs and the output.

$$\text{Output} = 245.6 + [3.56 \times (\text{Knob A})] - [14.3 \times (\text{Knob B})] + [23.1 \times (\text{Knob C})]$$

In the second formula, both Knob A and an interaction between Knob A and Knob B have an effect on the output.

$$\text{Output} = 114.5 + [2.1 \times (\text{Knob A}) \times (\text{Knob B})] [5.7 \times (\text{Knob A})]$$

The third formula represents output that is affected by Knob B and proportional to the square of Knob A, but there is no interaction between the two knobs.

$$\text{Output} = 25.6 + [16.7 \times (\text{Knob A})^2] - [2.5 \times (\text{Knob B})]$$

For the purpose of simulation, these formulas are mathematical descriptions of real processes. The knob settings are components of the model.

Using multiple regression on the 20 samples in Table 8.2, the following model was created. The model shows K1 and K3 interact.

Displacement $= 0.40 + (4.49 \times K4) + (1.17 \times K1 \times K3)$

Monte Carlo Task 3: Characterize Knob Fluctuations

Once a model is developed, the next step is to describe how each important knob fluctuates. In statistical language, this means describing the nature of frequency distributions for knob settings. Based on their respective distributions, randomly selected values for the knob settings provide the input data for the Monte Carlo simulation. For example, for a knob that naturally fluctuates between 95 and 105, a computer might generate five random settings of 97, 103, 101, 98, and 100. Figure 8.2 illustrates the various ways knob values can be distributed depending on how the knobs naturally fluctuate.

Some knob values are uniformly distributed across the knob's operating range, like the distribution in Figure 8.2a. Uniform distributions are common when different operators run a process

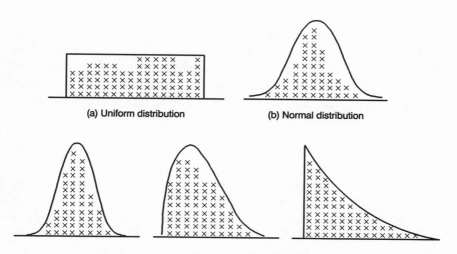

(a) Uniform distribution   (b) Normal distribution

(c) Lognormal, Weibull and exponential distributions

Figure 8.2   How knob values are distributed based on knob fluctuations

based upon their own opinions of correct knob settings. Or, time-dependent uniform distributions are seen in processes with a tool wear condition. A new tool is set so the output falls at one side of the specified tolerance. The process is allowed to run as the tool wears until the output reaches the other side of the tolerance. As a result, approximately equal amounts of product will be produced throughout the tolerance range over the life of a single tool.

Some feedback systems will also produce a uniform frequency distribution as they constantly adjust the process output to the target. These distributions are uniform typically over a narrow range. Grinding and honing are examples of precision operations that often result in uniform distributions controlled over a very narrow range.

Often when knobs fluctuate, their values are tightly distributed around a target value. The influence of many small sources of variation causes the knobs to change, but their values never move far from the target. Such knobs create a normal frequency distribution, as shown in Figure 8.2b. In this context, *normal* describes a distribution that is symmetrical and falls off rapidly as it moves away from the average value. It does not mean natural or usual.

Many process variables are normally distributed. For example, some feedback systems produce normal distributions of fluctuating knob values. The metal temperature in a die casting process falls below a set value, triggering a signal to raise it. The rising temperature will pass the target value before a control turns off the heat source. As the temperature rises and falls through this cycle, it creates a time-dependent normal distribution. Other examples are fabricating processes that produce normally distributed dimensions. In turn, important knobs in assemblies are often dimensions that result from an upstream process whose output is normally distributed.

With the fluctuations of still other knobs, most of the values fall around a target value and trail off nonsymmetrically. To reflect these various types of fluctuations, different frequency distributions are used to simulate knob behavior. These include the lognormal, Weibull, and exponential distributions, as depicted in Figure 8.2c.

Finally, some knobs are constant. Once they are set to a specific value, they do not change their setting unless someone turns them. For Monte Carlo simulation, constant knobs are set to single values, instead of simulating settings based upon a frequency distribution.

The appropriate distribution to use for a given knob can be discovered in three ways. First, data from the process under study or a similar process can be examined to see which distribution most closely resembles the knob fluctuations. Second, when data are not available, interviewing operators or engineers often provides clues about the knob distribution. Finally, reviewing the fundamental physics governing the process can help determine which distribution to use.

In our gas valve example, all three knobs were normally distributed. Table 8.3 shows the process capability and specifications for each of the knobs. To simulate the knob values for the confirmation, random numbers were generated from the normal distributions for K1, K3, and K4. Random values represent the expected values of knob settings if actual hardware were used. For each distribution, averages and standard deviations must be identified. Each knob's specification target was used as the average (2.00, 4.80, 3.00, respectively). Standard deviations were

Table 8.3 Capability summary and specifications for
Knobs K1, K3, and K4

Knob	Capability	Specification
K1	$\bar{X}$ = 2.015 6s = 0.654	Target = 2.00 Tolerance = 0.60
K3	$\bar{X}$ = 4.835 6s = 2.040	Target = 4.80 Tolerance = 2.10
K4	$\bar{X}$ = 2.970 6s = 0.588	Target = 3.00 Tolerance = 0.60

$\bar{X}$ = average
s = standard deviation

estimated as one sixth of each knob's tolerance range (0.1, 0.35, and 0.1, respectively).

Monte Carlo Task 4: Confirm the Model

Next, the model being used for the simulation is confirmed. Failure to confirm the model can lead to false conclusions and expensive mistakes. By simulating the process with all knobs at their current settings and ranges, the output should approximate the existing output. If there is a big difference between the simulated output and the actual output under similar conditions, the model may not be valid. The model-building steps should be retraced and the new model reconfirmed.

For the gas valve example, the confirmation showed the displacement average was 24.99 and the capability range (6 standard deviations) was 6.76. Thus, the estimated upper and lower limits of the needle displacement were 28.37 and 21.61. These results confirmed that some displacements do not meet their requirement even when each knob is within its specified range. This is a common condition in product assemblies with three or more components. Rigorous application of the SPS optimization step can remove the inconsistencies between individual component requirements and assembly requirements.

Monte Carlo Task 5: Explore Knob Effects on Output

The Monte Carlo technique itself is performed by generating numerous simulated observations of each knob. Simulated knob values are then entered into the model to determine the simulated process output. Using a personal computer makes simulation a manageable activity. Software packages are available to help the investigator through the simulation. Spreadsheet programs can also be used to perform a simulation.

In our example, the team discussed how they might improve the needle displacement capability. All agreed that the range of Knob K3 could be controlled to 1.5, an improvement over 2.1. A second simulation was performed with K1 and K4 unchanged. The standard deviation for K3, however, was reduced to 0.25, reflecting the tighter specification.

Monte Carlo Task 6: Assess Simulated Results

Output from a simulation is assessed to see if it meets requirements. Table 8.4 shows four possible outcomes of simulation. Possibilities 2, 3, and 4 indicate problems of nonconformance due to excessive dispersion, an off-target condition, or both. Based on the outcome, further simulation may be necessary. Knob target settings and ranges are changed to explore their effects on the output. Knob exploration, however, should be based on what changes are feasible to implement given the existing technology and resources.

The second simulation in our example predicted an average displacement of 25.06 and a capability range of 5.06. These results yielded minimum and maximum values of 22.53 and 27.59, marginally acceptable when compared to the required range of 22 to 28.

Monte Carlo Task 7: Continue Simulate/Assess Cycles

Cycles of simulate/assess continue until the simulated output displays the desired result. When the outcome fits Possibility 1 in Table 8.4, 100% of the output meets the specified requirements. At this point the optimization step is complete and the team can move on to implementation.

For our gas valve example, the team decided to perform a third simulation. Further discussion led to the conclusion that the capability of K1 and K4 could be improved slightly. For the purpose of simulation, the standard deviations of each knob

Table 8.4   Simulated output possibilities

	On-target	Off-target
Capable	Possibility 1	Possibility 3
Incapable	Possibility 2	Possibility 4

were reduced from 0.10 to 0.075. Using the same targets, a third set of simulated values for each knob was generated and used in the model. The average displacement became 25.13 with a capability range of 4.33, producing an expected minimum and maximum of 22.97 and 27.30. These results met the 22–28 mm displacement requirement. The team then moved on to implementing the solution—tighter control of K1, K3, and K4.

Other Uses for Monte Carlo

Even when the output meets requirements, ongoing improvement can be pursued by continuing to explore knob settings and ranges. Further reduction in output variation might be possible. Whether or not to act on the knowledge gained through simulation is a business decision. The cost to control the knobs is weighed against the corresponding benefit.

Monte Carlo simulation can also help discover opportunities to reduce operating costs or increase equipment life. It might be found, for instance, that acceptable output is possible at lower temperatures if other knobs are set to new levels. Lower temperatures reduce energy costs. Similarly, lower pressures help prolong equipment life. Simulation is an inexpensive way to explore quality and productivity improvement possibilities.

Planned Experimentation

Authors' Note: The material in this section was simplified for general reading. If it seems too complex for your needs, keep in mind that only a few problem situations meet the conditions for planned experimentation described below. For those few problems, we recommend you seek technical help in conducting the experiments.

When the following execution conditions are met, the most efficient and accurate form of optimization is planned experimentation:

- All knobs are easily turnable.
- All knobs are turnable without disrupting operating efficiency.

- The amount of nonconforming product produced is not likely to increase by turning the knobs.

In an actual production setting, these conditions are usually difficult to meet. Opportunities do arise occasionally, however, to use planned experimentation. The three conditions often exist during product and process development or in the laboratory environment.

Optimization through planned experimentation has been applied most successfully in the chemical industry, where it is known as *evolutionary operation* or *EVOP*. George Box and his associates developed EVOP methods in the 1950s. Along with wide use in the chemical industry, EVOP has also been applied beneficially in other industries. Reference 2 surveys EVOP applications in several industries.

Understanding RSM Optimization

Consider a plating process where two knobs—current and electrolyte concentration—have a strong effect on plating thickness. The knob settings can be plotted on two axes and the plating thickness plotted on a third axis. If enough combinations of current and concentration are tested, their combined effect can be plotted. The plot would generate a surface showing the different thicknesses at various settings of the two important knobs. Figure 8.3 shows such a surface, called a *response surface*.

The planned experimentation techniques discussed below are called response surface methods (RSM). While RSM is a general term for an empirical optimization strategy that explores surfaces, EVOP is the specific strategy of applying RSM in a production environment.

Figure 8.3 resembles a topographical map. Altitude represents plating thickness. The north-south direction represents the knob setting for current, while the east-west direction represents the electrolyte concentration knob setting.

When optimizing any response surface, investigators are searching for the "perfect" altitude. If a higher output value is better, investigators must search for the top of a mountain or the crest of a ridge, topographically speaking. Output such as yield, density of a forging, or weld strength are examples of processes

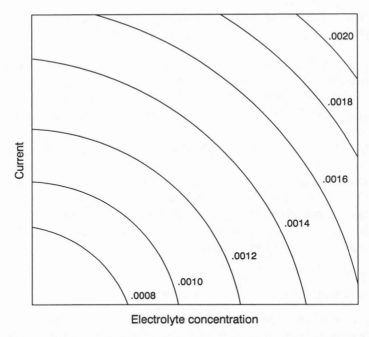

Figure 8.3   A typical response surface with contour lines showing plating thickness

where higher values are better. A lower output value is better, however, for surface finish, out-of-round parts, or the percentage of impurities. In such cases, the surface is explored for valleys. Finally, a specific target value may be the desired response. For these cases, the optimum lies at a specific altitude on the surface.

Because knobs are actively turned, planned experimentation is very similar to the SPS evaluation step, with two important differences. First, knob changes during optimization are typically over narrower ranges than in an evaluation experiment. Second, several experiments are conducted during optimization, while evaluation is accomplished through one experiment. The result of each small experiment guides later experiments. For this reason, RSM and similar methods are sometimes described as *sequential* design of experiments.

A method similar to EVOP is the simplex method,[3] developed before calculators and personal computers. The simplex method relies on simple graphical techniques to guide experimentation. Although easy to use, the simplicity of this method limits its range of applications. The availability of numerous software products today facilitates the use of the more complex RSM and sequential design of experiments.

Conducting RSM Optimization

Like Monte Carlo simulation, response surface methods use several techniques requiring mathematical and engineering skill. The description that follows is very general. Problem solvers should seek the help of a statistical expert or consult suitable references.[4] The procedure for conducting RSM experimentation can be summarized as follows:

1. Determine a starting point based upon the results of the SPS evaluation step.
2. Design and conduct the first experiment.
3. Analyze the experiment and plan the next experiment.
4. Continue experiment/analyze cycles until the conditions for optimum output are discovered.

To explore the response surface, problem solvers must understand RSM logic. When near an optimum point, a surface is typically more irregular and—like natural topography—surrounded by steep slopes, with closely spaced contour lines. When far from the optimum, slopes tend to be gentler—broad and flat. Since the first experiment is usually conducted fairly far from the optimum, its surface is rather flat. In its flat regions, simple experiments are effective in describing the surface. Nearer the optimum point, the greater curvature in the surface requires more sophisticated experimental designs to discover surface details. The tasks of optimization through planned experimentation are guided by these considerations.

The first task in using RSM is to settle on a starting point for exploring the response surface. Typically, the first optimization experiment will be in the region of those settings discovered during the evaluation step to be *approximately* the best. This experiment is usually a two-level factorial experiment with the settings varied over a narrower range than used during evaluation.

For the sake of example, consider the problem of optimizing chemical process yield. Evaluation found temperature and time to be the interacting guilty knobs. Figure 8.4 shows four combinations of temperature and time used for the first optimization experiment. "X" marks the starting point around which experimental settings for the two guilty knobs were selected. Percentages indicate the average yield for the four experimental conditions.

The next experiment is planned only after analyzing the first. Analysis helps determine which direction on the surface to look for further improvement. Since the goal in our example was to maximize yield, the direction explored was that of steepest ascent. In Figure 8.5, the straight, parallel lines—far from the optimum—represent an approximate response surface based on the first experiment. When the butt of an arrow is placed at the center of the experimental settings and pointed perpendicular to the parallel lines, the arrow falls along the line of steepest ascent.

The second experiment was a set of tests conducted along the path of steepest ascent. The objective was to observe the yield at

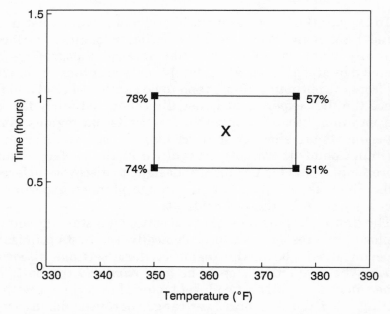

Figure 8.4   A simple experiment using a 2^2 factorial

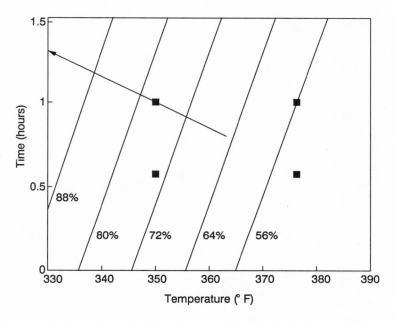

Figure 8.5   Level curves based upon the first simple experiment

several points along that path. These tests are represented by triangles in Figure 8.6. The yield ordinarily increases as the exploration moves away from the region of the first experiment, and then it begins to decrease. Since the optimum is usually found near the highest point along the steepest ascent line, the third experiment was conducted in that region.

Seven additional tests (the circles in Figure 8.6) made up the third experiment. The yield for each test is noted in Figure 8.6. Experiment/analyze cycles continue until the SPS team is satisfied they have discovered the conditions for optimum output. Response surface explorations are rarely as simple and straightforward as our example. Our intent was to illustrate the basic strategy and steps of optimizing with planned experimentation. Problem solvers should consult the references cited in this section for the mathematics and technical details of RSM.

The Teamwork Factor

POINT ONE: Optimization can be a long-term effort occurring before, during, or after solution implementation. The SPS team

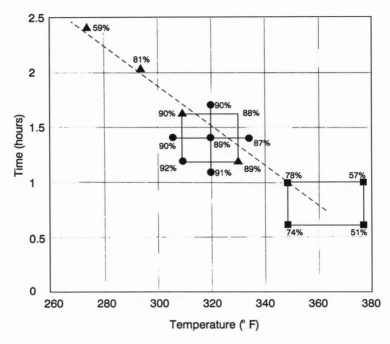

= Simple first experiment
▲ = Tests along path of steepest ascent (second experiment)
● = Tests in optimal region (third experiment)

Figure 8.6   Overview of tests done during EVOP optimization

must consequently *sustain* improvement activity over time. When SPS Step 5 begins, team membership should be adjusted according to the remaining investigative tasks. Because optimization usually requires specialized product or process knowledge, the number of people needed is usually fewer than needed for the first four SPS steps. In addition, a smaller team can actually work more efficiently at this stage. Team members who are no longer needed should be released to work on other improvement projects.

POINT TWO: During the SPS optimization step, data are generated that must be carefully analyzed and understood. Even at this last stage of the problem investigation, teamwork remains essential in reviewing optimization results. Team members should work cooperatively to answer questions like: Do the results make sense? What *new* permanent knowledge about the product or process has been gained? How can this knowledge help in related problems?

POINT THREE: Once the problem is solved, what happens to the SPS team? The answer depends on the type of teams a particular company opts to form. Two general types of teams are commonly used: temporary (ad hoc) and permanent (ongoing). Temporary teams are formed to work on specific projects and then disband when the projects are completed. Membership largely changes from project to project. The SPS approach advocates team membership based on the requirements of the specific problem.

The second type of team is fixed; its membership remains basically the same from problem to problem. *Continuous improvement team* is one popular label for the permanent team. In using SPS, staff with specialized knowledge are added to the core team for a limited time, as projects demand.

A case can be made for each type of team. Company strategy is probably the deciding factor for which type of team is most workable. Many companies may decide on a combination of team types to meet their various goals. Regardless of team type in use, however, the SPS process is the most productive route to permanent problem resolution for any team to follow.

Conclusion

Optimization is the activity that squeezes additional improvement out of a product or process. It continues the exploration begun during the evaluation step.

Optimization is only fruitful if preceded by the first four SPS steps. Problem solvers sometimes jump the gun and begin optimizing their favorite knob before it is proven guilty. Time and effort are wasted—with no improvement in the problem situation—if the wrong knobs are optimized.

Despite the initial complex appearance of many problems, the SPS evaluation step reveals straightforward solutions. Additional improvement is then often possible through common sense, engineering judgment, and experience *alone*. This optimization route is referred to as common sense experimentation.

On the other hand, some problems remain complex even after the top few knobs are known and understood. Monte Carlo simulation is then necessary to improve the process further. Under the right execution conditions, however, planned experimentation in the form of response surface methods (RSM) is more efficient for optimizing processes.

Both simulation and RSM are manageable only if just a few knobs are being optimized. Successful optimization is thus dependent on the proper focus resulting from the first four SPS steps.

Optimization is often closely related to implementation, the subject of the next chapter. The solution to a powdered metal problem illustrates this relationship. Manual agitation of the metal powder in a hopper was found to improve density. Although manual agitation was the SPS solution, it was not a viable option for the permanent solution. To automate the agitation, the SPS team decided to add mechanical vibrators to the stand. Several implementation factors, however, were not known. How many vibrators should be used? Exactly where should they be placed? What amplitude and frequency of vibration should be used? Optimizing the agitation parameters could occur only *as* the automated solution was implemented.

For many problem solutions, changes to process hardware and knob settings continue to be refined as time passes. In a word, implementation breeds optimization.

References

1. Reuven Y. Rubinstein, *Simulation and the Monte Carlo Method*, New York: John Wiley & Sons, 1981.

2. W. G. Hunter and J. R. Kittrell, "Evolutionary Operation: A Review," *Technometrics*, Vol. 8, No. 3, August 1966.

3. Robert L. Mason, Richard F. Gunst, and James L. Hess, *Statistical Design & Analysis of Experiments*, New York: John Wiley & Sons, 1989, pages 221–230. Also, Thomas P. Ryan, *Statistical Methods for Quality Improvement*, New York: John Wiley & Sons, 1989, pages 390–393.

4. George E. P. Box and Norman R. Draper, *Evolutionary Op-*

eration: A Statistical Method for Process Improvement, New York: John Wiley & Sons, 1969. Also, John A. Cornell, *How to Apply Response Surface Methodology*, Vol. 8 of the ASQC Basic References in Quality Control: Statistical Techniques, Milwaukee: American Society for Quality Control, 1984.

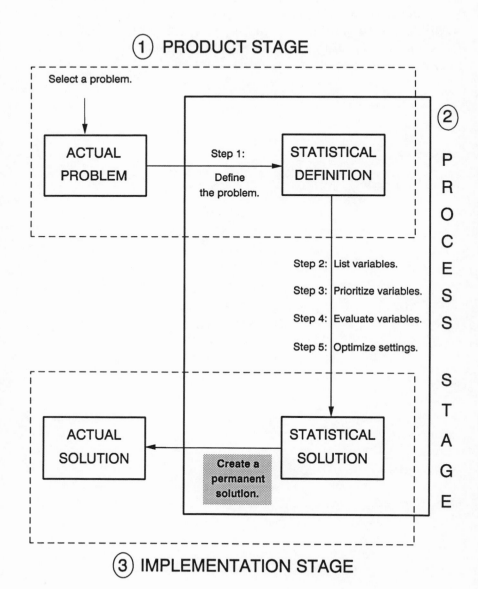

224

Chapter 9

Implementing
SPS Solutions

Issue:	Problem solving efforts often falter at implementation. Without an overall strategy and workable tactics to guarantee permanency, even solid solutions will fail to bring about lasting improvements.
SPS Response:	Once the team has settled on a *statistical* solution to the problem, they apply their creativity to translate it into an *actual* solution. They then proceed with implementation confident that their solution will correct the problem and yield the desired improvement.
SPS Result:	An effective problem solution that becomes a permanent part of the process.

From Statistical Solution to Actual Solution

As a doctor precedes treatment with diagnosis, the SPS team identifies problem symptoms during the problem definition step. In subsequent SPS steps, the knobs (variables) guilty of affecting the problem are revealed. The statistical solution of SPS Steps 4 and 5 is analogous to the doctor's final diagnosis and planning of a treatment. Knowledge of the disease and a plan to cure it by themselves do not improve the patient. An effective treatment must be put into action. Implementation is taking the pill.

The outcome of an SPS investigation is a statistical solution to the problem, identifying which knobs and settings will improve the process output. The statistical solution is the *knowledge* of how to correct the problem. Implementation is the *translation* of that knowledge into specific actions, closing the gap between knowledge and results.

The actual solution is composed of process changes or

other actions taken during the implementation stage. Ideally, actual solutions should set the important knobs to their new settings automatically and irreversibly. Practically, some solutions involve a one-time change of a knob, while other solutions require continued monitoring to assure a guilty knob remains at its new setting.

For instance, a problem with a malfunctioning assembly required a redesigned spring with a different spring rate. Purging the assembly line of the old spring and stocking it with the new spring was a one-time change that created a permanent solution. In contrast, a forging operation required a certain quench oil temperature to solve a problem. Since the oil temperature was affected by the ambient temperature, production rate, and size of the parts, it had to be continually monitored and controlled. Monitoring may be done by an operator or may be automated to varying degrees. To assure a permanent solution, monitoring and control should be automated.

Implementing Permanent Solutions

The primary determination of implementation success is the permanence of the solution. Juran describes a universal sequence for quality improvement that includes two major elements: breakthrough and control. Breakthrough moves a process to a new quality level, while controls must be instituted to hold the gains.[1] In SPS, the breakthrough is the discovery of the statistical solution. Control is established during implementation, when actions are taken to establish a permanent solution.

Many solutions can be implemented with a single change. The solution may be a different dimension, a new material, or a component change in an assembly. No monitoring is needed to assure that proper process conditions are maintained. Typically, one-time changes are the most permanent of all solutions and therefore the most desirable.

With design problems, design specifications are changed and the problem is solved. Process problems may be solved with a single change to a key knob in a variety of ways. For example, the evaluation of a crimping operation problem revealed that the crimp tool shape was the guilty knob. A change to the tool permanently fixed the problem and even removed the need to monitor the process. Similarly, a roundness problem in a machining operation was solved by changing a fixture configuration. A change in the sequence of operations may also yield a permanent solution. Equipment is physically moved, creating a new material flow pattern. The new sequence requires no monitoring.

When the team decides on the implementation action, clear responsibility must be assigned. A person to follow up should also be designated. Although it may sound obvious, *inaction* is frequently the cause of failing to solve a problem. Verification of needed changes is therefore essential to successful solutions.

Changes that implement an actual solution independent of continued action are the most permanent solutions. Not all solutions, however, can be implemented through a single change.

Implementing Monitored Solutions

The goal of implementation is always the same: permanent improvement of the process output. Often improvements that are not one-time changes must be monitored to assure some degree of permanence. At the low end of the permanence scale is the revision of standard operating procedures (SOPs). Such changes rely on the continual conformance of human action to the new SOPs. Table 9.1 summarizes implementation strategies for monitored solutions according to their degree of permanency.

To illustrate how each implementation strategy works, we will use a common example: maintaining the proper concentration of a soluble machining coolant. When the coolant concentration falls below a certain level, the surface finish of the process output deteriorates to an unacceptable level.

Human Intervention

One way to implement a solution is to change a standard operating procedure (SOP). Preventive maintenance practices, periodic process interventions, or process monitoring protocols can all be modified. Changing SOPs is a versatile and flexible means of implementation.

This type of actual solution can usually be implemented immediately after the statistical solution is discovered—a major advantage. Changes to SOPs, however, may not be permanent—

Table 9.1 Implementation strategies and tactics for monitored solutions

Implementation Strategy	Implementation Tactics	Actual Solutions			Degree of Permanency
Human intervention	Change SOP and audit	Follow standard procedure; check it periodically.	Use SPC on process OUTPUT; audit periodically.	Use SPC on process KNOB; audit periodically.	▮
	Warning plus audit	Install an automatic signal to indicate required action; check periodically that the required action is being taken.			▮
Partial automation	Dual warning	Install two signals: one to indicate required action, the second to reinforce the first.			▮
	Warning plus shutdown	Install an automatic signal to indicate required action; install mechanism that prevents further operations until the required action is performed.			▮
Full automation	System upgrade	Fully automated system monitors process and automatically changes process knobs to correct settings. Removes need for any human action to sustain improvement.			▮

a major shortcoming. Nevertheless, because they can be implemented quickly, changes to SOPs can be an interim solution until a final and permanent solution is found.

When a solution is implemented by changing a standard operating procedure, success depends upon continued human action. All human beings have difficulty changing their habits, however, even when they recognize the need to do so. Changes to SOPs must thus be periodically audited for conformance and effectiveness.

Changing an SOP can vary in its effectiveness as a solution. For our coolant concentration example, Table 9.1 proposes three variations of this implemented solution. First, the operator follows a standard procedure that requires regular action, but no monitoring. For instance, the coolant is changed once per week. Second, SPC is used to monitor a product characteristic affected by coolant concentration, such as the finish of the machined surface. When the control chart indicates the surface finish is deteriorating, the operator takes appropriate action to restore the coolant to its correct concentration. The third variation monitors the condition of the process knob itself using a control chart. When the chart signals a change in concentration, the operator adds concentrate.

This coolant concentration example also suggests appropriate use of the *permanent* control chart. SPS follows this logic path: First, the statistical solution reveals a critical process or product characteristic. Second, the team concludes that a successful implementation must monitor the characteristic. Finally, the team decides automated monitoring (discussed in the next section) is not feasible, either technically or economically. Only then is a permanent control chart justified.

As described in Chapter 4, SPS uses the control chart primarily as a problem definition tool. Situations calling for control charts as a permanent part of the process are infrequent. Yet permanent charting has been popular and even viewed as the main solution to process problems. Since they rely on continual human action, however, permanent control charts are the least desirable option for an actual solution.

In fact, because SOPs rely on people, the procedures described above for monitoring and correcting coolant concentration can break down at several points. The operator may forget or neglect to monitor the coolant concentration. Even when monitoring takes place, corrective actions may be omitted. A periodic audit of SOP conformance is thus important. The audit can be performed by a supervisor or an independent third party, such as a quality control auditor.

A final point on using the human intervention strategy deserves mention. Deming maintains if 80% of personnel are not following an SOP, something is wrong with the procedure—not the people.[2] The system is inadequate. Improving the system by finding a solution that can be *integrated* into the product or process insures effective and permanent solutions. The new knowledge gained through SPS helps achieve that end.

Partial Automation

Moving up the permanence scale, automated monitoring is added to enhance human action. This implementation strategy still relies on human intervention, but personnel are automatically alerted to the necessity for action. As is true for standard operating procedures, either a process knob or a process output characteristic is monitored to trigger the automatic signal. There are several variations on how partial automation can improve the permanence of a solution.

The simplest variation prompts operator action through an automated signal. In our coolant concentration example, a probe in the fluid monitors the concentration and signals when it falls below an acceptable level. If the alarm is heard only by the operator, however, it might be ignored. Thus, a supervisor or QC auditor should check periodically that required action is being taken.

Follow-up signals can be added to reinforce the need for action. For example, if no action is taken after an initial brief signal, identical signals go off at regular intervals until the concentration is restored. Or, each signal following the first gets incrementally louder; if ignored, the signal is soon heard all over the shop. A second signal could also be added in another location, such as a supervisor's office or the quality control lab. However the signal is reinforced, the objective is to give the operator continued reminders until the required action is completed.

Moving one step further up the permanence scale, automated monitoring can trigger a machine shutdown when action is required but not taken. Such an arrangement prevents the option of ignoring a signal, assuring that the need for action is known.

Full Automation

The most reliable implementation strategy for solutions that require ongoing attention is automated monitoring with automatic process intervention. In our coolant example, the concentrate is automatically dispensed whenever the signal of the automated monitoring device sounds. Thus, reliance on continued human performance is eliminated. In other cases, automating the required action may be technically more difficult.

In a problem with joining two fibrous substrates, SPS revealed that a buildup of adhesive on a guiding roller caused misalignment of the input materials. An interim solution was implemented as a change to the standard operating procedure; the operator was to clean the rollers every four hours. A permanent solution was later implemented by adding a system that automatically cleaned the rollers as the process ran.

In a precision grinding operation, holding size was a problem. SPS revealed that the machine drifted two-and-a-half millionths of an inch (0.0000025") in size with each cycle. While that may not sound like much, it meant every 40 cycles the machine drifted through one tenth of the specification. Since the capability was just about equal to the tolerance, any drift at all risked making product beyond the tolerance. The machine could be adjusted only in 0.00005" increments, so the operators had to make an adjustment about every 20 cycles. The interim solution was a new set of inspection and adjustment rules (SOPs) for the operator.

While this new procedure was being followed, the SPS team considered how to create a more permanent solution. The grinding machine moved through a dress-load-grind-unload cycle. Several team members suggested reworking the dressing system or the main ball screw. These solutions would have been very expensive, would have put the machine out of service for a long time, and were not guaranteed to work. It was unlikely that the dimensional discrepancy causing a 0.0000025" change per cycle could even be found.

Another suggestion was to add automatic gaging to monitor

the drift and increase compensation as required. Like the machine repairs, however, automatic gaging would be expensive and might require extensive debugging. Then one team member came up with a simple solution. If the machine controller counted the cycles, an extra compensation step could be added every 20 cycles. That solution was implemented and was permanent.

Actual solutions that are fully automated can be thought of as system upgrades. The solution becomes part of the original problem-plagued system. In fact, many fully automated solutions lead to technological innovation. A well-known example of a system upgrade is the frost-free refrigerator. Frost-free refrigerators gained a competitive advantage due to their innovative convenience.

Another familiar example of system upgrade is the cooling system on today's automobiles. Formerly, the owner had to check the antifreeze level in the car's radiator periodically and add fluid if necessary. The improved system has a fluid reservoir and a valve that allows fluid to enter and leave the radiator as needed. The owner only checks the fluid—at longer intervals—for its rust-inhibiting quality and freezing point. Now some cars even have an optional sensor that detects the need for a fluid change.

Confirming Solutions

The statistical solution provides strong evidence for the effectiveness of the actual solution before implementation dollars are spent. Nevertheless, after implementation, data should be collected to confirm the effectiveness of the actual solution. If it is effective, the problem symptoms identified in SPS Step 1 (problem definition) will have disappeared.

During problem definition, data are collected to answer four questions: WHERE is the problem? WHAT are the problem symptoms? WHEN do the symptoms occur? HOW EXTENSIVE is the problem? As recommended in Chapter 4, the most useful tool for answering these questions is an appropriate control chart.

Once the actual solution is implemented, the control chart is also the tool for confirming problem symptoms have disappeared. For instance, if there was an off-target condition, a control chart will show whether the process is now on target. If the process was incapable, the control chart will reveal the new capability. However implementation is handled, the process must be monitored for a sufficient time to insure the implemented solution is effective.

Sometimes the implementation effort reveals the need to start another SPS investigation. A heat treating problem illustrates this point. Its statistical solution indicated the need to better control the temperature in one zone of the furnace. During an implementation attempt, it was discovered that the heat treat furnace was not capable of the level of control required. Understanding the many variables affecting temperature became the subject of a new SPS investigation.

Cost-effective Implementations

Team members may be tempted to jump to solutions during the defining or listing steps. If they prematurely consider possible solutions, the team may take the wrong path, squandering valuable time and resources. During the SPS investigation (Steps 1–5), therefore, the team should not get sidetracked by implementation ideas.

Of course, the general feasibility of possible solutions should be considered. Ease of knob turnability, for instance, is a feasibility concern. But before the guilty knobs are known, it is wasteful to begin discussing implementation details for all possible solutions. Once the team formulates a statistical solution, they naturally enter the implementation stage of problem solving. The knowledge and creativity of the team are then turned loose on the challenges of implementing the solution.

In Chapter 1 we contrasted the important differences between conventional hunch-based problem solving and scientific problem solving. Figure 1.1 stresses how conventional problem solving often implements several unsuccessful "solutions" before arriving at a workable one. Following one hunch after another can be very costly, very time-consuming, and still not produce a lasting, effective solution. Statistical Problem Solving is designed specifically to prevent the wasted time and resources common with nonscientific problem solving.

Figure 9.1 depicts how SPS conserves both implementation

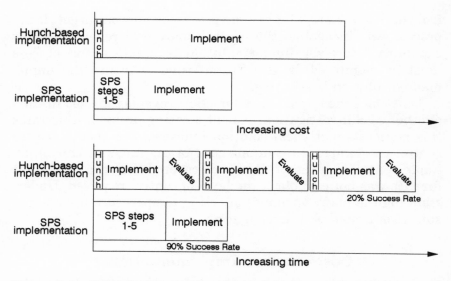

Figure 9.1   Graphical approximations of the cost and productivity of implementing hunch-based solutions versus SPS solutions

time and expense. As we have been emphasizing, SPS is cost-conscious at every point in the problem investigation. Because the SPS statistical solution helps to assure a successful actual solution, implementation dollars are consequently spent more predictably, more reliably, and more profitably.

In terms of time, the SPS investigation certainly requires a commitment for careful problem definition and analysis. And we have stressed not taking any shortcuts in following the SPS process, especially during the planned evaluation of Step 4. Still, SPS seeks the shortest path to problem resolution. (Refer to Table 2.2 in Chapter 2.) Because of its systematic, disciplined approach to problems, time devoted to an SPS investigation is typically productive from start to finish.

The real timesaver with SPS is realized at implementation. With conventional problem solving there is neither the certainty nor the specifics needed to implement a solution confidently and efficiently. Loose ends are common. The statistical solution of SPS is so precise, however, that creating and implementing an actual solution is straightforward, productive activity. Time put into the investigation thus saves valuable time at the implementation stage. And, as everyone knows, time is money.

The Teamwork Factor

POINT ONE: Whenever a solution is implemented, something is changed. In some cases, the change will create undesirable side effects. Thus, when considering the specifics of implementation, the team should include everyone with knowledge about the solution's impact on existing operations. Team members may be added even at this final stage. The objective is to anticipate and minimize any new difficulties that the actual solution might create.

POINT TWO: The SPS team itself naturally supports the implementation because they arrived at the solution. For effective implementations, however, *all* affected people must buy in to the solution, not just the SPS team.

Despite efforts of the team to avoid it, the implementation may increase someone's work or require major adaptations. In some instances, automated changes may eliminate someone's job. Such human relations challenges require the team to brief all affected personnel on the problem and the benefits of its solution to the company.

We began this chapter by describing implementation as a pill that must be taken. Pills may be sugar coated, may be in easy-to-swallow capsule form, or may be forced down the throat. Patients will usually take pills willingly, however, if they understand the pill is far less distressing than a continued illness.

Behavioral scientists Robert Blake and Jane Mouton offer much insight into how Americans react to changes in their work setting. The following excerpt is from their 1981 book *Productivity: The Human Side*:

> When two or more people gather and share their thoughts, attitudes, or feelings, or do not gather but take one another's thoughts, feelings, and attitudes into account, their viewpoints tend to converge. Once such convergence occurs, it takes on the character of a norm. When a norm has been established, group members feel the need to conform to it.[3]

Conclusion

Problem solving is not complete until an actual solution is effectively implemented. Ideal implementations are based on a one-time change and need no monitoring. Unfortunately, the permanency inherent to ideal implementations is not always possible.

Whenever solutions require continued monitoring, there are basically three implementation strategies: human intervention, partial automation, and full automation. The last is the most reliable and thus most closely meets the goal of permanent solutions.

With any actual solution, the problem definition of SPS Step 1 should be reviewed and data collected to *confirm* that the problem is solved. If the solution is effective, the original problem symptoms will be eliminated.

As mentioned in Chapter 2, Deming and other quality experts observe that greater than 85% of quality problems belong to the system. And the responsibility for improving the system is management's. Fewer than 15% of quality problems can be solved without management intervention.

SPS addresses the 85%. When properly applied, SPS helps to improve the system by successfully attacking difficult and chronic problems. Once the SPS team discovers a statistical solution, however, management must insure that an actual solution is implemented quickly, economically, and permanently.

References

1. J. M. Juran and Frank M. Gryna, editors, *Juran's Quality Control Handbook*, fourth edition, New York: McGraw-Hill Book Company, 1988, Section 22.

2. W. Edwards Deming, *Out of the Crisis*, Cambridge: Massachusetts Institute of Technology, Center for Advanced Engineering Study, 1986, page 375. Also, William Glasser, M.D., *The Quality School*, New York: Harper & Row, 1990, page 116.

3. Robert R. Blake and Jane Srygley Mouton, *Productivity: The Human Side, A Social Dynamics Approach*, New York: AMACOM, a division of American Management Associations, 1981, Chapter 8.

Epilogue

For us, Statistical Problem Solving is still a dynamic and developing experience. We are students as well as teachers, learning something new with each problem we encounter. Writing this book prompted us to refine our often artful approach to problems, transforming it into a more consistently disciplined and scientific process.

In the foregoing pages we have detailed this process for your own use, plus offered guidance for the productive application of available problem solving tools. Still, no book, no classroom can fully prepare you to become an effective problem solver. To really learn about problem solving, you have to solve a few problems.

> One must learn by doing the thing; for though you think you know it, you have no certainty until you try.
>
> –Sophocles

Each problem poses new challenges and results in new lessons. Because of vested interests, you may face resistance to solve a problem or opposition to a specific solution. Overcoming all the barriers to solving problems is part art and part science. Science can be taught. Art must be practiced.

Because problems are not in short supply, there are unlimited opportunities for practice. Find one problem and begin. If you stick with it, you will become a successful problem solver.

Case Study 1: Design Problem -- Electromechanical Device

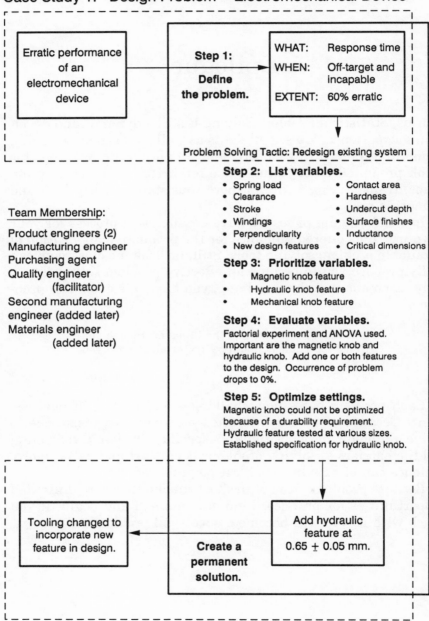

Erratic performance of an electromechanical device

Step 1:

Define the problem.

WHAT: Response time

WHEN: Off-target and incapable

EXTENT: 60% erratic

Problem Solving Tactic: Redesign existing system

Step 2: List variables.
- Spring load
- Clearance
- Stroke
- Windings
- Perpendicularity
- New design features
- Contact area
- Hardness
- Undercut depth
- Surface finishes
- Inductance
- Critical dimensions

Team Membership:

Product engineers (2)
Manufacturing engineer
Purchasing agent
Quality engineer
            (facilitator)
Second manufacturing
engineer (added later)
Materials engineer
            (added later)

Step 3: Prioritize variables.
- Magnetic knob feature
- Hydraulic knob feature
- Mechanical knob feature

Step 4: Evaluate variables.
Factorial experiment and ANOVA used.
Important are the magnetic knob and
hydraulic knob. Add one or both features
to the design. Occurrence of problem
drops to 0%.

Step 5: Optimize settings.
Magnetic knob could not be optimized
because of a durability requirement.
Hydraulic feature tested at various sizes.
Established specification for hydraulic knob.

Tooling changed to incorporate new feature in design.

Create a permanent solution.

Add hydraulic feature at 0.65 ± 0.05 mm.

Appendix A:
SPS Applications

Case Study 1:
Design Problem—
Electromechanical Device

PRODUCT STAGE

Select:

A customer was having a problem in their system with the operation of a supplier's product, an electromechanical device. The problem was experienced on prototype hardware prior to the product being introduced into production. To resolve the problem, the supplier formed a team consisting of two product engineers, a manufacturing engineer, a purchasing agent, and a quality engineer as the SPS facilitator. As the investigation progressed, a second manufacturing engineer and a materials engineer were added to the team.

Define:

Erratic operation of the device in the customer's system was the primary problem. The team had to define the problem in operational terms and translate it into tests that they could perform in their own laboratory. By analyzing the customer-returned prototype samples that operated erratically, a useful performance characteristic was identified and agreed upon, which the team called response time (WHAT). The problem was defined as incapability due to a combination of an off-target condition and excessive dispersion of the response times (WHEN). The problem magnitude was quite large, with almost 60% of the devices displaying erratic performance in the customer's system (HOW EXTENSIVE). Since the product was not yet in production, the issue of WHERE the problem occurred in the process was not relevant. *Problem solving tactic: Redesign the existing system.*

PROCESS STAGE

List:

Using brainstorming, the team listed knobs suspected to affect the response time. The list included spring load, a critical clearance, stroke of a moving part, number of turns in the windings, perpendicularity of two surfaces, contact area of two mating surfaces, material hardness, depth of an undercut, finish of several surfaces, inductance of the device, a number of critical dimensions, and several ideas for new design features.

Prioritize:

Because the design was under development, there were no existing data available to prioritize the knobs. Further, many of the listed knobs were new ideas that had never been tried. The team attempted to prioritize the list using the subjective rating and ranking method, but they reached an impasse. Then one team member suggested that they organize the various knobs on a cause-and-effect diagram. Three main branches accounted for all the listed knobs: one branch for mechanical forces in the device, one for magnetic forces, and one for hydraulic forces. Classifying the knobs reduced the long list to three primary knobs that could be used to evaluate how the forces combine to cause the problem. The team then selected one subknob to change each of the three primary knobs.

Evaluate:

The team decided to use the current design to provide a setting for each of the three knobs to be evaluated. An alternative design configuration was created for each knob to provide a second setting. Since new knobs had to be created, the evaluation was performed by conducting a factorial experiment. With the experiment replicated once, 16 total experimental trials were conducted. Table A.1 shows the experimental layout with the actual test order (random) in the third column. Knob settings are identified in the fourth through sixth columns. Performance data appear in the last column. The faster the device (i.e., the lower the response time), the better. ***Statistical Solution:***

Table A.1   Layout of a factorial experiment for an electromechanical design problem

Standard order	Replication	Test order	Magnetic knob settings	Hydraulic knob settings	Mechanical knob settings	Response time
1	1	2	Current	Current	Current	8.00
1	2	9	Current	Current	Current	8.20
2	1	3	New	Current	Current	5.54
2	2	7	New	Current	Current	5.44
3	1	5	Current	New	Current	7.20
3	2	14	Current	New	Current	6.34
4	1	6	New	New	Current	5.46
4	2	11	New	New	Current	5.44
5	1	1	Current	Current	New	9.30
5	2	15	Current	Current	New	9.74
6	1	13	New	Current	New	5.36
6	2	16	New	Current	New	5.70
7	1	8	Current	New	New	6.34
7	2	2	Current	New	New	7.70
8	1	4	New	New	New	5.36
8	2	10	New	New	New	5.46

(1) The ANOVA results of Table A.2 indicate the relative contribution of each knob. The most important knob was the magnetic knob. The hydraulic knob had the next largest effect. An interaction between the magnetic and the hydraulic knobs also had a significant effect on the problem.

Table A.2   ANOVA results for evaluation of response time

Source of variation	Sum of squares	Degrees of freedom	Mean square	F-ratio	Critical F-value
A. Magnetic	22.71	1	22.71	122.7 *	5.3
B. Hydraulic	3.98	1	3.98	21.5 *	5.3
C. Mechanical	0.70	1	0.70	3.8	5.3
A x B	3.37	1	3.37	18.2 *	5.3
A x C	0.70	1	0.70	3.8	5.3
B x C	0.40	1	0.40	2.1	5.3
A x B x C	0.30	1	0.30	1.6	5.3
Error	1.48	8	0.18		
Total	33.64	15			

*Statistically significant

(2) The interaction plot of Figure A.1 suggests the best device would have both the magnetic and hydraulic design features added.

(3) It was expected that adding the new design features would totally eliminate the erratic performance in the customer's system since the average response time was reduced from 8.8 to 5.4 milliseconds.

Optimize:

During optimization, the team attempted to select proper materials and dimensions for the new design features. In addition to

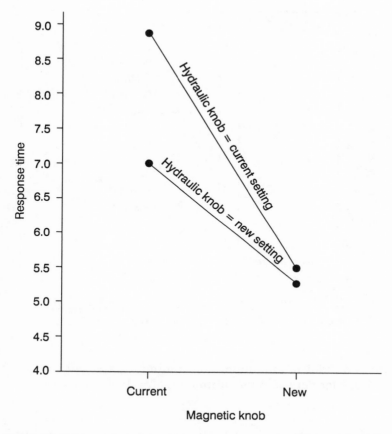

Figure A.1   Interaction plot of response time as a function of magnetic and hydraulic knobs

achieving the desired response time performance, the product had to meet a durability requirement. The team had concerns about the durability of both the magnetic and hydraulic knobs. Attempts to meet the durability requirement using various sub-knobs for the magnetic design feature were unsuccessful. Once that had been learned, the team concentrated on optimizing the hydraulic design feature *alone* for the actual solution. This feature was tried at several sizes. Figure A.2 plots the response time as a function of the feature size. Two lines are plotted, the maximum and minimum of several repeated tests. Ideally, the response time should be as low as possible and as repeatable as

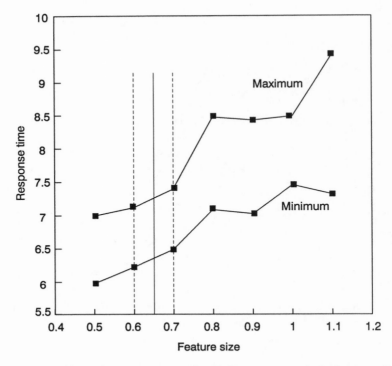

Figure A.2   Plot of maximum and minimum response times versus feature size for determining optimum hydraulic knob size

possible. The team decided to specify 0.65 ± 0.05 mm for the new design feature. Although a smaller size would have further improved performance, the team was concerned about the durability of a smaller feature. Tests of the hydraulic feature across its tolerance range proved it to be sufficiently durable.

IMPLEMENTATION STAGE

The affected part drawings were updated and the prototype components appropriately changed. Samples were given to the customer and the erratic performance in the customer's system was eliminated. The production tooling was changed to incorporate the new design feature.

Conclusions

With the conventional problem solving path:

1. The problem was not clearly defined due to the different expectations and goals among the problem solvers.
2. No clear performance characteristic was identified, compounding the confusion.
3. Many different ideas were being tried independently, creating a proliferation of design ideas and excessive experimental costs. Laboratory time and equipment availability became a real problem.

Statistical Problem Solving:

1. Focused the team's efforts by starting with a complete problem definition.
2. Used a clearly defined performance characteristic to reduce the amount of data that needed to be collected and analyzed, saving both time and money.
3. Through the prioritization step, transformed confusion (following too many hunches) into a single experiment that ultimately led to the solution.
4. Through the evaluation step, provided data that assured the team they had found a solution.

Case Study 2: Design Problem -- Crimp Joint

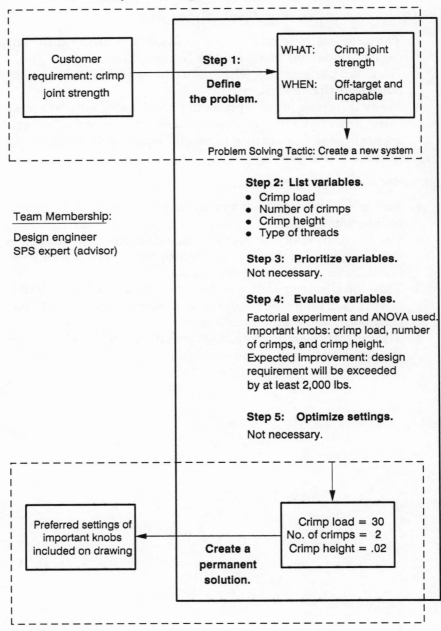

Customer requirement: crimp joint strength

Step 1:

Define the problem.

WHAT: Crimp joint strength

WHEN: Off-target and incapable

Problem Solving Tactic: Create a new system

Team Membership:

Design engineer
SPS expert (advisor)

Step 2: List variables.
- Crimp load
- Number of crimps
- Crimp height
- Type of threads

Step 3: Prioritize variables.
Not necessary.

Step 4: Evaluate variables.

Factorial experiment and ANOVA used.
Important knobs: crimp load, number
of crimps, and crimp height.
Expected improvement: design
requirement will be exceeded
by at least 2,000 lbs.

Step 5: Optimize settings.
Not necessary.

Preferred settings of important knobs included on drawing

Create a permanent solution.

Crimp load = 30
No. of crimps = 2
Crimp height = .02

Case Study 2:
Design Problem—
Crimp Joint

PRODUCT STAGE

Select:

A new product required a crimp joint with a minimum strength of 15,000 lbs. load resistance. The design engineer sought the help of an SPS expert to reach the best design as quickly as possible.

Define:

Develop a design to meet the 15,000 lbs. minimum joint strength (WHAT). The objective was to be on-target with acceptable capability (WHEN). In design problems, WHERE a problem occurs is not pertinent. HOW EXTENSIVE the problem is cannot usually be known until some prototypes are tested. *Problem solving tactic:* Create a new system.

PROCESS STAGE

List:

Brainstorming identified these knobs (variables): crimp load, number of crimps, crimp height, and type of threads.

Prioritize:

The prioritization step was unnecessary since all four knobs could be investigated in the development environment.

Evaluate:

An experimental matrix showed the combination of knob settings for each test. Data was gathered on only one sample per

Table A.3   Load data in 1,000 lbs. for 2^4 experiment

				Number of crimps			
				1		2	
				Crimp load		Crimp load	
				15	30	15	30
Thread type	A	Crimp Height	.01	4.7	12.0	8.8	17.7
			.02	5.1	11.6	10.65	21.0
	B	Crimp Height	.01	5.9	11.3	9.9	17.55
			.02	7.2	12.35	11.9	20.1

test since the samples were expensive and evaluation required a destructive test. Table A.3 shows the test data on the performance characteristic, joint strength. Yates algorithm was used to calculate the contributions of each knob and knob interactions. *Statistical Solution:*

(1) The major contributors to joint strength in order of importance were crimp load, number of crimps, and crimp height. These knobs did not interact, but contributed to joint strength independently.

(2) The best settings for these knobs were determined to be: crimp load = 30 lbs., number of crimps = 2, and crimp height = .02 inch.

(3) With these settings, average joint strength would be 20,550 lbs. Using only the three important knobs, a second ANOVA table was calculated in order to predict the joint strength capability. The ANOVA results are shown in Table A.4. The lower limit of the process capability was computed using the mean square error from the ANOVA table. The standard deviation of the design variation was

Table A.4   ANOVA for three important knobs

Variables	Sum of squares	Degrees of freedom	Mean squares	F-ratio	F-table
Crimp load	220.5	1	220.5	157.5 *	4.75
Number of crimps	140.4	1	140.4	100.3 *	4.75
Crimp height	9.2	1	9.2	6.6 *	4.75
Error	16.6	12	1.4		
Total	386.7	15			

*Statistically significant

calculated by taking the square root of the mean square error in the ANOVA table ($\sqrt{1.4} \times 1000 = 1180$ lbs.). By subtracting three standard deviations (3×1180) from the estimated average value of 20,550 lbs., a minimum strength of 17,010 lbs. was predicted. The expected minimum would meet the requirement of 15,000 lbs.

Optimize:

The SPS team felt the optimization step was unnecessary for two reasons. First, the design requirement was adequately met by putting each important knob at its preferred setting. Second, interactions did not contribute to variation in any practical way, and, as a result, it was unnecessary to develop a response surface.

IMPLEMENTATION STAGE

The best settings were made part of the design specifications and included in the drawing.

Conclusions

The conventional problem solving path would approach a design problem in this manner:

1. Create a design from the first best guess.
2. Generally, if the first best guess fails to meet the requirements, the design engineering process considers just one factor at a time for improvement of the design requirement.
3. The process continues in an irreversible fashion by successively adding new design features until the design exceeds the requirements, often adding unnecessary costs.
4. Knowledge of interactions among design variables is not gained.

The Statistical Problem Solving path takes this approach:

1. Create a design by simultaneously considering many knobs that may affect performance.
2. Through this more disciplined approach, less effort is used to deliver the optimum results.
3. New features are reversible during creation of the design. The important knobs are retained; the unimportant ones are dropped, often resulting in less cost.
4. Knowledge of interactions among knobs is an integral part of the design process.

Case Study 3: Manufacturing Problem -- Glass Blemishes

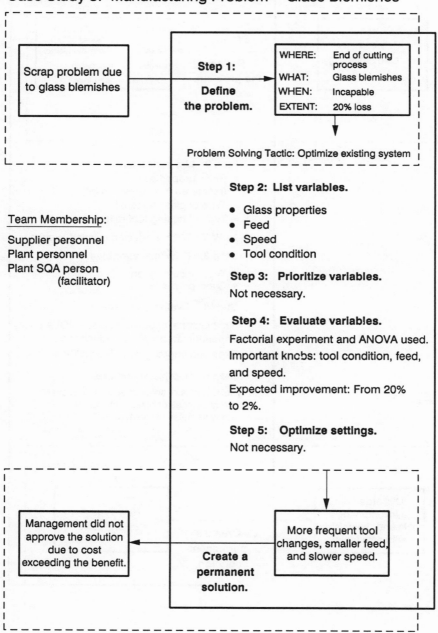

Case Study 3: Glass Blemishes -- Second Try

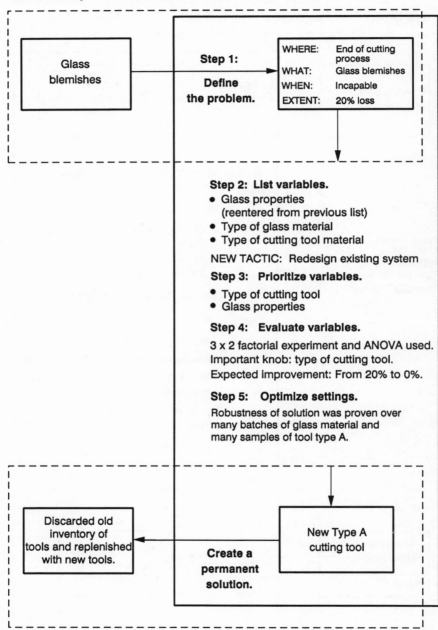

Step 1: **Define the problem.**

Glass blemishes

WHERE:	End of cutting process
WHAT:	Glass blemishes
WHEN:	Incapable
EXTENT:	20% loss

Step 2: List variables.
- Glass properties
  (reentered from previous list)
- Type of glass material
- Type of cutting tool material

NEW TACTIC: Redesign existing system

Step 3: Prioritize variables.
- Type of cutting tool
- Glass properties

Step 4: Evaluate variables.

3 x 2 factorial experiment and ANOVA used.
Important knob: type of cutting tool.
Expected improvement: From 20% to 0%.

Step 5: Optimize settings.
Robustness of solution was proven over
many batches of glass material and
many samples of tool type A.

Discarded old
inventory of
tools and replenished
with new tools.

Create a permanent solution.

New Type A
cutting tool

Case Study 3:
Manufacturing Problem—
Glass Blemishes

PRODUCT STAGE

Select:
A manufacturer of TV monitors was losing market share. Each of its plants was to improve quality and productivity by solving one major problem. A plant that routinely collected Pareto chart data selected a scrap problem due to glass blemishes.

Define:
A p-chart at the end of the cutting process (WHERE) to monitor the blemish problem (WHAT) showed a random pattern (WHEN) with an average defective level at 20%, a medium-sized problem (HOW EXTENSIVE). The problem was one of incapability. Nobody, including the glass manufacturer, understood how the blemishes were created.

PROCESS STAGE
Since about 80% of output was acceptable, the plant felt there must be a reason for the 20% bad parts. It was insisting that the quality control of the glass supplier improve. The supplier, on the other hand, felt that its quality control procedures were adequate. To reach agreement, an SPS team was formed consisting of both supplier and plant personnel. ***Problem solving tactic:*** *Optimize the existing system.*

List:
A focused brainstorming session identified four knobs: glass properties, feed, speed, and tool condition.

Prioritize:
Unnecessary since it was feasible to investigate all four knobs.

Evaluate:
The glass supplier provided two batches of material with sufficiently different but acceptable machinability properties. To

minimize investigative expenses, it was decided to try a dull tool (tool condition just before a normally scheduled tool change) and a sharp tool (condition just after a change). Feed and speed were operator-controllable knobs. With the four knobs each at two settings, a factorial experiment was run. The performance characteristic used was the proportion of product that had glass blemishes. Data analysis brought surprises. *Statistical Solution:*

(1) In order of importance, the guilty variables were tool condition, feed, and speed. All were controlled by the plant. No interactions were found significant.
(2) A slower speed, smaller feed, and more frequent tool changes were the preferred settings.
(3) The data analysis showed that the expected reject rate would go from 20% to less than 2%.

Management considered this solution impractical from a business perspective because reduction in feed and speed would significantly reduce productivity and increased tool change frequency would significantly increase the tooling cost. The loss of productivity and increased tool cost were greater than the benefit gained by reducing the defects. *The team was consequently directed to look for another solution.*

List—Second Try:

Since management wanted a solution that didn't affect productivity, feed, speed, and tool change interval could no longer be considered. Only glass material properties remained on the list. The team considered additional knobs. They thought of two new knobs, changing glass material or changing the type of cutting tool. Since the glass supplier did not have the research capabilities to develop a new glass formula, changing material was dropped from the list. *Problem solving tactic: Redesign the existing system.*

Evaluate—Second Try:

The team had to identify a cutting tool type that would perform well for the range of glass properties expected in production.

Three different tool types were selected for evaluation, all obtained from tool suppliers as free samples (no cost). The team decided to evaluate the three new tool types using two batches of glass material. All combinations were tested in a 3×2 factorial experiment. Types B and C produced almost the same result as the existing tool type. *Statistical Solution:* Type A of the new tools was significantly better and completely eliminated the problem, reducing the glass blemishes to 0%.

Optimize:

To test the robustness of the new tool type against variation in glass material and the tool itself, the team tried samples of Type A from different lots with several different batches of glass material. The tool type proved to be robust with no defectives created regardless of the tool type lot or batch of glass material.

IMPLEMENTATION STAGE

The new tool cost was almost the same as the existing tool cost. As repeated tests showed, the tool change interval was not affected by the adoption of the new tool. The new tool was adopted as a permanent change. All the old tools were discarded from the inventory.

Conclusions

With the conventional problem solving path:

1. Haphazard experiments with the glass cutting process offered no solutions.
2. Badgering the supplier about its quality control procedures produced no improvement.

Statistical Problem Solving:

1. Revealed that variation in glass properties did not contribute to the problem.
2. Looked for and inexpensively investigated new variables.
3. Accepted the business reality that degrading productivity and increasing tooling cost were not feasible.
4. Found an inexpensive solution within the existing process.

Case Study 4: Design/Manufacturing Problem -- Servomotor

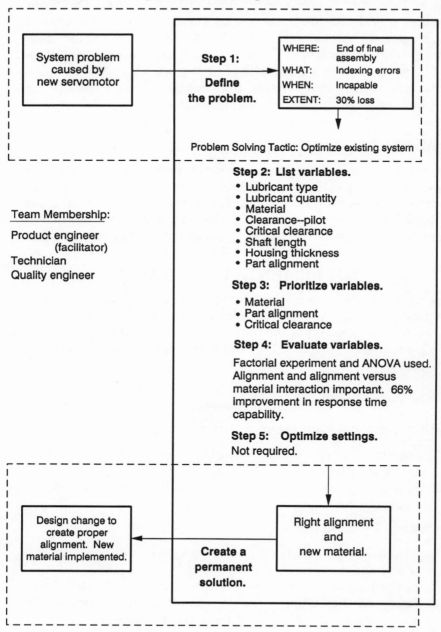

System problem caused by new servomotor

Step 1:

Define the problem.

WHERE:	End of final assembly
WHAT:	Indexing errors
WHEN:	Incapable
EXTENT:	30% loss

Problem Solving Tactic: Optimize existing system

Team Membership:

Product engineer
 (facilitator)
Technician
Quality engineer

Step 2: List variables.

- Lubricant type
- Lubricant quantity
- Material
- Clearance--pilot
- Critical clearance
- Shaft length
- Housing thickness
- Part alignment

Step 3: Prioritize variables.

- Material
- Part alignment
- Critical clearance

Step 4: Evaluate variables.

Factorial experiment and ANOVA used. Alignment and alignment versus material interaction important. 66% improvement in response time capability.

Step 5: Optimize settings.
Not required.

Design change to create proper alignment. New material implemented.

Create a permanent solution.

Right alignment and new material.

Case Study 4:
Design/Manufacturing
Problem—Servomotor

PRODUCT STAGE

Select:

A controls supplier was developing a new servomotor, a spin-off of a motor already in production. The customer experienced trouble in its system and blamed it on the motor. Since the customer was working with two suppliers, the business was awarded to the competitor. The supplier was told that if the problem was fixed, the business would be restored. Company management assigned the problem to a small SPS team consisting of a product engineer, a technician, and a quality engineer.

Define:

Several motors suspected to cause the problem in the customer's system had been returned. The supplier requested some motors from fully functioning systems also returned. Both "good" and "bad" motors were subjected to a number of engineering tests. A major difference was identified as errors in indexing accuracy within the range of frequencies used to drive the motor (WHAT). Since the new design was a spin-off, the team decided to work on the existing motors, which were readily available and less expensive than the prototypes. From sample motors obtained from production lots over several days, the indexing problem was discovered to be a stable condition, inherent to the design and process (WHEN). The team concluded the design was incapable of functioning in the customer's system, although it worked successfully in existing applications. The problem was attacked at the end of final assembly (WHERE) since the problem location could not be discovered until a completed motor was tested, revealing the actual cause. Since there was no established specification for motor indexing accuracy, the EXTENT of the problem was estimated at 30% unacceptable motors in the new application. ***Problem solving tactic:*** *Optimize the existing system.*

PROCESS STAGE

List:

Brainstorming identified eleven suspect knobs, including process and design knobs and one knob in the customer's system. These were lubricant type, lubricant quantity in two places, material of one component, two piloting clearances, a critical clearance, shaft length, housing thickness, mating part alignment and driving frequency. The customer was approached about changing the driving frequency in its system, but was unwilling or unable to make any changes. The supplier then turned its full attention to working with the knobs under its own control.

Prioritize:

Several knobs could be examined by taking existing motors apart. The team compared "good" and "bad" motors for each suspect knob condition. After the results were placed in a contingency table, two knobs were identified as strong suspects. Knobs that could not be inspected in a disassembled motor were ranked subjectively after discussing motor function. A total of three knobs were chosen for evaluation: a critical clearance, the alignment of two components, and the material of one component.

Evaluate:

The team first decided on the settings for each knob. Two of the three knobs were subject to process variation for which the process capability was known. The first knob was the clearance between two parts, one of which was a stamping. The parts could be easily hand-tailored to represent the maximum and minimum conditions seen in production. The second knob was the relative alignment of two parts. The process could result in a range of alignment varying in two directions from the design intent. The team decided to evaluate three alignments: centered (intended), biased left, and biased right. The third knob was a pending material change to solve another problem. Early production samples of the new material were already available. The team laid out the designed experiment shown in Table A.5 with a total of 12 (2 × 3 × 2) combinations. Each test combination was replicated once, for a total of 24 motors. Motors were assembled by hand to assure the proper clearance and alignment in the assembly. The performance characteristic chosen for evaluation was indexing error, expressed as the total number of errors occurring during a severe test. The raw data is shown in the cells of Table A.5; the results of the ANOVA are shown in Table A.6. *Statistical Solution:*

(1) The most important knob was alignment, with the alignment versus material interaction also significant. Material change alone showed a small significance, but was not very important relative to the other important knobs. Clearance did not significantly contribute to the problem. The evaluation also revealed the exact location of the

Table A.5 Experimental layout for indexing error evaluation

		Current material			New material		
		Alignment left	Alignment center	Alignment right	Alignment left	Alignment center	Alignment right
Small clearance		177	78	28	105	78	36
		75	60	24	61	87	42
Large clearance		250	53	47	65	39	39
		153	56	46	99	64	35

Table A.6   ANOVA results for indexing error evaluation

Source of variation	Sum of squares	Degrees of freedom	Mean square	F-ratio	Critical F-value
A. Alignment	30907	2	15453	15.45 *	3.88
B. Material	3675	1	3675	3.67	4.75
C. Clearance	376	1	376	.38	4.75
A x B	9589	2	4794	4.79 *	3.88
A x C	3605	2	1802	1.80	3.88
B x C	2223	1	2223	2.22	4.75
A x B X C	1092	2	546	.55	3.88
Error	12006	12	1000		
Total	63474	23			

*Statistically significant

problem in the process—the operation where the two parts with the critical alignment were joined.

(2) Right-biased alignment gave the fewest index errors. A plot of the alignment-material interaction (Figure A.3) indicated that the difference between the materials at the centered and right alignments was very small. At the left alignment there was a big difference in performance. The new material desensitized the part to alignment, an opportunity to exploit the forgiving principle. The preferred knob settings were thus right-biased alignment and new material.

(3) For expected improvement, the data was pooled to incorporate the clearance variation with the error, with the

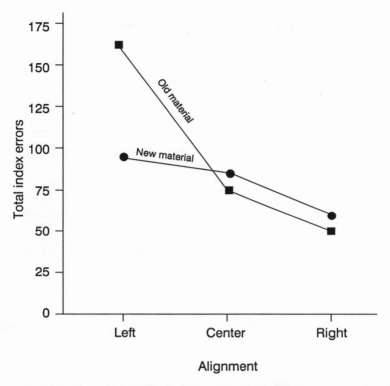

Figure A.3   Interaction plot of the combined effect of material and alignment on index errors

associated ANOVA results shown in Table A.7. The standard deviation of the improved design was estimated by taking the square root of the mean square residual in Table A.7. Three times the estimated standard deviation was added to the average for the new knob settings to provide an estimate of the new capability, an upper limit of 79 index errors. The new settings promised a major improvement over an estimated 230 errors for the current production design.

Optimize:

Improvement was so substantial that the team decided they could skip the optimization step and immediately provide sam-

Table A.7   ANOVA results for pooled data

Source of variation	Sum of squares	Degrees of freedom	Mean square	F-ratio
A. Alignment	30907	2	15453	14.41
B. Material	3675	1	3675	3.43
A x B	9589	2	4794	4.71
Error	19303	18	1072	
Total	63475	23		

ples to the customer. Testing in the actual system environment confirmed the solution was fully effective.

IMPLEMENTATION STAGE

The team saw two possible routes to correcting the alignment problem. Either the tooling could be changed to bias the alignment to the right during the assembly operation, or features could be added to the aligning components to positively locate the two mating parts. The team chose to add the new design features because it was a more permanent solution. Drawings were made and samples tested. The locating feature worked effectively and was permanently added to the design. The material change was already being implemented; but with the proven additional benefit, its incorporation was expedited.

Conclusions

1. Unless clearly justified otherwise, knobs should be evaluated at two settings. In this case, the alignment knob was evaluated at three settings since it was not known how

movement in either direction from the assumed optimum would affect the problem. Because the prioritization step identified only three strong suspects, the experiment could include a knob at three settings. It was still manageable and allowed all possible combinations to be evaluated. Thus, with no confounding the results were clear.

2. This case illustrates the "element of surprise," as discussed in Chapter 7. The engineers involved were very surprised that the centered alignment was not the best setting. It was also surprising that the critical clearance had no effect on the problem since it had been blamed in the past. Further, the multiknob approach revealed an interaction that made the design more robust. The objectivity of SPS evaluation allows the team to be open to revealed benefits without feeling the need to defend a pet theory or an already implemented solution.

Case Study 5: Manufacturing Problem -- Unacceptable Gears

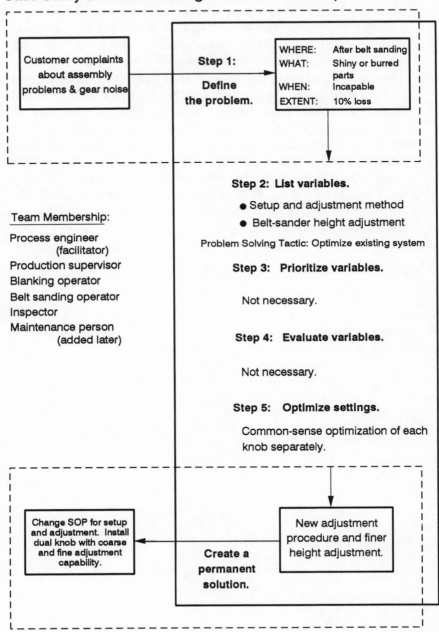

Customer complaints about assembly problems & gear noise

Step 1:

Define the problem.

WHERE:	After belt sanding
WHAT:	Shiny or burred parts
WHEN:	Incapable
EXTENT:	10% loss

Step 2: List variables.

- Setup and adjustment method
- Belt-sander height adjustment

Problem Solving Tactic: Optimize existing system

Team Membership:

Process engineer (facilitator)
Production supervisor
Blanking operator
Belt sanding operator
Inspector
Maintenance person (added later)

Step 3: Prioritize variables.

Not necessary.

Step 4: Evaluate variables.

Not necessary.

Step 5: Optimize settings.

Common-sense optimization of each knob separately.

Change SOP for setup and adjustment. Install dual knob with coarse and fine adjustment capability.

Create a permanent solution.

New adjustment procedure and finer height adjustment.

Case Study 5:
Manufacturing Problem—
Unacceptable Gears

PRODUCT STAGE

Select:

A burred gear produced by a blanking process either created difficulty in assembling a final product or resulted in a noisy assembly for the customer. Sometimes the gear was shiny and reduced the life of the product significantly. The supplier of the blanked parts was notified that neither burred nor shiny gears were acceptable.

Define:

Almost all parts at the end of the blanking process have burrs. It is an industry-wide problem and the belt-sanding process as a secondary operation is considered an acceptable solution. After belt-sanding (WHERE), the parts fell into three categories: 90% acceptable, 5% shiny (WHAT), and 5% burred (WHAT). A p chart which included both defects indicated a stable and incapable process (WHEN) chronically producing an average of 10% (HOW EXTENSIVE) unacceptable parts. The plant management assigned the problem to an SPS team consisting of a process engineer, a production supervisor, one operator each from the blanking and belt-sanding processes, and an inspector.

PROCESS STAGE

List:

SPS team members began with the premise that the blanking process itself could not be made burr-free because almost 100% of blanking output has burrs. In addition, the belt-sander was designed for consistent part heights during a run. When a thin part passed through the belt-sander, the burrs were not removed; when a thick part passed through, the part became shiny. A knob on the machine could be adjusted to accommodate groups of parts with different thicknesses. It was a coarse knob (discussed in Chapter 7) and not designed to handle minor fluctuations around the average thickness in a group. The operators used this knob for setup and process control by sampling only one part at a time. If they found the part to be shiny or to have incomplete burr removal, they adjusted the knob. Despite being instructed not to touch the knob after the initial setup, the operators were continuously adjusting it. Initially the team considered an expensive new belt-sander with a pulley system that automatically moved the sanding belt up and down based on the amount of resistance felt while removing burrs. But it was not proven to be any more capable than the existing machine. After reviewing all this information, the team could list only two knobs—the thickness adjustment knob and the setup and control procedure. They decided both knobs needed to be optimized. **Problem solving tactic:** *Optimize the existing system.*

Evaluate:

Not necessary. It was physically impossible for the two knobs to interact, so each could be optimized independently.

Optimize:

Because of the thickness variation within a group of parts, the team concluded that basing setup and adjustments on a single part was statistically unsound. The SPS team decided on an improved procedure for setting up and adjusting the belt-sander:

1. Take a periodic sample of five gears from the incoming stock.
2. Measure the thickness of all five parts.
3. Compute average thickness.
4. Adjust the thickness adjustment knob corresponding to the average thickness of the subgroup.
5. Repeat steps 1 through 4 periodically. (The frequency of

part-thickness checks would be refined after implementation.)

The team realized, however, that effective adjustments could not be made with the present thickness-adjustment knob. The knob could only make very coarse adjustments, plus there was no way to identify the current setting or the amount of adjustment. The team decided to add both fine adjustment capability and markings on the knob to indicate different settings. A maintenance person joined the SPS team at this point to assist in the changes.

IMPLEMENTATION STAGE

The maintenance person on the team was able to convert the adjustment knob into a dual knob—one for coarse adjustments and one for fine adjustments. The team calibrated markings on the knobs. Once finer adjustments could be made, the team found that the adjustment mechanism could not respond to the finer adjustments. The pulley sliding tracks on the machine were improved. Defectives dropped from the 10% average to a 0.5% average as a result of these changes in the procedure and hardware.

Conclusions

Conventional problem solving:

1. Based setup and adjustment on a single part.
2. Tinkered with the adjustment knob too frequently and used unsound adjustment rules.
3. Concluded a new machine was needed, although no new machine had better capability.

Statistical Problem Solving:

1. Based setup and adjustment on the average thickness of five parts, a statistically sounder procedure.
2. Improved process hardware by changing to a dual knob to allow for finer adjustments and by adding calibration markings to the knob.
3. Optimized existing hardware, a lower-cost and more effective solution than investing in new hardware.

Using Statistical Problem Solving on Administrative Problems

The SPS approach to quality and productivity improvement can be equally valuable when the process output is a service instead of a product. Not only consumer services such as banks, schools, restaurants and insurance companies, but also the operations support systems within a company—finance, production control, purchasing, etc.—would benefit from the SPS approach.

Fundamental differences between administrative problems and technical problems affect the SPS process at several steps. Because design and manufacturing problems involve physical products or processes, their investigation is a scientific search for unknown physical causes. In administrative problems, however, the source of the problem is usually known. What is not known is the action or combination of actions that will be most effective in creating a satisfactory solution to the problem.

During the product stage (problem selection and definition), applying SPS to administrative problems is essentially the same as for technical problems. Differences emerge during the process stage.

For the listing step, the knobs of an administrative problem are possible actions for solving the problem. Data cannot always be collected for the prioritization step since the knobs are often untried actions. Consequently, subjective rating and ranking is the most frequently used method.

During the evaluation step the team relies on its combined knowledge and experience to predict how the possible actions might help the problem. Typically no tests are conducted, and thus hard data is not usually available. Instead, each team member expresses a subjective preference for a given combination of possible actions.

Since the evaluation process for an administrative problem is less precise than for a technical problem, expected improvement cannot be estimated. Only implementation itself can quantify the effectiveness of the solution. Implementation therefore involves some risk that money will be spent without solving the problem. Any economic risk, however, is still not as great as it is with conventional problem solving due to the unbiased team approach of SPS.

The evaluation step determines a statistical solution in the form of a preferred combination of actions. Optimization of administrative solutions means deciding on the details of implementation and taking action. As the solution is implemented, ideas for action are refined.

SPS execution principles call for a low-cost investigation. For administrative problems, however, the distinction between investigation and implementation is often not as clear-cut as it is for technical problems. For example, a bank decides to try out a new checking account scheme to attract more customers. They will go through the expense to design and print checks, write software, talk with potential customers, and train staff. Even though the scheme is experimental, implementation money must be spent. Because of this cost risk with administrative trials, initial implementation may be limited, then scaled up if successful.

For some administrative problems, investigation costs may be minimal if the knobs to be tried are part of current activities. For example, in trying to reduce accounts receivable, one company decided to use letters, followed up by phone calls, in which they offered incentives for immediate payments. It was possible to integrate these knobs into existing procedures at practically no cost and very little additional burden for the employees involved.

Understanding underlying physical principles is not an issue in solving administrative problems. Instead, psychological and sociological factors are important. The problem solving process must not only find a solution, but it must guarantee that those affected by the solution support and participate in its implementation. The best way to accomplish both goals is to create a team environment where members can openly express their ideas and preferences. In turn, the SPS process is ideal for facilitating a productive team effort.

Case Study 6: Administrative Problem -- Customer Service

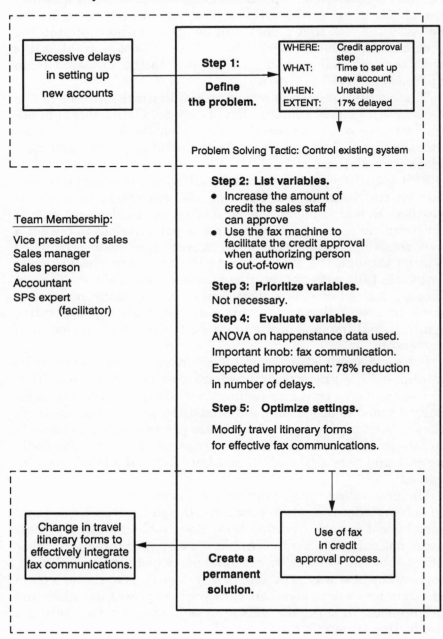

Excessive delays in setting up new accounts

Step 1:

Define the problem.

WHERE:	Credit approval step
WHAT:	Time to set up new account
WHEN:	Unstable
EXTENT:	17% delayed

Problem Solving Tactic: Control existing system

Team Membership:

Vice president of sales
Sales manager
Sales person
Accountant
SPS expert
　　　(facilitator)

Step 2: List variables.
- Increase the amount of credit the sales staff can approve
- Use the fax machine to facilitate the credit approval when authorizing person is out-of-town

Step 3: Prioritize variables.
Not necessary.

Step 4: Evaluate variables.

ANOVA on happenstance data used.
Important knob: fax communication.
Expected improvement: 78% reduction in number of delays.

Step 5: Optimize settings.

Modify travel itinerary forms for effective fax communications.

Change in travel itinerary forms to effectively integrate fax communications.

Create a permanent solution.

Use of fax in credit approval process.

Case Study 6:
Administrative Problem—
Customer Service

PRODUCT STAGE

Select:

A sales department was losing potential accounts. In reviewing customer complaints and surveying customers about the quality of service, they became aware of a major problem: It was taking too long to set up a new account. The sales vice president assigned an SPS team consisting of himself, the sales manager, a sales person, and an accountant. An SPS expert coached the team along the way.

Define:

Setting up a new account involved four major steps: (1) Contact three references. (2) Review the Dunn & Bradstreet report. (3) Approve a line of credit. (4) Execute administrative tasks. The SPS team decided to collect data on new orders for a while, recording the total time required on an X chart and the time for each of the four steps on a Pareto chart. A representative sample of six new accounts is shown in the X + Pareto chart of Figure A.4. The X chart revealed obvious instability (WHEN) in the primary problem of total time to set up a new account (WHAT). The time to set up a new account sometimes took ten times the average of three hours (HOW EXTENSIVE). One of the steps (time spent in credit approval—WHERE) accounted for the instability. Credit was authorized by one of three individuals. Many accounts could be approved by the salesperson, higher credit amounts required the sales manager's approval, while the highest amounts required the vice president's approval. The team decided to review the history of recently approved accounts to find which of the three levels of approval created the most de-

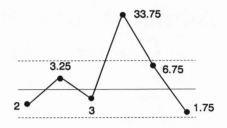

Total hours ⟍ Category	2	3.25	3	33.75	6.75	1.75	Total
Check 3 references	1	1.5	.25	.5	2	1	6.25
Review Dunn & Bradstreet report	.25	.25	.25	.25	.25	.25	1.50
Approve credit	.25	.5	2	32	1.5	.5	36.75
Execute paperwork	.5	1	.5	1	3	0	6.00
New account transaction no.	1	2	3	4	5	6	

Figure A.4   Use of X + Pareto chart to analyze the time involved to set up new sales accounts

lays. Figure A.5 shows the results of this investigation. Most delays were at the vice president's level. Further analysis revealed that the majority of delays caused by either the manager or vice president were due to their out-of-town travel. The subproblem to solve was thus defined as approval delays due to out-of-town travel. ***Problem solving tactic:*** *Control the existing system.*

PROCESS STAGE

List:

Focused discussion on the pertinent subproblem suggested two possible actions (i.e., knobs) to remove or reduce the number of

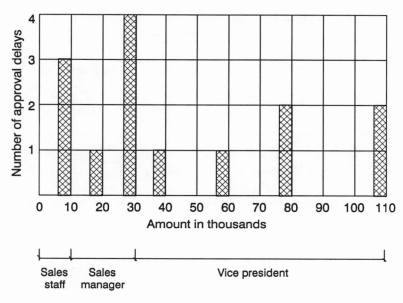

Figure A.5 Charting credit approval delays by their source

delays: (1) increase the amount of credit that the sales staff can approve and (2) use the facsimile machine to facilitate the credit approval process when the manager or vice president are out of town.

Prioritize:

This step was unnecessary since there were only two knobs.

Evaluate:

The team used the same data (see Figure A.5) for evaluation that they used to define the problem. They considered what outcome would have resulted if credit approval amounts were increased, approvals were obtained by fax, or both. (The maximum authorization amount was increased from $10,000 to $30,000 for salespersons and up to $55,000 for the sales manager.) The number of delays was chosen as the performance characteristic. In Table A.8, Cell 1 represents the status quo in which 14 approval delays occurred during the data collection period. If authoriza-

Table A.8 Evaluation of observational data for two knobs
affecting credit approval delays

		Fax communication	
		Not used	Used
Approval amount	Stayed the same	1 14 delays	2 3 delays
	Increased	3 6 delays	4 3 delays

tion by fax had been used, only 3 delays would have occurred
(Cell 2). If credit approval amounts had been increased, the
number of delays would have been reduced to 6 (Cell 3). If both
actions had been implemented, the number of delays would have
been 3 (Cell 4), no better than the use of the fax alone. *Statistical Solution:*

(1) The most important knob is the use of the fax.
(2) The team decided the use of fax communication would be
    an effective solution without changing credit approval
    amounts.
(3) Based on available data, use of the fax could have resulted
    in about a 78% reduction in delays.

Optimize:

The team further discussed how to optimize the faxing procedure. They thought of modifying travel forms to include relevant
fax numbers, plus arrival and departure times at all locations in
the itinerary, and developing secret codes to protect confidenti-
ality.

IMPLEMENTATION STAGE

Action items were formulated to implement the new procedure, including the design of new itinerary forms, distribution of fax codes to all persons routing approval requests for new accounts, removal of old forms from the system, documentation of the new procedure, and education for all affected employees. Completion of items were assigned to each department. The team monitored results for a few weeks after the changes were instituted, and the average approval time had significantly dropped. The improvement focus then shifted to the reasons for delays attributed to the sales staff.

Conclusions

With the conventional problem solving path, there was:

1. No sensitivity to customer needs.
2. No formal recording or use of existing data for improvement purposes.
3. No thought of using fax technology to improve service.

Statistical Problem Solving:

1. Focused on the direct relationship between customer needs and sales department actions.
2. Identified the actions responsible for instability in the system for setting up new accounts.
3. Used new technology to create improvement in the system.

Case Study 7: Administrative Problem -- Plant Productivity

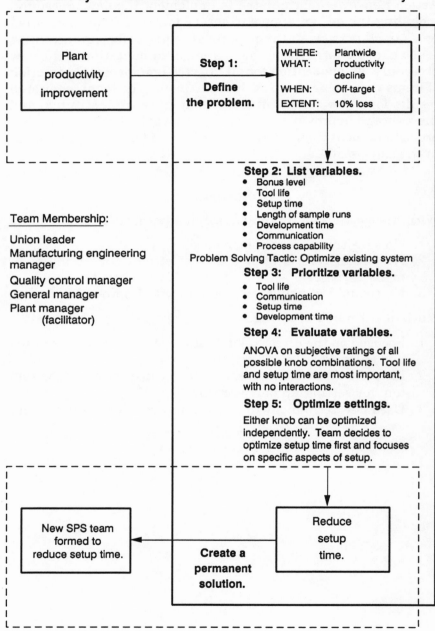

Plant productivity improvement

Step 1:

Define the problem.

WHERE:	Plantwide
WHAT:	Productivity decline
WHEN:	Off-target
EXTENT:	10% loss

Step 2: List variables.
- Bonus level
- Tool life
- Setup time
- Length of sample runs
- Development time
- Communication
- Process capability

Problem Solving Tactic: Optimize existing system

Step 3: Prioritize variables.
- Tool life
- Communication
- Setup time
- Development time

Step 4: Evaluate variables.

ANOVA on subjective ratings of all possible knob combinations. Tool life and setup time are most important, with no interactions.

Step 5: Optimize settings.

Either knob can be optimized independently. Team decides to optimize setup time first and focuses on specific aspects of setup.

Team Membership:

Union leader
Manufacturing engineering manager
Quality control manager
General manager
Plant manager
    (facilitator)

New SPS team formed to reduce setup time.

Create a permanent solution.

Reduce setup time.

276

Case Study 7:
Administrative Problem—
Plant Productivity

PRODUCT STAGE

Select:

Plant productivity was affected by a recent strike. After the strike ended, productivity improved, but not to the previous level. The plant staff struggled for some months to raise the productivity level, with no success. Finally, the plant manager suggested that they take an SPS approach to improving overall productivity. A team was formed consisting of a union leader, the manufacturing engineering manager, the quality control manager, the general manager, and the plant manager as the SPS facilitator.

Define:

During the recent strike, plantwide (WHERE) productivity shifted downward (WHAT) from 90% to 70%. After the settlement, it rose back to 80%. Productivity was stable and off-target (WHEN) by 10% (EXTENT).

PROCESS STAGE

List:

Before forming an SPS team, management suspected a new bonus formula adopted after the strike may have caused dissatisfaction among workers. The formula, however, could not be changed until the next contract negotiations. Brainstorming revealed additional possible contributors to the decline in productivity as follows: tool life, setup time, length of sample runs, development time, communication, and process capability. A cause-and-effect diagram (see Figure A.6) was used to organize

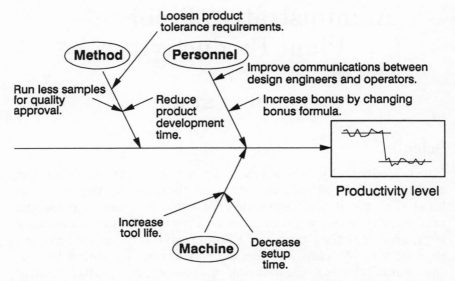

Figure A.6   Use of a cause-and-effect diagram to organize list of possible actions

the list as possible actions. **Problem solving tactic:** *Optimize the existing system.*

Prioritize:

Subjective rating and ranking was used to identify four knobs for evaluation: tool life, communication, setup time, and development time.

Evaluate:

A table was laid out showing two options for each of the four knobs, resulting in 16 combinations to choose from. Team members rated each combination on a 1–10 scale, 10 being their strongest preference. The results of this rating procedure were consistent within combinations (see Table A.9), indicating general agreement among team members. The median rating for each combination was selected as the performance characteristic to analyze. ANOVA was used to determine which combinations were most strongly preferred. **Statistical Solution:** The analy-

Table A.9 Summary of team member preferences for combinations of four knobs

				B — Communication			
				B1 Improve		B2 Adequate	
				A — Tool life		A — Tool life	
				A1 Improve	A2 Adequate	A1 Improve	A2 Adequate
D Engineering trial time	D1 Reduce	C Setup time	C1 Improve	10 (10) 10	8 (8) 7	10 (9) 8	8 (6) 6
			C2 Adequate	6 (7) 8	4 (6) 6	6 (6) 7	(4) 2 5
	D2 Not an issue	C Setup time	C1 Improve	9 (9) 8	7 4 (7)	8 (7) 7	7 4 (6)
			C2 Adequate	(6) 5 8	2 (3) 5	(5) 4 6	1 (1) 5

Note: Median ratings encircled.

sis showed two major preferences among team members. Setup time reduction was the top preference, followed by an increase in tool life as a close second. Other knobs and their interactions were not found to be significant.

Optimize:

Because setup time and tool life were independent, the team elected to work on setup time reduction first. Progress could be monitored more quickly since setup changes occur frequently, while tool replacements occur at longer intervals. Setup time consisted of three parts: (1) administrative/scheduling aspects, (2) staging logistics, and (3) actual setup. Discussion revealed that the first two parts used up most of the time. The team directed their efforts at reducing those elements for each product line. Tool life optimization was deferred until after the setup time optimization results were known.

IMPLEMENTATION STAGE

A new SPS team was formed to study each setup element in detail and track results. Setup time reduction became a problem itself, with the team beginning a new SPS investigation.

Conclusions

Conventional problem solving strongly suspected one obvious variable (the bonus formula) and did not seriously consider other possible causes for the productivity decline.

Statistical Problem Solving examined all possible variables—both the subtle and the obvious—that could have been affected by the strike. Began positive team action to improve overall plant productivity by focusing on a high-priority improvement project.

Appendix B

SPS Execution Principles

Statistical Problem Solving is characterized by an adherence to economical execution principles in the problem environment. These principles are based on the belief that experimentation should be practical, efficient, and productive.

SPS investigations are based on four principles:

(1) **Variables (knobs) initially selected for investigation should be inexpensively turnable.** This principle is central to the SPS goal of zero-cost investigations. Since only easily turnable knobs can be tested for free, they should always be investigated first. Experimenters should be able to turn knobs from one setting to another and back again. Temporary changes (reversibility) in knob settings are almost always inexpensive or free.

   As basic as turnability is to the SPS evaluation step, it is also an important concern for implementation. If a solution cannot be implemented due to technical or financial roadblocks, then the preceding investigation wasted time and resources. However, if easily turnable knobs are investigated first, the odds are in the team's favor that the solution will be feasible to implement.

(2) **Knobs should be turned as far as possible during the evaluation without damaging product or process equipment.** Involving operating personnel in determining the range of settings over which to turn the knobs can guard against violation of this principle.

(3) **When changing knob settings during experimentation, the historical level of defects should not be exceeded.** Knowledge of the process is needed to fulfill this principle. If a given combination of settings creates more defects than normally allowed, the experimentation should be stopped before completing the sample size.

(4) **Data collection on existing processes should not adversely affect normal production operations.** Through their knowledge of the process, the team should create sampling methods that maintain operating efficiency. Production should not be interrupted to finish the investigation at one time. If a few normal production runs take place in between the stages of experimentation, the integrity of the investigation will not be jeopardized.

Method-driven investigations are often unnecessarily expensive. Instead, the method used should depend upon the execution challenges of a particular problem. Investigative decisions during SPS are based on economy and the ease of execution, as guided by the four principles above. When the principles are followed, the cost of investigation is minimized.

After the investigation is complete, it's possible that the cost to translate a statistical solution into an actual solution would outweigh any benefits gained. When SPS execution principles are carefully followed, however, implementation costs are also minimized.

Appendix C

The Teamwork Factor

Indicated chapters discuss each point in greater detail. The training of SPS team members is described in Chapter 1.

POINT #1: **Successful problem solving is dependent on a team approach.** Synthesizing the experiences within the group provides the most accurate problem definition. Throughout the ensuing investigation, team effort protects against individual bias. Finally, recognizing the value of personal experience leads to full support of the solution implementation. (Chapter 2)

POINT #2: **Careful selection of team members insures a sufficient base of knowledge to solve the problem.** Team formation is a crucial point because SPS relies on the team's combined experience with the problem. Executing SPS requires different information at each step. Team membership is consequently dynamic, with members added and released as need dictates. (Chapter 3)

POINT #3: **The SPS facilitator's role is threefold: guide the team in using the SPS process, keep the team focused on the problem, and moderate any possible disputes among team members.** (Chapter 3)

POINT #4: **When defining the problem, the team should neither make assumptions about possible causes nor suggest solutions.** To create an effective definition of the problem, the team must focus on the process output characteristic manifesting the problem. (Chapter 4)

POINT #5: **SPS team members need only a general understanding of the statistical methods used in SPS.** The facilitator guides their use of appropriate methods and is their resource for any necessary statistical knowledge. (Chapter 4)

POINT #6: **The SPS facilitator must be skilled in statistical methods, problem solving strategies, and group dynamics.** While functioning as technical advisor to the team, the facilitator must also be aware of interaction among team members and intervene when necessary. (Chapter 4)

POINT #7: **Besides being a teacher of SPS, the facilitator is a student of the team in learning about the problem.** Team members are also both teachers and students in exchanging information on the problem. These dual roles help to create an atmosphere of mutual respect within the group. (Chapter 4)

POINT #8: **The facilitator must maintain an open, accepting atmosphere.** Only in an uncritical setting will team members share their individual knowledge freely and productively. Effective team interaction can uncover the many possible variables affecting a problem. (Chapter 5)

POINT #9: **Any recognition should be equally shared by all team members to reinforce the objective of working together towards a common goal.** (Chapter 5)

POINT #10: **SPS facilitators should be carefully selected for their personal characteristics and professional capabilities.** The ideal facilitator is a generalist who can be flexible in dealing with the complexity common to problem situations. Adaptability extends to the use of statistical techniques. The facilitator cannot be biased towards a specific technique but must be ready to use a variety of statistical tools. Finally, the facilitator's communication skills must effectively encompass the roles of leader, teacher, and moderator. (Chapter 5)

POINT #11: **For successful use of the subjective prioritization method, it may be necessary to draft new team members with special knowledge.** If key people are missing, certain suspect knobs might get too much or too little attention. (Chapter 6)

POINT #12: **Team members should equally influence the outcome of the investigation.** Consequently, the facilitator must not allow strong personalities to dominate the group. The private rating of knobs frees team members from possible pressures to agree with others on the team. (Chapter 6)

POINT #13: **The facilitator must be alert to the possible use of biased or invalid data, questioning when and how data were collected.** (Chapter 6)

POINT #14: **Consensus on the results of prioritization insures the support of team members during the evaluation step.** Because evaluation is a costly effort, team satisfaction with the top knobs is an important concern for the facilitator. (Chapter 6)

POINT #15: **Facilitators actively participate in the SPS process.** They contribute to each step according to how much they know about the problem under investigation. (Chapter 6)

POINT #16: **A careful verbal rehearsal helps the team avoid potential difficulties in conducting an evaluation experiment.** The team should plan in detail how knobs will be changed. In addition, any instability created by changes in materials, operators, or shifts should be anticipated and factored into the experiment. (Chapter 7)

POINT #17: **Teamwork discourages impulsive changes in direction during the investigation.** Team members should reinforce each other in sticking to the evaluation plan. (Chapter 7)

POINT #18: **Contributions from the entire team help to interpret and understand the results of the evaluation.** The synergy of several minds working together is highly effective in creating new understanding from new information. (Chapter 7)

POINT #19: **The number of team members needed to pursue optimization is usually fewer than needed earlier in the SPS process.** Team members not involved in the optimization effort can begin work on new improvement projects. (Chapter 8)

POINT #20: **Teamwork remains essential in reviewing results of the optimization step.** Team members should work cooperatively in understanding and using any new knowledge. (Chapter 8)

POINT #21: **SPS is adaptable to the various types of teams in common use.** The SPS approach advocates team membership based on the requirements of the problem, implying a temporary team structure. When ongoing teams use SPS, persons with special knowledge are added to the team for a limited time, as projects demand. (Chapter 8)

POINT #22: **When planning implementation, anyone who can anticipate the solution's impact on existing operations should be added to the team.** The goal is to minimize any difficulties the actual solution might create. (Chapter 9)

POINT #23: **The team should brief all affected personnel on the problem and the specifics of its solution.** For a successful implementation, everyone involved must support the solution. (Chapter 9)

Appendix D

Glossary for Statistical Problem Solving

The intent of this glossary is to clarify terms that might be unfamiliar or confusing to our various readers. The definitions are not intended for universal reference but are offered to aid problem solvers.

Actual solution   Changes or other actions that become a permanent part of the process to significantly reduce or completely eliminate the problem.

Acute problem   A problem due to instability in a process. Although usually of short duration, acute problems develop suddenly and demand immediate attention. In the field of statistical quality control, acute problems are linked to *special cause variation*, which experts believe responsible for approximately 15% of all quality problems.

Analysis of covariance (ANCOVA)   A method similar to analysis of variance (ANOVA) but takes into account a third component, variation assignable to a covariable. A *covariable* is a variable that cannot be controlled but whose value is recorded as it changes during an investigation.

Analysis of means (ANOM)   A graphical method to examine several subgroups of data simultaneously for significant statistical and engineering differences. Developed by Ellis R. Ott in 1958, ANOM is similar to analysis of variance (ANOVA) but is simpler.

Analysis of ranges   A method of investigation to determine if ranges of different subsets of data are significantly different. It is primarily used to analyze dispersion effects in factorial experiments.

Analysis of variance (ANOVA)   A method to divide the total variation in the data gathered during investigation into two components: (1) between test group variation or that which can be controlled and (2) within test group variation or that which cannot be controlled or is not being studied.

Attributes charts   The type of control charts that deals with attributes data. They either express the proportion of sampled output that does not conform to requirements or the number of nonconformities per unit of sampled output.

Attributes data   The type of data that identifies process output in discrete categories. For example, output is either acceptable or unacceptable. The degree of acceptability is not indicated.

Average   A summary statistic that estimates the central tendency of the population from which a sample is drawn. It is computed by summing all the data in a sample and dividing by the number of data points.

Average and range charts   A pair of variables control charts designed to be used with heterogeneous output. Both the location (average) and the spread (range) of the process output are revealed.

Average chart   A control chart that displays averages of samples over time to show where a process is running relative to a target value. It is usually displayed along with a range chart for processes with heterogeneous output.

Backward thinking   An investigative approach that begins with the troublesome output and then "backs into" the process. It enhances forward thinking. SPS is the science of executing backward thinking.

Bartlett's test   A statistical procedure to check for significant differences among dispersions within multiple sets of data, also referred to as homogeneity of variance. Bartlett's test is useful for checking whether the output ranges of parallel streams in a process are equal. See Chapter 4, Reference 9.

Basket checks   The random sampling of product at different, easily accessible locations in a process. Basket checks are used to quickly pinpoint the largest source of problem variation.

Brainstorming   A creative thinking technique to encourage a free flow of ideas within a group. The objective is to generate a maximum number of potentially usable ideas in a minimum of time. During SPS, brainstorming can be used to select the problem and to list suspect variables.

Capability   The ability of a process to repeat a task expressed as a range. Statistically, capability is defined as six standard deviations. Capability is only meaningful when measured under stable conditions. It is assumed to reflect the best process understanding at the time.

Capability study   A study to determine the expected range of process output (capability) under stable conditions. Typically, the location, dispersion, and shape of the process output distribution are described.

Capable process   A process is capable when its expected output range (capability) is smaller than its specification range and the output is targeted so that no out-of-specification output is produced.

Cause-and-effect diagram   A problem analysis tool that depicts the variables affecting a problem, usually according to the common categories of people, materials, methods, environment, and equipment. It is also referred to as the Ishikawa diagram, for its originator, or the fishbone diagram, due to its appearance.

c chart   An attributes control chart that displays nonconformities per unit. The *nonconformities* can be incidents, defects, headaches, and accidents. A *unit* can be one product unit, one day, one hour of production, several feet of production, a batch, etc. The c chart is used to identify the defect categories or sub-problems that contribute to both incapability and instability.

Chi-square value   A statistic that is a measure of the difference between observed and expected frequencies of attributes data in a contingency table. The larger the chi-square value, the stronger the association between a suspect variable and a problem.

Chronic problem   A problem due to an incapable process. Because chronic problems are always or frequently present, they usually become accepted as normal or unavoidable. In the field of statistical quality control, they are equated with *common cause variation*, believed responsible for at least 85% of all quality deficiencies.

Common cause variation   The variation in process output that exists under stable conditions. It may result from the unknown effects of process variables and their interactions. Statistical control charts separate process variation into two types, common cause variation and special cause variation.

Confounding   Confounding occurs when the effects of two process variables or their interactions are inseparable during data analysis. Confounding can occur due to poorly planned data collection, but it also occurs in planned screening experiments when many variables are studied in relatively few experimental trials.

Contingency table analysis (CTA)   A tool for analyzing attributes data to determine the strength of association between a suspect variable and a problem. Both the variable and the output must be classified into at least two categories. CTA is used during the SPS prioritization step.

Continuous knob   A knob that can take any value along a scale and can be adjusted incrementally within its operating range. Speed, pressure, temperature, and feed rate are examples of continuous knobs.

Control chart   A graphical display of a summary statistic derived from output samples over time. It includes a centerline plus control limits that provide a boundary between what is natural and expected for the process and what is unnatural. A control chart allows the study of process stability. Any discernible patterns within limits or points outside of the limits indicate the presence of special cause variation.

Controlling upstream   Attempting to solve a problem by tightening the quality control of input variables (e.g., incoming material).

Correlation analysis   An analysis of two or more variables to determine if they are related. A helpful means of determining the strength of the association between an individual suspect variable and the problem during the SPS prioritization step. Using a graph called a scatterplot, the problem output characteristic is plotted as a function of the suspect variable when both are available in the form of variables data.

Correlation coefficient   A statistic that measures the degree of relationship between any two variables when available in the form of variables data. Its smallest possible magnitude is zero, indicating no relationship, and its largest possible magnitude is $+1$ or -1, indicating a perfect correlation.

Data stability   Any plot of data summaries that shows a random pattern with respect to time and is within the natural limits of its distribution can be considered stable. Any out-of-control points or trends on a control chart will indicate instability.

Data sufficiency   Number of samples required for the SPS evaluation step that represents the full operating range of each variable under study, assures that variables are statistically independent of one another, and represents the full range of process output.

Degrees of freedom   The number of independent conclusions that can be derived from any set of data. It is computed differently depending on the investigative situation.

Designed experiment   A well thought-out plan that (1) lists all the questions to be answered at the end of the investigation, (2) creates a data collection procedure to answer all the questions, and (3) specifies the analysis methods needed for all the answers. Well-designed experiments are a productive means to investigate many variables and their interactions simultaneously to identify which are creating undesirable process variation.

Discrete knob   A knob that can be set only at a finite number of distinct values and cannot be adjusted incrementally. For example, a method could be a discrete knob as in processing by either Method 1 or Method 2. There are no Methods 1.1, 1.7, 1.9, etc.

Dispersion   The range or spread over which data are scattered from the average. Usually measured by the standard deviation.

Distribution   The shape of a data set as depicted by a plot. The horizontal axis shows the value of each data point while the vertical axis represents the frequency that a value appears. Its theoretical shape is called a frequency distribution.

Evaluation   An investigative procedure for developing a full understanding of how important process variables and their combinations affect output variation. The investigation either actively changes variable settings or observes random changes for variables that cannot be easily changed.

Evolutionary operation (EVOP)   An optimization exercise in which a series of small changes in variable settings are made during production to map out process response.

Experimental error variation   The variation that occurs within an experimental test combination. It is the variation we do not understand either because the variables contributing to it were not part of the investigation or because it is inherent to the process being studied.

Experimental noise   Same as experimental error variation.

Factorial experiment   A designed experiment in which two or more variables are studied simultaneously at two or more levels. For example, a 3 × 2 factorial experiment studies one variable at three levels and another at two levels for a total of six experimental combinations.

Feedback system   With this arrangement, process behavior is measured immediately *after* output is produced; knobs are then adjusted to return the process to target. See Figure 7.16, Chapter 7.

Feed-forward system   With this arrangement, knobs are measured *before* the operation and forgiving adjustments then made so the target is hit more consistently. See Figure 7.15, Chapter 7.

Forgiving downstream   Solving the problem by improving process knowledge and thereby preventing the many naturally varying inputs to the process from affecting the output.

Forgiving principle   A philosophy that advocates investigating how to make downstream processes forgiving of the problem first, before tightening control of upstream processes to solve the problem.

Forgiving process   A process that is insensitive to changes in either process conditions or input materials by design or by its ability to compensate for the changes.

Forward thinking   Reliance on process expertise or engineering judgment alone to resolve problems.

Fractional factorial   A fraction of a factorial experiment, reducing the number of experiments required for full investigation. A fractional factorial assumes that either higher order interactions are negligible or do not matter in ranking suspect variables.

F-ratio statistic   A ratio that compares two variations. In ANOVA it is the ratio of the variation we understand to the variation we do not understand (experimental error).

Guilty knobs   Variables that are proven contributors to undesirable variation.

Heterogeneous processes   Processes that produce consecutive units of output that are not exactly alike. For example, assembly processes are heterogeneous.

Histogram   A pictorial representation of a frequency distribution composed of vertical bars whose areas are proportional to the frequency of the values in the distribution.

Homogeneous processes   Processes that produce consecutive units of output that are identical. For example, grinding processes are homogeneous.

Implementation   Translating knowledge of how to correct the problem (see **statistical solution**) into specific actions (see **actual solution**), closing the gap between knowledge and results.

Incapability   The status of a process when its output range under stable conditions is wider than the specification range.

Incapable process   A process is incapable when, under stable conditions, it produces some portion of output that does not meet the requirements. Either the output range may be greater than the specification range, or the output average may deviate from the specified target, or a combination of both.

Inherent variation   The variation in a controlled, stable process that cannot be reduced or eliminated.

Instability   The condition when process output shows a discernible pattern on a control chart or one or more points outside the statistical control limits.

Interaction   Two or more process variables jointly affecting the process output. The effect of one variable cannot be accurately described without knowing the setting of the second variable.

Investigative SPC (ISPC)   Using statistical process control (SPC) to define the process output problem condition and discover complex causes of instability. ISPC methods include the p + c + Pareto chart, multistation analysis, the multivariate chart, and the multi-vari chart.

Knob   Any suspect variable or possible action that, when changed or adjusted, has a positive or negative effect on the problem. For example, temperature (a variable) or writing a letter (an action).

Knob reversibility   The ability to turn knobs and return them to their original settings while exploring how they affect process output.

Knob turnability   A knob property that describes the degree of ease with which a knob can be tried (investigated). Some knobs are easily turnable over their full ranges, other knobs can be turned over only a limited range, and still others are difficult or even impossible to turn.

Location   Where most measurements in a distribution are concentrated. Location can be represented by the average (mean), median, or mode.

Mean square   A measure of variation that indicates how much experimental variables contribute to the problem variation. It is computed by dividing the sum of squares by the degrees of freedom in the ANOVA table.

Median   A measure of the location of a distribution. It is the middle value that divides the data into two groups of equal size. For example, the median of the data set 2, 4, 5, 9, 10 is 5.

Monte Carlo simulation   A computer-based procedure to explore how changes in the target and range of important process variables affect the target and range of the process output. The purpose is to determine the values of process variables that will deliver the desired output.

Multiple regression analysis   An analysis to derive a mathematical relationship between a process output variable (dependent variable) and two or more process variables (independent variables).

Multi-vari chart   A control chart that graphically dissects problem dimensions. It exhibits both size and shape variations, allowing them to be quantified and attacked in a strategic order.

Narrow limit gaging (NLG)   A gaging technique devised to warn the user that the process is changing to the point of producing out-of-specification parts unless action is taken. The narrow limit is generally selected to be 50% of the specification range. It is also referred to as PRE-control, stoplight control, or rainbow charting.

Natural process behavior   Behavior of a process output characteristic over time with no discernible patterns and no observations falling outside the statistical control limits. Natural behavior is how the process operates under stable conditions.

np chart   A control chart that displays the number of nonconforming units. Similar to the p chart except that the np chart reports the number nonconforming instead of the proportion.

Observational data   Data derived from observing and recording naturally occurring changes in the process and product.

Off-target   An output condition in which there is a difference between the achieved target and a desired target. A nominal dimension on a blueprint may be considered a desired target.

Operating ranges   The extreme settings for process variables between which the process operates.

Optimization   Continued investigation of important process variables, as confirmed by the SPS evaluation step, to maximize process performance.

Orthogonal   The property of a data set when all the variables are statistically independent. It is the most mathematically efficient condition present in a multifactor evaluation. Orthogonality insures that the widest possible coverage is given to the experimental space. Orthogonal comparisons are balanced so that each variable can be evaluated independently of every other variable. For example, Factor A has two levels: $-$ and $+$. Factor B has two levels: $-$ and $+$. The arrangement $(-,-)$, $(-,+)$, $(+,-)$, and $(+,+)$ is an orthogonal array.

Pareto chart   A bar chart that ranks subproblem categories according to their frequency of occurrence. The Pareto chart assumes a stable system. It is based on the Pareto principle, or the 80/20 rule, that suggests 20% of the subproblem categories contributes to 80% of the primary problem.

p chart   A control chart that displays the proportion of non-conforming process output. It is used for attributes data. The plotted value, p, is computed by dividing the number of nonconforming units by the total number of units in a sample.

p + c + Pareto chart   An investigative use of SPC that combines three charts to define a problem. The p chart separates overall instability from incapability. The c chart dissects the nonconforming units by the category of defect and distinguishes those categories that cause instability from those that cause incapability. The Pareto chart identifies which problem categories occur most often.

Performance characteristic   The process output characteristic under investigation during the SPS evaluation step. Common performance characteristics include the average, median, range, signal-to-noise ratio, and proportion defective.

Planned experimentation   Systematically exploring how changes in important variables and their combinations relate to process output. As a succession of experiments, it is the most efficient and accurate form of optimization when all the knobs are easily turnable without disrupting operations or increasing defective output.

Planned observational study   The observation and notation of naturally occurring changes in the process variables and output. Also referred to as the planned collection of observational data.

Primary problem   The primary problem is a description of the problem that is broad enough to include all potential sub-problems.

Prioritization   Ranking suspect variables as a means of reducing the variables list to a workable number for investigation. Only the top-ranked suspects are fully evaluated to determine their effect on the problem.

Probability number   A number representing the chance that a given result could occur by coincidence. Also referred to as *significance level*. The smaller the probability number, the greater the contribution a variable makes to variation in the process output. Probability numbers can be associated with almost any statistical procedure, including contingency table analysis, correlation analysis, and ANOVA.

Problem solving skills   The set of skills necessary to successfully resolve problems. Included are the ability to define the problem, to identify factors possibly contributing to the problem, to collect and analyze relevant information, to conduct tests for confirming the key contributors, and to create a plan that effectively controls or eliminates the problem.

Problem solving tactic   The approach taken for dealing with a problem and implementing its solution. SPS advocates selecting the tactic for problem solution as early in the problem solving process as possible since knowing it can shorten problem solving time. There are four basic tactics: (1) control the system, (2) optimize the system, (3) redesign the system, and (4) create a new system.

Process   Any activity or set of activities designed to produce a given result or a usable output.

Process capability   See capability.

Process capability analysis   An analysis carried out to compute the expected range of the process output. The analysis must include investigating the stability of the process since only a stable process has predictable output.

Process control   Maintaining known process variables on preferred targets and within acceptable ranges.

Process flow diagram   A planning tool that graphically depicts the steps or activities in a process. It can also display the controllable variables and intermediate output variables leading to the final output.

Process improvement   Positive changes to a process that reduce variation in the output by removing instability or improving process capability.

Process output   Whatever is produced by a process. See product.

Process output characteristic   An attribute of the output that may be of interest due to product function, process control, or problem solving.

Process variables   The controllable factors in a process that are responsible for the resulting condition of the output.

Product   The outcome of any process. Goods, services, information, and performance are all considered products.

Proportion defective   The number of nonconforming units of output divided by the total units checked. See p chart.

Range   The difference between maximum and minimum values in a data set. It measures the spread or dispersion in the data.

Range chart   A control chart in which the ranges of samples are plotted over time to show the degree of output consistency. It is usually used in combination with an average chart for heterogeneous process output.

Replication   A repeated test in an experiment done at another time. Provides an estimate of experimental noise (error variation). Differs from *repetition,* when two consecutive samples are not separated by a time interval.

Residual variation   The variation within test groups, not attributable to changes made during experimentation, or the variation that cannot be understood. Also known as error variation or experimental noise.

Response surface methods (RSM)   A collection of mathematical and statistical techniques for analyzing problems in which several variables interact to affect the output. The output (response) can be a process output characteristic or product characteristic. The objective is to optimize the response.

Robustness   The characteristic of a product or process that is insensitive to variation in components, to variations in process parameters, and to environmental influences. Ideally, processes and products should be designed to be robust against changes in variables that cannot be inexpensively controlled or are impossible to control.

Scatterplot   A graph that depicts the relationship between two variables. Corresponding values of each variable are plotted on rectangular coordinates. There are multiple uses of these plots. For example, when X is a process variable and Y is a product variable, scatterplots can be used to establish suspect rankings of different process variables. When X and Y are both process variables, scatterplots reveal the operating characteristics of the process. Also called a *scatter diagram.*

Screening experiments   A planned experiment in which a large number of variables are tested with the objective of choosing only a few for further investigation. Fractional factorial experiments, Plackett-Burman experiments, and Taguchi experiments fall into the screening experiments category. Screening experiments are orthogonal, but confound variable effects with interaction effects.

Settings   Knob positions or values.

Shewhart principle   Dr. Walter Shewhart, a pioneer in the field of statistical quality control, reasoned that no valid conclusion about a system of causes can be reached in the presence of instability. Causes of unnatural behavior must thus be removed—or at least understood—before process capability can improve.

Special cause variation   Instability in a process is typically caused by substantial changes in process conditions (called special causes) that are relatively easy to discover through the use of statistical process control. Special causes of variation must be removed from a process before the capability of the process can be determined. Also known as assignable cause variation.

Spread   The stable dispersion in a distribution. It is measured by the range or the standard deviation.

SPS rules of selection   Three guidelines applied during the SPS listing step to reduce the variables list to a manageable number.

Stable process   Output for a stable process shows only random patterns on a control chart with no individual points outside the statistical control limits.

Standard deviation   A measure of spread or dispersion. As the variation in the data increases, the standard deviation gets larger.

Statistical problem definition   A four-part problem diagnosis that decides on a point of attack (WHERE), describes the problem symptoms (WHAT), identifies symptom patterns (WHEN), and determines the size of the problem (HOW EXTENSIVE).

Statistical Problem Solving (SPS)   SPS is a systematic process for finding the most efficient path to problem resolution and permanent improvement. It consists of five steps: define the problem in statistical terms; list the variables suspected of affecting the problem; prioritize the variables; evaluate the top few variables and their interactions; and optimize the settings of the important variables.

Statistical process control (SPC)   The science of monitoring output data with respect to its natural limits and directing appropriate actions when unstable patterns or out-of-control conditions occur. Process behavior is expressed by plotting on a chart, in time order, a summary statistic of repeated samples of output, such as the proportion defective. Limits are calculated and drawn on the chart, providing boundaries between what is considered natural and what is considered unnatural.

Statistical significance   A large difference between experimental groups relative to the variation within experimental groups is statistically significant. The difference in output is believed to be due to the effect of the variables, and not due to chance. The level of significance depends partly upon the amount of data collected. Statistically significant means there was sufficient data gathered to claim that the conclusions are valid. Practical significance does not necessarily follow from statistical significance.

Statistical solution   The outcome of the SPS evaluation step that (1) confirms which variables and their interactions are causing the undesirable process output variation, (2) discovers how each variable should be set for improved output, and (3) quantifies the expected improvement.

Statistical thinking   A problem solving orientation that relies on data to clarify and analyze complex situations. Statistical principles guide decisions during all problem solving activity. The focus of statistical thinking is the identification of variables that combine favorably or unfavorably to create good or bad product.

Statistic   A summary of sample data that is useful for making an inference about a population.

Statistics   The science of assembling, analyzing, characterizing, and interpreting collections of data.

Suboptimization   An improvement effort at a local level that does not have a favorable impact at the global level.

Subjective rating & ranking   A group method to prioritize suspect variables for further investigation. Team members individually rate each suspect based on their experiences. After all ratings are tabulated, variables are rank-ordered according to their median ratings.

Subproblem   A component of a primary problem with its own unique system of causes.

Sum of squares   A mathematical summary that quantifies the degree to which the data deviates from its average.

Symptom   Evidence of a problem. Many symptoms are experienced through the senses; other symptoms are revealed through measurement.

Target   The most desired single value of an output characteristic. An achieved target is an average of output data. A desired target is an output value where the product optimally meets its requirements.

Tolerance   An acceptable range of either process or product variables that will not jeopardize either process operations or product integrity.

Top few knobs   Those variables identified by the SPS prioritization step for full investigation during the SPS evaluation step.

u chart   An attributes control chart that displays average defects per unit. Similar to the c chart except that the u chart has a different sample size from subgroup to subgroup.

Unnatural process behavior   Unnatural process behavior occurs when there is instability, revealed as runs, trends, or points out of limits on a control chart.

Unstable process   A process that shows unnatural behavior.

Variable   Anything—controllable or uncontrollable—that can influence the condition of process output. Sometimes referred to as a factor or a parameter. SPS uses the term **knob**.

Variables charts   The type of control charts designed to plot variables data. They display summaries of data from process output that can be measured on a continuous scale, such as temperature.

Variables data   Output data that is continuous between any two points and can be represented as a number.

Variation   Inconsistency. Differences among two or more supposedly identical things. Scatter in process output. A problem occurs when the variation in process output exceeds the required range. Excessive variation can be due to instability or incapability. Reducing variation is synonymous with improving quality.

WHAM processes   Manufacturing processes that produce several product characteristics simultaneously. Stamping, forging, screw machining and casting are examples. Output from a WHAM process exhibits relationships among multiple characteristics because they are produced simultaneously. For example, in a process where powder is converted into a tablet, the weight and height of tablet are simultaneously produced and have a definite relationship. That is, when the height is higher, the weight is higher, and vice versa.

X chart   A control chart that plots the value of a single sample. The X chart is used for homogeneous processes where one output observation sufficiently represents the process condition. Also called an individuals chart.

Yates algorithm   A simple mathematical procedure to calculate ANOVA in factorial experiments where all factors have an equal number of levels.

Index